CHURCH & STATE

for Eric & Michael
from
Myles Shuslael
Aug. 2, 2003

CHURCH
&STATE

LUTHERAN PERSPECTIVES

EDITED BY

JOHN R. STUMME AND ROBERT W. TUTTLE

FORTRESS PRESS

MINNEAPOLIS

CHURCH AND STATE
LUTHERAN PERSPECTIVES

Cover and book design: Zan Ceeley

Library of Congress Cataloging-in-Publication Data
Church and state: Lutheran perspectives / edited by John R. Stumme and Robert W. Tuttle.
    p. cm.
Includes bibliographical references and index.
    ISBN 0-8006-3604-X (pbk. : alk. paper)
    1. Church and state—Lutheran Church. 2. Two kingdoms (Lutheran theology) 3. Lutheran Church—Doctrines. 4. Church and state—United States—History. 5. Lutheran Church—United States—History.
I. Stumme, John R. II. Tuttle, Robert W.
    BV630.3.C47 2003
    261.7—dc21   2002156639

Manufactured in the U.S.A.
07   06   05   04   03   1   2   3   4   5   6   7   8   9   10

Contents

PART II
THE LEGAL CONTEXTS OF CHURCH-STATE INTERACTION

Contributors

MARIE FAILINGER is Professor of Law, Hamline University School of Law, St. Paul, Minnesota.

MARY JANE HAEMIG is Associate Professor of Church History, Luther Seminary, St. Paul, Minnesota.

GARY M. SIMPSON is Professor of Systematic Theology and Chair of the History / Theology Division, Luther Seminary, St. Paul, Minnesota.

MYLES C. STENSHOEL is Professor Emeritus of Political Science, Augsburg College, Minneapolis, Minnesota.

JOHN R. STUMME is Director for Studies, Division for Church in Society, Evangelical Lutheran Church in America, Chicago, Illinois.

ROBERT W. TUTTLE is Professor of Law, George Washington University Law School, Washington, D.C.

SUSAN KOSCHE VALLEM is Associate Professor of Social Work and Chair of the Social Work Department, Wartburg College, Waverly, Iowa.

Preface

John R. Stumme and Robert W. Tuttle

Wherever the church of Jesus Christ exists, it stands in some relation to civil community and its governing institutions. For its own integrity as well as for the well-being and instruction of the faithful, the community that confesses and proclaims "Jesus is Lord" must define its relation with civil governance. Governments, in turn, must account for the fact that at least some of their citizens belong to a community that relies on an authority that transcends that of civil authority. Readers of a book on "church and state" know they are being invited to take part in an inescapable and enduring conversation.

History reveals various patterns of relationships: church withdrawal from public affairs, church support for government, church opposition to government, church control of government, government persecution of the church, government support of the church, government discrimination toward the church, government control of the church, as well as friendly and hostile divisions of spheres and responsibilities between these two actors. Be it through cooperation, conflict, compromise, coercion, or collision, both church and government have to come to terms with the other in practice and in theory. The many variables that shape these patterns in particular contexts—the society's religious composition and history; the church's theology, size, and organization; and the form of government and its political philosophy—are a reminder that church and state relations have been and continue to be complex and dynamic.

This book has its particular setting in the Lutheran tradition in the United States at the beginning of the twenty-first century. On the one hand, then, the book arises from a Christian tradition that believes that God is at work in both church and civil community; the two have distinctive mandates and identities, but both carry out God's purposes. On the other hand, this book arises from a political tradition that affirms a constitutional order that places governments' relation to churches and all religious bodies in the context of religious freedom. The chief norm of this political tradition is found in the First Amendment of the United States Constitution, which strictly limits what government actors can do in relation to religion: "Congress shall make no law respecting an establishment of religion, or prohibiting the free exercise thereof. . . ."

Forty years ago the Lutheran churches that later became the Evangelical Lutheran Church in America (ELCA) broke new ground in reflecting on the relationship of church and state. Criticizing a history of Lutheranism that did not take seriously the church's responsibility for public life, they called upon Lutherans and their churches to participate critically in public affairs. These churches left their mark in the formation of the ELCA in 1988, whose constitution pledges to "work with civil authorities in areas of mutual endeavor, maintaining institutional separation of church and state in a relation of functional interaction."

The last forty years have witnessed momentous changes in the relationship between religion and civil government in the United States. The de facto "Protestant establishment" has given way to a pervasive religious pluralism and, in the eyes of many, a growing secularism. Decisions by the U.S. Supreme Court set the tone by forbidding Bible reading and prayer in public schools, eliminating many forms of public funding for parochial schools, and removing religious symbols from public facilities. Along with important court decisions on moral issues—abortion being foremost—the forced bifurcation of religion and civil government has provoked a sharp response from religious conservatives, who contend that this separation undermines the nation's moral and religious foundation. This response engendered a backlash from those who protest the involvement of religion leaders in politics and has led to an increasingly polarized political and civic discourse.

For the sake of both church and civil community, the contributors to this book take up the challenge of continuing and enriching the reflections of our predecessors in the context of this polarized public debate over the role of religion and government. They were called together by the Division for Church in Society of the Evangelical Lutheran Church in America to think through church and state issues and to write essays to stimulate conversation in this church body and beyond. The authors write both as Christians and as citizens, aware of their responsibility to the church's witness and to the civil community's well-being. They place their formation in different academic disciplines—church history, systematic theology, ethics, social work, political science, and law—in service to the church's calling to be a faithful and responsible participant in society.

This book has two parts. The chapters in part I, "The Tradition Revisited," explore the church's identity, beliefs, and history, and show how they shape a Lutheran perspective on our topic. Part II, "The Legal Contexts of Church-State Interaction," examines Supreme Court rulings on the First Amendment, describing and evaluating their meaning for church and society.

In chapter 1 Mary Jane Haemig draws on Martin Luther's theology and the Lutheran Confessions to offer a theological framework for addressing contemporary questions of church and state. Her chapter introduces readers to important theological concepts and distinctions that Lutherans use in their church's approach to government, including the distinction between law and gospel, the uses of the law, the "two kingdoms," and the orders of creation. Haemig concludes by illustrating how confessional perspectives help us face some key challenges today.

Gary M. Simpson also turns to Luther and the Lutheran Confessions for direction amid our society, which differs so dramatically from that of the sixteenth century. Simpson carefully examines crucial confessional texts to elaborate the relation of God's agency to political authority, comparing this understanding with other conceptions. He highlights in Luther the often-ignored theme of political resistance and brings to light early Lutheran resistance theory, which, he argues, was one factor in the development of Western political thinking and structures. Simpson traces the emergence of civil society as a public sphere, shows how its emergence changes the ways in which church and governments relate, and calls for congregations to be "companions" in civil society.

In his chapter, John R. Stumme addresses how the Lutheran tradition took shape in the United States during the twentieth century. He documents a significant change in Lutheranism that began in mid-century, from a posture of absolute separation to one that affirmed both the freedom and integrity of church and state as well as their legitimate interaction in areas of mutual concern. Examining the official documents of church bodies that formed the ELCA, Stumme interprets the meaning of the phrase "institutional separation and functional interaction of church and state," which came to represent the new Lutheran posture. Finally, he suggests the continuing significance of this dimension of the church's "public witness."

Susan Kosche Vallem writes out of and about Lutheranism's long tradition of social ministry endeavors. She concludes part I by looking at one area of "functional interaction" between church and state: addressing human need, especially of people who are poor, and promoting the general welfare. Vallem describes the biblical and Lutheran call to care for people who are poor and in need, discusses the basis of the American public welfare system in the Elizabethan Poor Law of 1601, and outlines the development of church and state cooperation in responding to social need. She reviews constitutional questions involved in this cooperation and places her discussion in the context of effects of the welfare reform legislation of 1996. Vallem calls for a Lutheran response that includes both serving those in need and prophetically advocating to hold government accountable to its obligations for all citizens.

Myles C. Stenshoel opens the section "The Legal Contexts of Church-State Interaction" with a comprehensive review, accessible for the non-expert, of the Supreme Court's interpretation of the "religion clauses" of the First Amendment during the last sixty years. He discovers in the Court's opinions four competing rationales for religious freedom, which account for the court's contradictory decisions and lead him to conclude that the court's quest for religious freedom is unfinished. In addition to introducing the reader to significant court decisions and offering categories to interpret them, Stenshoel also sets out criteria for evaluating an adequate rationale for religious liberty.

The following two chapters take up constitutional questions in two controversial arenas of interaction between church and state. Marie Failinger focuses on education, where battles on religion and government are often fought. She draws on Luther to describe Lutheran themes related to education and brings these themes to bear on her analysis of Supreme Court rulings on education. Failinger considers state regulation of religiously based education, the place of religion and values in public schools, and the state's duties to provide education for all school children. Failinger's chapter both introduces readers to constitutional issues related to education and religion and shows how Lutheran insights help to understand and find alternatives to current dilemmas.

Robert W. Tuttle deals with one of the least understood yet most significant areas of conflict between church and state, land use regulation. In the past when a church wanted to acquire land for building or to expand an existing structure, zoning boards tended to defer to church plans. Today, however, zoning boards for various reasons have become more restrictive, including attention to the concerns of surrounding neighbors. In facing increasing difficulties in attempting to locate new construction sites, receive building permits, or secure exemptions for historical preservation laws, churches have found relatively little legal protection. Tuttle explores the legal questions in zoning disputes by carefully examining federal and state court rulings and legislative efforts to protect religious land uses. He argues against churches appealing to "a broad religious privilege" in their dealings with government, reminding churches of their obligations to their neighbors. Instead, Tuttle develops a hierarchy of free exercise of religion claims to offer guidance to churches and the courts in religious land use contexts.

With its combination of theological and legal approaches, we hope that this book will advance the Lutheran community's understanding of its public vocation and also contribute to the broader conversation on church and state relations in a time when these relations are in significant flux.

PART I

THE TRADITION REVISITED

1

The Confessional Basis of Lutheran Thinking on Church-State Issues

Mary Jane Haemig

The Lutheran tradition, founded in the very different social and political world of the sixteenth century, now must use its theological heritage to address contemporary questions of church and state in the United States. Its heritage offers a framework and resources for this endeavor. This chapter seeks to outline such a basic framework and to identify some resources from Luther's theology and the Lutheran Confessions that relate to church and state issues today. Instead of attempting a complete description of all relevant parts of Martin Luther's theology or the Lutheran Confessions, I will seek to focus on central guiding principles. I will also consider briefly some contemporary issues that turn out to be not so new. The major focus will be the *church's,* not the individual Christian's, relationship with the state or government, although the individual's relationship with the state will also come into the picture.

I will first examine how the Lutheran confessional perspective defines both church and state,[1] then consider the doctrine of God's twofold rule as a basis for discussing how church and state interact. That will lead to some theological guidelines in the Lutheran tradition that illuminate the interaction and involvement of the church with the state. These include (1) the positive yet limited valuation of reason, (2) a realistic anthropology that affirms both human possibilities and limitations, and (3) a theology that recognizes the difference between civil righteousness and the righteousness of God. Finally, I will apply the confessional perspective to some issues today.

Church and State Are Established
by God for Specific Purposes

The Church

The true church is not a human creation but the work of God the Holy Spirit. The Holy Spirit "calls, gathers, enlightens, and sanctifies the whole Christian Church on earth and keeps it in union with Jesus Christ in the one true faith. . . ."[2] Thus the church is not simply a group of people who decide to gather (a voluntary organization); it is an assembly called together by the Holy Spirit.[3] It is not of human origin. The true church is not coextensive with the empirical church but is hidden and thus not immediately apparent to the observer.

The outward identifying marks of the church are word and sacrament. Thus the church is "[t]he assembly of all believers among whom the Gospel is preached in its purity and the holy sacraments are administered according to the Gospel."[4] This definition of the church is twofold. The church is the *assembly* of all believers, but not merely any assembly of such believers. Rather, it is the assembly among whom God the Holy Spirit is active by the preaching of the gospel and the administration of the sacraments. The church is defined in terms of God's activity rather than in terms of a particular institution, structure, or function shaped by humans. In order to be the church, certain things must happen in the assembly of believers. No contradiction exists between the two parts—assembly and activity—of this definition, for one cannot exist without the other. As Luther said, God's word cannot be without God's people, and God's people cannot be without God's word.[5] Thus any entity claiming to be the church must first ask whether it is in fact where the gospel is purely preached and the sacraments rightly administered before proceeding to consider its position vis-à-vis the state.

The proclamation of the gospel,[6] God's word, entails the proclamation of both law and gospel. The law reflects what God expects us to do.[7] More broadly, "law" is any sort of expectation that meets us in our lives and demands our action. The law is demand; it is directed at us. The gospel is the good news of what God does for us. The gospel is God's gift of forgiveness; it is given freely to us.

The law has two uses, a civil use and a theological use. The civil or "first use" of the law expresses God's good intention that evil be curbed and human society enabled to live in some degree of order and safety. The law has a preservative rather than a salvific function. Humans can to some extent keep the law. Thanks to this "civil righteousness," human societies live in varying degrees of outward peace and justice. The theological or "second use" of the law is God's mirror, showing us our sin and driving us to the gospel. The essence of the law is the expectation that we live our lives in absolute trust in God. We should "fear, love, and trust in God above all things."[8] Obedience to any commandment flows out of this basic orientation expressed in the First Commandment. Serious consideration of the law reveals that we never meet this standard of fear, love, and trust, even if we do attain some measure of civil righteousness. The second use of the law makes us aware that we are continually inclined to fear, love, and trust someone or something other than God and thus even our best moral efforts fall short and are under God's judgment. The second use of the law keeps us from absolutizing or assigning too much value to our own efforts. God's expectations, taken seriously, drive us to look to the message of Christ's saving work for us.

The gospel proclaims that God in the person of Christ has taken the consequences of sin upon himself. God, for the sake of what Christ has done, forgives us our sin and grants us new life. Gospel is not a moral or ethical program or achievement; it is the proclamation of what God has done in Christ to renew his relationship with humans and all of creation. It is the righteousness (or justice) of God apart from the law. Gospel is qualitatively different from law. In response we confess: "I believe that Jesus Christ . . . is my Lord, who has redeemed me, a lost and condemned creature, delivered me and freed me from all sins, from death, and from the power of the devil."[9]

If the church fails to preach the law, it becomes antinomian and eviscerates the meaning of the gospel. Without the law (particularly the deep dimension of the second use that we "fear, love, and trust" God above all else), the gospel becomes less serious; without the law human problems seem more manageable and God's drastic intervention in Christ less necessary. A church that fails to preach the law may become quietistic and withdraw from the real problems of our world. It will also withdraw from the real spiritual problems of individuals and misrepresent God's love. On the other hand, if the church fails to preach the gospel, it is no longer the church. Other sources (including other religious and ideological heritages) may offer the law, at least in its first use, but only the church is shaped by the proclamation of God's gift of forgiveness for us in Jesus Christ. The church must avoid becoming merely the bearer of yet another moral program, yet another human plan for improvement. Such programs and plans may be helpful and necessary, but they are not the gospel. The church must always remember that it is the custodian of the distinction between law and gospel,[10] recognizing the depth of the law's demand, proclaiming the new life given by the gospel, and remembering the connection between law and gospel. This view of law and gospel is the basis for the Lutheran perspective on church-state matters and is what distinguishes it from some other Christian perspectives (discussed later).

The Lutheran tradition confesses that the proclamation of law and gospel is the vehicle of God the Holy Spirit. It is the instrument God chooses to use and thus bears all the power of God. This word of God also defines the sacraments and makes them means of grace. The temptation is to despair and see the

proclamation of law and gospel as "mere words," ineffective to accomplish anything. The word appears weak and improbable, just as the other means of
grace—water, bread, wine—appear weak and unlikely vehicles of God's grace.
Yet Lutherans believe that the means God has chosen are strong—stronger
than the principalities and powers of this age. The proclamation of the word as
law and gospel in public preaching and the sacraments is the most powerful
tool the church has. The word of God is the church's prize possession. To give
up on this is to become merely another institution, merely another interest
group within our society, rather than the church of Jesus Christ. The church
experiences the apparent weakness of the word in this age but is sustained by
its faith that this is God's word and thus ultimately definitive for our lives.

It may be difficult for the church to cling to its own self-understanding
when this is threatened by other concepts. Public opinion may want us to see
the church primarily as a preacher of ethics or moral values and may even see
the gospel in primarily moral or ethical terms. The Lutheran church must
resist this temptation, properly distinguishing the proclamation of law and
gospel, and proclaiming both.

Cultural attitudes may pressure us toward seeing the church simply as a voluntary organization, formed by humans for whatever purposes those humans
may determine is right. Again, the Lutheran church must resist this view,
remembering that it is "called, gathered, enlightened, and sanctified" by the
Holy Spirit.

The American legal system may force us to use a definition of the church
for certain legal purposes that is inadequate in theological terms. The church
must function for certain purposes within a legal system, and for those purposes it must live within that system's definition of the church. Yet the church
should never let this legal definition be definitive of its existence; it must
instead look to its confessional heritage for this definition.

The State

The state, in Lutheran terms, is instituted by God and defined in terms of
its function. "It is taught among us that all government in the world and all
established rule and laws were instituted and ordained by God for the sake of
good order."[11] [A note on terminology: Augsburg Confession 16 speaks of
"government" and "temporal authority" (Article 28). In this chapter, "temporal authority," "state," and "government" are used interchangeably unless
specifically stated.]

Government receives its authority and purpose from God. The explanation
of the Fourth Commandment in the Large Catechism states that the authority
of civil government is derived from that of parents. Just as he uses parents, so
God also uses government to give us "food, house and home, protection and
security."[12] Article 28 of the Augsburg Confession[13] notes that temporal
authority is "concerned with matters altogether different from the gospel.

Temporal power does not protect the soul, but with the sword and physical penalties it protects the body and goods from the power of others."[14] The sphere of civil government lies in keeping peace and order in a society (with force if necessary) and supporting and nourishing the lives of its citizens. This function is not inferior to that of spiritual government (the church), for Article 28 also notes that our teachers direct that both governments "be held in honor as the highest gifts of God on earth."[15]

The function of temporal authority is good and God-given.[16] Temporal authority is to uphold the law (in its first use) and thus function as an agent of God's struggle against the forces of sin and evil in God's creation. A particular person or entity placed in that function or the particular form of authority (government) may or may not actually fulfill the function well in Lutheran terms.[17] Though temporal authority is instituted by God, this does not declare every particular government good nor does it justify every government action. Luther recognized that the office was good while the people in it may be bad or incompetent.[18] Further, legitimacy and competence were not dependent on their being Christian. Non-Christian governments and officials can carry out the function of temporal authority just as well as or even better than governments and officials that identify themselves as Christian.

This view of the state and its functions does not automatically favor one particular form of government over another. Monarchy, democracy, or one-person rule—to name a few—are all systems that can *possibly* meet some divinely mandated functions. Lutheran churches have lived under many different political systems. While they do not automatically favor one form of government over another, the Lutheran Confessions, by describing the function of the state, offer a measuring stick for determining how well a particular form of government lives up to its mandate. The confessional perspective recognizes that order should not exist without justice and that justice cannot exist without order. The state is to uphold the law—no room exists for the state to consider itself above the law, an end unto itself.[19]

Lutherans recognize government as one of the "masks" of God. Though God is not always recognizable in its actions, government is one of the ways God rules the world. The confession that government is instituted by God was easier to accept in the sixteenth century. Today it appears to contradict the Enlightenment ideal that governments are chosen by humans. Lutherans do not resolve this apparent contradiction by assuming that God simply approves our choice (whatever it may be) of the form of a government or particular officeholders. Nor should officeholders or supporters of a government assume that they have a "divine right" to their positions. Such a view of "right" tends to be independent of the appropriate exercise of governmental responsibility and power and thus foreign to Lutheran thinking.

In Lutheran thinking, government is one of the divinely instituted orders or structures embedded in creation.[20] These orders are built into the created world; they do not derive from the Christian doctrine of redemption. Each order has specific functions and limitations; each is a place where the Christian can legitimately live out his or her vocation. Thought about the one order necessarily includes some reflection on the functions of the others and the relationships between the orders. Strictly speaking, references in Lutheran theology to the "secular realm," "temporal order," or "temporal kingdom," include not only the government but also other orders such as the family. The gospel does not overthrow these orders or structures but requires that they be kept.[21]

Government is a place where Christians can legitimately serve and carry out their vocation. Involvement with the government, whether as a civil servant, soldier, or merely a voter, is—in principle—good. Like all human activity, involvement in government is darkened by sin, but it is not inherently more sinful than other vocations. Augsburg Confession 16 points out that Christians may engage in the myriad of activities—for example, holding civil office, serving as a judge, or engaging in just wars—commonly associated with government and the life of this world. It condemns those who teach that "Christian perfection" cannot be obtained by those who participate in these activities.[22] As the Apology explains, "lawful civil ordinances are God's good creatures and divine ordinances in which a Christian may safely take part."[23] The Lutheran Confessions strongly countered those (such as the Anabaptists) who thought involvement with the government was not Christian, and those (such as Catholic monastic orders) who thought that other pursuits were more Christian or more holy than service to or with the government. Luther and the Lutheran Confessions saw service to or with government as an opportunity for the Christian to serve others. Christian love motivates Christians to acquire the appropriate knowledge, skills, and experience for such service and also motivates Christians to use their capacities for critical thought to determine the best way to serve the neighbor. At the same time, Christians should not pretend that Christian love governs the world. Government is still the arena of law, not gospel.

The Confessional Perspective Distinguishes and Upholds the Functions of Church and State and Recognizes Their Interactions

The Twofold Reign of God

God rules the world in two ways: temporally and spiritually. These two ways correspond to God's two ways of dealing with the powers of sin, evil, and death: law and gospel. This way of thinking is sometimes called the doctrine of the "two kingdoms"; sometimes the terms God's "twofold rulership" or "twofold reign" are preferred.[24]

It must be constantly kept in mind that the Lutheran doctrine of the twofold reign of God is not the same thing as the American legal doctrine of the separation of church and state. First, the secular or temporal rule referred to in Lutheran theology today includes not merely the government but all things related to earthly, bodily existence. Thus temporal rulership (the secular kingdom) includes culture, economics, education, nature, and so forth. The doctrine of God's twofold reign is a profound statement about the relationship of the proclamation of Christ to a myriad of human endeavors, one of which is government. Government is not the entire secular or temporal kingdom. Second, God's spiritual government (the spiritual kingdom) is not identical with any particular institutional form that claims to be church. As discussed above, the true church is defined by the activity of God the Holy Spirit in word and sacrament in the assembly of believers. Thus a particular institutional expression may fail to be the church in Lutheran terms though it may still continue to be the church in the eyes of American legal doctrine. Third, the legal doctrine of the separation of church and state refers to the separation of two *institutions*. The political separation of institutions is not the same as the theological distinction of realms or kingdoms.

It is important not to use "two kingdoms" language in such a way that the two kingdoms are identified with the kingdom of God and the kingdom of the devil. In Lutheran theology both the spiritual and the temporal kingdoms are God's; one is not "more" the kingdom of God than the other, nor in this life is one assigned to rule over the other. Rather, God rules over both, which is why the terminology "twofold reign of God" may be preferable to "two kingdom" terminology. Lutherans grant a status to government and political endeavors that some other religious, even Christian, groups do not. The temporal realm remains God's creation and subject to God's law. Though it is the arena for the ongoing battle against the powers of sin and evil, the temporal realm never stops being God's creation and subject to God. (Lutherans sometimes discuss the twofold reign of God by referring to the right and left hands of God—the right hand being the spiritual reign and the left hand the temporal reign.)

God's twofold reign will continue as long as this age continues. Human effort cannot merge the two; humans cannot abrogate the temporal reign and bring about the actualization or fulfillment of the spiritual reign. Only God does that. Presently we experience God's spiritual reign in the preaching of the gospel and the administration of the sacraments. We experience his temporal reign in government and other structures of our society.

Church and State: Not Separated but Interacting

For the above reasons, Lutherans distinguish church and state and recognize their God-ordained functions; they do not separate them.[25] Theologically,

Lutherans cannot separate church and state, for they realize that both are among God's ways of dealing with the world. Christians live in both realms—spiritual and temporal government—simultaneously. The gospel does not remove Christians from involvement with civil government but rather subjects them to it.[26] Inevitably, then, church and state interact. The state, by curbing evil, preserving order, and providing for some measure of civil righteousness, creates conditions conducive to the good of all its citizens and thereby enables—perhaps unintentionally—the unhindered preaching of the gospel.

The church reminds the state of what its function is and encourages all citizens to be involved with their state. The preaching of the law provides a constant standard by which a society and its government are judged. Sixteenth-century Lutheran preachers criticized their ruling authorities for failure to protect their citizens, use tax dollars to benefit society, and otherwise fulfill their functions. By the preaching of the law, the church may admonish, proscribe, and criticize. It may challenge systems, individuals, and policies. It may even propose and give advice—Luther urged cities to establish and run schools in order to educate useful citizens. But a line (admittedly not always easily discernible) exists between admonishing the government to do its job as laid out in the Lutheran understanding of government and advocating for specific policy prescriptions. When the Confessions speak of the church and the church's proclamation of law and gospel, that proclamation does not include detailed policy prescriptions for a government. Augsburg Confession 28 points to limits on the church in this regard:

> Therefore, the two authorities, the spiritual and the temporal, are not to be mingled or confused, for the spiritual power has its commission to preach the Gospel and administer the sacraments. Hence it should not invade the function of the other [the temporal authority], should not set up and depose kings, should not annul temporal laws or undermine obedience to government, should not make or prescribe to the temporal power laws concerning worldly matters.[27]

The functions of church and state should not be confused: The church should not prescribe policy, and the government must not prescribe how or under what conditions the gospel is preached. It is not always easy for the church to discern where the line runs between justified admonition and unjustified interference in governmental affairs.

The distinction between the spiritual and temporal rule of God means that the preaching of God's word should never degenerate into the mere prescription of a specific political, social, economic, or cultural program. God's word does something different. The preaching of the law values the limited civil righteousness created by the law. By exposing specific injustices of human efforts and programs, it helps to correct those injustices and create greater jus-

tice within society. The preaching of the law also exposes the ultimate insuffi-
ciency of all human efforts and programs. The preaching of both the law and
the gospel frees us from seeing our particular agendas or policies as of ultimate value.

The distinction between church and state means that church and state will
interact. As described above, the church's preaching of the law is itself a type
of interaction with the state. Further, church institutions and individual members may interact with the state in the carrying out of their vocations. They
may bring particular expertise in various fields (for example, in immigration,
education, or social services) to the making and implementation of governmental policies. In doing this they are fulfilling their Christian vocation to
serve others. They do not claim special expertise springing from the gospel,
their status as Christians, or their connection to a church body. Their motivation may spring from their Christian faith, but their expertise springs from
their exercise of their human capabilities, including reason, capabilities that
are available to all people. The church as a body, its institutions, and its individual members must be careful never to claim, on the basis of the gospel, priority or special consideration for their policy suggestions or procedures.

In the Lutheran Confessions the church seeks neither to convert nor to
reign over the state. As the church is the custodian of the distinction between
law and gospel, so the church must remind the state of what the state's role is.
But reminding the state of what its job is does not mean the church is somehow "more" God's kingdom or a better version of God's kingdom. The doctrine of God's twofold reign acknowledges that God is at work in the world in
ways not directly related to the church. One of these ways is civil government,
and government should be allowed to do its job in accordance with its charge
from God. The church does not invent or control the function of government; it does however vigilantly proclaim what that function is.

Church and State according to Other Christian Traditions

The contrast to other Christian ideas of the relationship of church and state is
sharp. In medieval Europe, the Roman Catholic Church believed that the civil
authority derived its mandate from the church. Thus the state was reduced, at
least in theory, to an inferior adjunct or arm of the church. The state was sup-
posed to take its direction from the church. Lutherans took issue with this
because it distracted the church from its true function and failed to see God
at work in the state where the church was not involved. Further, the medieval
church believed that involvement in "spiritual" vocations—life as a priest,
monk, or nun—was superior to involvement in "secular" vocations such as
government, business, and the family. Lutherans rejected this and affirmed
that Christians are able to serve God and neighbor in almost any occupation.

In the Reformed stream of the Protestant Reformation, government
became an instrument to transform society in accord with a Christian vision.

While the Lutheran Confessions see civil government concerned with the first use of the law, Calvin states in regard to the office of secular magistrates that "no government can be happily established unless piety is the first concern."[28] Rather than having specific functions limited to the temporal order, civil government was also "to defend sound doctrine of piety and the position of the church."[29] Though many sixteenth-century Lutherans (and later Lutherans) agreed that the state should, precisely by establishing some measure of peace and justice in a society, provide favorable conditions for the preaching of the gospel, they were (and are) troubled by the attempt to have the civil government take over functions of the spiritual government. In essence, this proposal makes gospel into law, that is, it makes God's grace and mercy into a rule for governing human society.

Another result is that civil law becomes a sort of gospel, promising a version of salvation. Some later followers of Calvin saw the civil government as an instrument for the achievement of God's kingdom by humans within temporal society. In effect, the state was to convert society in accordance with a model prescribed by the church. Puritan New England followed this model, and this model still influences many groups (both religious and secular) in contemporary America. This vision has historically had tremendous dynamism for it has motivated individuals and groups to work on this earth toward their visions of God's kingdom. (It should also be noted that the failure of various such visions has led to despair and withdrawal.) This essentially theocratic vision has troubled Lutherans because it is a form of idolatry. It says that we humans know what God's kingdom will look like and how it should be attained—but Lutherans believe that only God knows the timing and future shape of that kingdom. While we await that kingdom, Lutherans believe the law both preserves our earthly society and exposes its faults and possibilities, making us aware both of the civil righteousness that nourishes and betters a society and of the ultimate imperfection of any human society. Lutherans cannot view any human effort, political or otherwise, as achieving or moving toward the salvation God has promised. The achievement of civil righteousness, not the preaching of the gospel, is the function of civil government.

Sixteenth-century Anabaptists generally saw government and any involvement with government as inherently evil. They advocated both institutional and personal separation from the state in order to preserve the purity of the church and the integrity of the individual Christian.[30] Anabaptists promoted a sort of utopianism that is inimical to the Lutheran belief that God's people in this world cannot be so pure as the separation from worldly involvements suggests. Anabaptists failed to see that God was at work even though the civil authority was not overtly Christian or even was anti-Christian. Anabaptists also did not value the opportunities for service to the neighbor that involvement with the government offered. In effect, Anabaptists underestimated the presence of God in the world and thus failed to understand the nature and extent of God's creative activity.

The Limits of the State and the Church

For Lutherans, church and state limit each other in a way meant to enable the full functioning of both. Both remain subject to God. A particular manifestation of temporal government is not an ultimate commitment, just as a particular manifestation of the spiritual government (an institutional church) is not an ultimate commitment. To recognize either as ultimate would be idolatry—recognizing something other than God as ultimate.

The Lutheran view of the state keeps the state within limits. Because the state is given its function by God, the state acts outside of its intended character when it claims to be God, that is, when it makes an absolute claim on the lives of its citizens. Disobedience to the state is justified when it fails to fulfill its function in relation to the law of God or when it oversteps its limits. The confessional tradition allows and even demands such disobedience:

> Accordingly Christians are obliged to be subject to civil authority and obey its commands and laws in all that can be done without sin. But when commands of the civil authority cannot be obeyed without sin, we must obey God rather than men. (Acts 5:29)[31]

In such a case, the civil authority places itself above the law instead of enforcing the law. Thus it steps out of its assigned place, and disobedience may be necessary. Sixteenth-century preaching makes clear that Lutheran preachers criticized their rulers for failure to do their jobs and called their rulers to account for such failure. Similarly, they told their congregations they did not have to obey a ruler who commanded them to do something contrary to God's command. Such disobedience, however, should not be confused with the modern notion of "standing up for one's rights." In the sixteenth century, Lutheran believers were admonished to endure injustices themselves but to act, disobeying a government if necessary, if such government did not fulfill its responsibility to others. Lutherans were admonished to stand up for others, not for their own interests or rights.

Just as a particular government is not absolute, so also a particular form of the institutional church can never be seen as absolute. Instead, an institutional church must be judged by the standard of Article 7 of the Augsburg Confession, that is, by whether it preaches the word of God (both law and gospel) in its purity and administers the sacraments rightly. Criticism of a particular institutional expression of the church may be justified (as it was in the case of Luther) in the interest of obedience to the word of God. Thus the Confessions also demand that believers, both as individuals and as the assembly, judge the institutional church. It may be necessary to call the institutional church to account when it either fails to preach the law, shrinking within its own domain, when it oversteps its bounds, infringing on the civil domain, or when it fails to do what only the church can do, preach the gospel.

Theological Guidelines or Limiting Principles

Law and Reason

God has not left humans without guidance in regard to the law that governs the civil order. Luther and the Lutheran Confessions believed in an unwritten universal law given by God that governs worldly affairs and is available to every human, Christian or non-Christian. This is sometimes known as "natural law."[32] "Law" in this sense includes not only written law and the formation of laws and administration of justice. "Law" includes the entire process of discerning what is right and wrong in a particular context. The Decalogue is one but not the only expression of this universal law. The Apology states that to some extent human reason naturally understands the Decalogue "since it has the same judgment naturally written in the mind."[33] The Large Catechism mentions that the Ten Commandments are "inscribed in the hearts of all men."[34] The uniquely Christian proclamation, the gospel, does not introduce any new laws governing the civil order but commands us to obey existing laws.[35]

Human reason has its proper role in ascertaining and applying this law, that is, in determining better and worse ways of running a human society, better and worse ways to serve one's neighbor. Human reason must also recognize that today's "better" way may look worse tomorrow. While Luther strongly rejected any role for reason in producing salvation, he emphasized repeatedly that reason was a good gift of God and meant to be used both in the life of faith and in service to one's neighbor. Such service included the functions of government. Yet the use of reason itself is darkened by sin. Thus reason may make mistakes in determining what the law is and how it should be applied. Human reason should never delude itself into thinking that it is either a neutral resource or itself the highest lawgiver or lawmaker. An implicit tension exists here: while humans must determine what the law is and apply it in concrete situations, they must also be aware that their own reasoning is more or less flawed and darkened and their best solutions are only proximate achievements. Assertions that legal or political proposals correspond to what the law demands always run the danger of becoming a pretext for adopting the particular agenda of an individual or group. At the same time, uncertainty and approximation of the ideal should not necessarily hinder an individual or government from acting. Individuals and governments must make and implement proposals in the knowledge that the consequences of such action may be surprising or even counterproductive. Changed contexts may make good proposals moot or even deleterious. Thus Lutherans must also recognize the need for continuing correction and renewal.

A corollary of this is that Christians (as individuals) and the church (as an assembly of believers or as an institution) have no guaranteed higher or better reason than other people. While encouraging the participation of Christians in the political realm, Lutherans differ from some other Christians in not claiming a special knowledge or special insight, based on the gospel, into policy matters. What Christians have is a perspective that acknowledges that humans are beings created by God and therefore valuable, that humans are not gods and therefore are subject to God, and that government does not exist to serve itself or a small group of people but rather exists under God to serve all its people. Even these perspectives may be shared with people of other faiths. The Christian faith may cause a special emphasis on compassion and an appreciation of the importance of the individual and the contextual solution. Yet these emphases may not be unique to Christians.

Sin and Human Possibilities

The Lutheran tradition remains conscious of human sin and is thus realistic concerning human possibilities; it also values the relative civil righteousness that individuals and societies can attain. The power of sin and evil in society cannot be denied or ignored. Lutheran support for any policy, program, or plan is always tempered by a knowledge of human limitations and a consciousness of how human sin can corrupt even the best intentions and deeds. Selfishness permeates all endeavors in which humans are involved, including both the state and the church. This sin, a manifestation of our unwillingness to accept our position as God's creatures, colors our evaluation of our own motives and our knowledge of the law. It makes us blind to violations of the law and seeks to justify, even glorify, our transgressions. This consciousness of sin restrains Lutherans from triumphalism, that is, from claiming the absolute rightness or purity of any policy or endeavor, and from utopianism, that is, from claiming the perfectibility of human endeavor.

Further, the Lutheran consciousness of sin makes us realize that even the highest and best moral agency of the human, sometimes called the conscience, is blighted by sin. The conscience is not "sacred" and thus exempt from sin; it is part of the created world and thus as subject to sin as any other part of that world. The view that the conscience is "sacred" can lead to the elevation of human conscience above the law and thus to an antinomianism inimical to the Lutheran Confessions.

Civil Righteousness

The Lutheran view of the human also allows us to value the civil righteousness (also called the righteousness of reason) that humans can achieve. This civil righteousness produces outward discipline and works that enable society to function and even to improve. This civil righteousness attainable by humans is qualitatively different from the righteousness that God gives us.[36] This qualitative difference does not make civil righteousness unimportant.

Civil righteousness is something that God wants. The law is evidence of God's love and care for human society. God desires obedience to that law, civil righteousness, to preserve and promote human life. The Apology makes clear that God requires this "righteousness of reason" and wants this civil discipline toward which "he has given laws, learning, teaching, governments, and penalties."[37] To some extent, humans, possessing reason and judgment, can achieve this civil righteousness. But the power of sin is so great that it overwhelms the natural weakness of reason, making even civil righteousness rare.[38]

The Lutheran Confessions give this righteousness of reason its "due credit; for our corrupt nature has no greater good than this. . . . God even honors it with material rewards."[39] But Lutherans are always careful to distinguish this righteousness from God's righteousness. In fact, the crux of the Lutheran Reformation was the distinction of this human righteousness from the righteousness that is salvific. In the Lutheran view, the medieval church had confused the two types of righteousness and given human righteousness an ultimate significance that it does not possess. The Lutheran Confessions emphasize that civil righteousness, the righteousness of reason, does not create, affect, complete, or define human salvation. Only the righteousness of God does that. Thus freed from the burden of achieving earthly or heavenly salvation through their own efforts, Lutherans can seek relative goods and limited goals and value their achievement. They can see that civil righteousness is God-pleasing simply because God cares for all humans on this earth and desires that they live in conditions of peace and justice.

The Lutheran Confessions see judgment and salvation not only at the end but also in the very midst of history. Every day God judges our motives, plans, and deeds as both adequate and inadequate. They are more or less adequate for our human relationships but inadequate as the basis for our relationship with God. In that relationship we need to depend on God's initiative rather than our own efforts. Every day in faith we can go out into life in family, community, and government and serve our neighbors by seeking civil righteousness, valuing the achievement of relative goods, setting limited but reachable goals, recognizing the sin that blights our individual and communal existences, and starting anew when our best plans and policies go awry.

Sixteenth-century Lutherans lived in this renewed knowledge of the two kinds of righteousness as well as in a vivid expectation of the end of the world.[40] They remained both engaged with and critical of temporal authority. They neither withdrew from involvement in the anticipation of a rapid end to this world, nor did they engage in a desperate attempt to convert the temporal order to the gospel. Instead, they preached both law and gospel, recognized the twofold reign of God through law and gospel, and sought to live as Christians in both realms.

New Issues Not So New

The Lutheran confessional perspective helps us face key challenges today. What follows is a brief example of how confessional thinking may be applied. One challenge in our times concerns the extent to which diversity is tolerated and encouraged. How much diversity is tolerable? Can a society tolerate diversity to such an extent that it overthrows the perspective that is the basis for tolerance? Is any attempt to set limits on human activity an impermissible intrusion of specifically Christian values into the secular realm? Is the preaching of the law an attempt to "christianize" society?

Diversity, Tolerance, and "Christianization"

The sixteenth-century society in which the Lutheran Reformation took place appears very different from the religiously and culturally diverse society of contemporary America. For example, sixteenth-century Germany knew religious diversity (Catholics, Protestants, and Jews) but tried to avoid it by mandating that subjects had to take the religion of their ruler. Given the fact that the Lutheran tradition grew up in a religiously homogeneous society, it is sometimes questioned whether and how it can deal with a diverse society. Can that tradition lead Lutherans today to tolerate, appreciate, and even work with those with whom it does not agree in matters of faith?

Luther and the Lutheran Confessions provided a framework for tolerance that went far beyond the actual practice of sixteenth-century Lutheran lands. The doctrine of the twofold reign of God provides a basis for civil tolerance that admittedly was not always carried out in Lutheran lands. As detailed above, the recognition that church and state have different jobs allows the state to be "non-Christian" and still do its job. Similarly, the high but limited valuation of human reason and civil righteousness mean a non-Christian neighbor may be valued for these qualities. We can even see God at work in these qualities of our non-Christian neighbors. Further, the doctrine of creation enables us to see all humans as God's creations. Because God creates and sustains all humans, every human has worth. God protects all people with his commandments. The structures (orders) of creation provide a place for each human. Thus every human has a God-given place, and the daily life and work of the Christian are not inherently more valuable than those of the non-Christian. The Lutheran perspective provides a framework for tolerance and appreciation of the non-Christian neighbor.

Though we usually do not think of the sixteenth century as a tolerant century, the possibilities for tolerance in Lutheran belief made their impact even then. Luther condemned the idea that Christians should not be allowed to marry non-Christians.[41] He commented favorably on non-Christian rulers. Unfortunately, Luther is also known for his intolerant attitude toward the Jews.[42]

A general assumption in the sixteenth century was that a certain common core of beliefs was necessary for social cohesion. One expression of this was the belief that religious uniformity was necessary for social order and cohesion. Lutherans were no different from other Christians in this regard. The sixteenth century had a greater fear of disorder than of order; contemporary American society tends to fear anything that seems to impose too much order. Given these differences in perspective, it is not surprising that sixteenth-century societies had less tolerance than we consider desirable. The fact that the possibilities for tolerance in the Lutheran heritage were generally not realized in the sixteenth century should not discourage us from thinking about them today.

Our heritage, however, does not allow us to forget that tolerance has its limits. Given Lutheran concern for the neighbor as expressed in the concrete commands of the law, it is appropriate to ask how much tolerance is tolerable. Can a society tolerate diversity to such an extent that it overthrows the perspective that is the basis for tolerance? What about a view that no longer sees some people as created by God and therefore as persons of worth deserving of protection, but rather sees these people as subhuman? What if this becomes the dominant view in a society? This has happened in our century in the name of Marxist and Nazi ideologies. The Lutheran understanding of law allows us to see that the law sets some limits on tolerance—love for the neighbor may mean that Christians should not tolerate some ideologies and movements but rather oppose them actively.

But here an objection may be raised. When individual Christians advocate for laws or social policies today, are they trying to impose their beliefs on society? Are they trying to "christianize" society? Is the church through its preaching of the law trying to "christianize" society? Once again the Lutheran distinctions between law and gospel and between the two reigns of God are helpful. As explained above, Lutherans believe that there is a fundamental law that is common to and beneficial to all creation. One expression of this law is the Ten Commandments. Its second table (commandments four through ten) is particularly applicable in the civil realm. Civil government is charged with upholding this law and thereby preserving and enhancing the life of its citizens.

When the church (within the framework set forth earlier) preaches and teaches the law, debates its content, and advocates its application, it is thus not attempting to christianize society. Similarly when individual Christians advocate for specific policies based on their own understanding of the law, they are not trying to christianize society. Only the preaching of the gospel makes Christians! As the universal law is accessible to all humans, Lutherans can join with non-Christians in learning, debating, and implementing that law. The law is an attempt both to prescribe and reflect the common values of a society; it is not an attempt to impose uniquely Lutheran or Christian values.[43] Lutherans are always aware that any attempt to impose on government or society what is uniquely Christian would turn the gospel into law and thus would destroy the Christian message. Further, Lutherans are aware that an attempt to make the gospel govern the secular realm would fail, for in this world the law is still needed to curb the power of sin and to organize the vast diversity of humankind for the mutual fulfillment of life in its temporal and physical aspects.

Conclusion

The relationship between church and state is one expression of the relationship between God's two ways of governing the world, the spiritual and the temporal realms. As such it is an inevitable relationship, one that will not end until God sets an end to this world. The perspective expressed in the Lutheran Confessions gives us a creative and realistic way of dealing with this relationship.

2

Toward a Lutheran "Delight in the Law of the Lord": Church and State in the Context of Civil Society

Gary M. Simpson

> Blessed are those who do not follow the advice of the wicked,
> or take the path that sinners tread,
> or sit in the seat of scoffers;
> but their delight is in the law of the Lord,
> and on that law they meditate day and night.
> —Psalm 1:1-2

God has endowed the Evangelical Lutheran Church in America (ELCA) and its predecessor bodies with a half-century of trustworthy theological reflection on our topic. This chapter builds on that endowment. The ELCA Constitution attempts to encapsulate this heritage in its "Statement of Purpose." Among the many ways to participate in the triune God's mission, the ELCA commits itself to "[w]ork with civil authorities in areas of mutual endeavor, maintaining institutional separation of church and state in a relation of functional interaction."[1] This formulation provides the imaginative horizon for my investigation.

At the beginning of the third millennium, Lutherans in the United States can harvest their heritage in order to face newer challenges, like the emerging shifts in the nation-state and the renewed appreciation for the public sphere of civil society. In the first section, "Our Originating Confessions," I outline the contours of Lutheran confessional reflections on the neuralgic theme of God and political authority as one contribution toward a Lutheran "delight in the law of the Lord."[2] These confessional contours appear succinctly in Article 16 of the Augsburg Confession. The vehicle that effectively hands these confessional convictions on from generation to generation is

Martin Luther's Small Catechism and Large Catechism. Here are the bases for a Lutheran predilection toward *critical participation* in political authority.[3] In "Luther's Critical Theology of Political Authority, Accountability, and Resistance," I investigate more fully the development of Luther's own critical theological reflection on political authority. Along with certain well-known aspects of Luther's thought, I highlight the question of political resistance. Lutherans as well as others have often minimized or even ignored political resistance in Luther, thereby diminishing a Lutheran "delight in the law of the Lord." This fuller account of Luther's reflections can still generate a fruitful imagination for the contemporary relationship of church and state. In the third section, "The Nascent Heritage of Lutheran Resistance Today," I explore the rise of Lutheran resistance theory as one factor in the growth of Western political thinking and institutional structure. In "The State, Civil Society, and Congregations as Public Companions," I (1) describe briefly how civil society emerges in Western civilization and contributes to more democratic forms of the state; (2) suggest how civil society "delights in the law of the Lord" and, thus, critically participates in the triune God's ongoing work of creating the world through political authority; and (3) propose how the church and particularly congregations of the church might imagine themselves as civil society companions and, in this way, can engage God's creative activity.

Our Originating Confessions

The Augsburg Confession

Article 16 of the Augsburg Confession (hereafter abbreviated as *CA* XVI, from the Latin *Confessio Augustana*) and the Fourth Commandment of Luther's Small Catechism and Large Catechism stand as the classic Lutheran confessional sources for subsequent Lutheran theological reflection on the nature of political authority in relation to divine agency exercised as law.[4] The simple, basic question that *CA* XVI addresses is whether Christians can occupy political offices of various sorts, or even make use of any civil laws whatsoever, without such activity being per se ungodly and sinful. This question arose because some forms of Anabaptist theological reflection, virulently anti-papist, and claiming Luther's theology as their inspiration, considered such political-civil participation to be by its very nature totally under satanic rule. For such Anabaptists, political authority and divine agency are incompatible and, indeed, antithetical agencies. Jesus' injunction in the Sermon on the Mount means, according to these Anabaptists, that God works only through those who do not use the sword in order to resist evil. This theological conviction forbids any Christian in political authority from bearing the sword. The confessors at Augsburg distinguished themselves from that kind of theology.

In *CA* XVI, the Augsburg confessors also distinguished themselves from the medieval Christian monasticism then dominant. This monasticism insisted that progress toward Christian moral perfection happens most fully in a life lived outside of the more ordinary, everyday modes of marriage, family, and civil-political communities.[5] *CA* XVI, by distinguishing itself from the theology and practice of medieval monastic perfection, with its proximity to "works righteousness," shows how close its spirit is to the Augsburg Confession's fundamental testimony of justification by faith alone. *CA* XVI employs a five-fold strategy in order to reform catholic Christianity in the field of political authority.[6]

The confessors' assertion that Christians can "licitly" and "without sin" hold political offices, participate in political affairs, and use civil laws rests on their primary truth claim that such offices and activities "were created and instituted by God" (the German text of *CA* XVI). The Latin text of *CA* XVI produces an even brisker tone by denoting these civil-political activities as themselves "good works of God" (Latin: *bona opera Dei*). As I explore in more depth below, Romans 13, along with other texts, presents the biblical reason for the confessors' claim. This claim supplies the participationist predilection to our confessional heritage precisely because God, as an active agent, joins in the work of political authority. Later I expand on this participationist heritage, most prominently by retrieving its "critical" dynamic. Rightfully, we can describe our heritage as "critical participationist."[7]

In some highly secularized arenas today, speech that is rooted in any claim whatsoever about the conjunction of divine agency and political life appears quite outlandish. This does not happen only in the academy. Ordinary Christian congregations hesitate to correlate civil affairs and divine action, in order to guard against particular political decisions as unequivocally and unquestionably identifying God's will. But total silence amounts to mere agnosticism, if not atheism. When people break the silence, they regularly do so in one of three ways. In the first way—often denoted as "liberal"—the relationship between civil-political affairs and God's action remains under the influence of generic deism. In this scenario divine agency remains confined to the original creation of the institution of government in a far distant past. Since that time, way back when, the activity of God in political affairs seems to be on a perpetual sabbatical. According to this deistic confinement of divine agency, all ongoing, present-day political agency remains always and only human agency. At most the deity perhaps affects the intentions, motivations, abstract principles, or general vision of human agents through specifically "religious" means. In the second—"theocratic"—way, people imagine that God operates primarily or even exclusively by way of explicit, "born again" Christian agents. Political affairs as good works of God depend on the election and participation of a critical mass of Christians in control of such affairs. This theocratic view can undergird a spectrum of agendas ranging from the "right" to the "left," and its roots in the United States go back to one type of Calvinist Puritan. In the third way—often denoted as "fundamentalist"—people recognize that God acts in civil-political realities principally in the contemporary legal encoding of particular and precise biblical injunctions, which are themselves inerrant and immutable. Sometimes the second and third ways intertwine.[8] *CA* XVI supplies a theological imagination different not only from Anabaptist sectarianism, monastic perfectionism, and modern secularism in its atheistic extremities but also from the three popular contemporary proposals. The fruitfulness of *CA* XVI's claim regarding civil-political affairs depends on the constellation of four additional aspects of its theological strategy.

The second strategy in *CA* XVI is to group political-governmental affairs alongside other types of activity less strictly understood as governmental-political, like buying and selling, owning property, being married, or raising children. In this way the confessors recognize that these diverse activities and institutions share the common feature that they are all *bona opera Dei*. It is significant that the proclamation of the gospel, the administration of the sacraments, and the office of the keys are not activities grouped among *CA* XVI's *bona opera Dei*, though certainly the gospel and sacraments are "good works of God." The point of this deliberate omission is that the gospel and sacraments are "redemptive" works of God.[9] By bundling the *bona opera Dei* of governing, buying and selling, and marrying, the confessors intentionally claim that these activities embody in an exemplary way God's continuing "creational" agency in and for the temporal world and its flourishing. To norm these relationships and activities by the civil use of God's law is, quite emphatically, to delight in the law of the Lord for creational purposes. More vividly still, Article 16 of the Apology of the Augsburg Confession bundles political-governmental affairs together with medicine and architecture, food and drink, even "air," as God's ongoing creational activity. All these affairs are "God's good creatures and divine ordinances" *[bonae creaturae Dei et ordinationes divinae]* comparable in this sense to the change of seasons as creational "divine ordinances" (*BC* 232.6).[10] I return to this theme in section two in examining Luther's critical theology of political authority.

Another, latent implication of this second strategy now emerges. The activities, institutions, and orders[11] other than political-governmental affairs also possess a distinct integrity. Each has its own integrity because each embodies God's ongoing creational activity of temporal earthly life. Stated negatively, and perhaps more provocatively, the confessors do not make the integrity of these other orders of God's creational agency necessarily dependent on a hierarchical subjection of them under the more narrowly defined sphere of political affairs and governmental agency. On the other hand, *CA* XVI does not offer an explicit theological warrant prohibiting such a hierarchical arrangement. This otherwise significant issue simply was not a question during the Diet of Augsburg in 1530. Historically, Lutherans have rightfully highlighted the "creational" significance of this second strategy in distinction from redemption and sanctification. However, Lutherans have not usually focused vigorously on the more latent "integrity" implication. At certain times and places, some Lutherans have so neglected the distinct "integrity" of the nongovernmental, nonpolitical orders that they have wrongly claimed a confessional rationale for political absolutism.[12] The constructive significance of this "integrity" implication will surface in sections two and three below in relation to political accountability and resistance in Luther and his theological heirs, and in section four in relation to the emergence and character of "civil society" and its significance for political accountability. By highlighting the concept of integrity, we place political authority within a constellation of integrity of God's active civil use of the law for continually creating a thriving world. In this way the constellation as a whole and each integral part renders delight in the law of the Lord.

As its third theological strategy, *CA* XVI prominently displays the so-called "Peter's clause"—*clausula Petri*—Acts 5:29: "But if a command of the political authority cannot be followed without sin, one must obey God rather than any human beings (Acts 5 [:29])" (*BC* 50.7). In this way, the confessors boldly reintroduce the reality of sin and evil within the arena of governmental rule, having already clarified that sin and evil do not constitute the essence of the political. On the contrary, sin and evil represent the antithesis to civil-political agency since political agency is rooted in the activity of God. As infiltrating, alien agents, sin and evil take up residence in a domicile constituted properly by God's creational agency and, indeed, become the true resident aliens. With the *clausula Petri*, the confessors acknowledge creational realities as contested terrain. The *clausula Petri* embodies the biblical warrant for the critical dynamic within our participationist heritage. This warrant also propels us to investigate critical competencies and criteria as we will in Luther's critical theology of political authority.

CA XVI's fourth strategy is to testify that the triune God initiates two ways to contest for the contested creation. The confessors most often employ the biblical notions of "law" and "gospel" (or "promise") as fundamental categories that encapsulate two distinguishable modes of divine agency whereby the triune God rules the world. The meaning and validity of these two terms as theological categories remain, of course, a lively interpretive conversation far beyond the scope of our brief inquiry. Nevertheless, the ELCA formulation of "institutional separation of church and state in a relationship of functional interaction" remains a valid implication and outgrowth—though not at all an equivalence!—of the Augsburg Confession's hermeneutical distinction of law and gospel as that hermeneutic takes linguistic form in *CA* XVI.[13] There exists a unique, constitutional integrity of political authority and "state" grounded in God's law and a unique, constitutional integrity of the church grounded in the proclamation of the gospel and the administration of the sacraments according to the gospel. The distinction between law and gospel, however, can in no way be reduced to the constitutional integrity of state and church. The constitutional integrity of political authority and "state" in God's law means that "[t]he Gospel does not overthrow [Latin: 'undermine'] secular government, public order, and marriage" (*BC* 49-50.5), as some sectarian Anabaptists had claimed. "Neither does the gospel introduce new laws for the civic realm" (*BC* 231.3), whether such laws be the particular judicial laws of Moses as Andreas Carlstadt and others had asserted or the so-called "evangelical counsels of perfection" of Jesus' Sermon on the Mount, as the dominant medieval monastics had argued. The church's unique integrity means that, through the Holy Spirit's public media of word and sacrament, a congregated people is constituted with a righteousness in Christ—"alien righteousness"—appropriate for eternal salvation, which issues in the Spirit's fruit of love and good works through a plurality of vocations of life. What the law uniquely constitutes is a righteousness normatively appropriate for temporal civil existence along the entire breadth of creational orders and institutions.[14] Such constitutional integrity of both creational orders and the church remains the inspiration for the ELCA's "institutional separation" formulation.[15]

By means of the basic hermeneutical distinction of law and promise, the confessors testify that the gospel in its proper relation to the law and creational realities "requires [Apology 16 has 'approves'] that all these [civil authority, the state, and marriage] be kept [Latin: 'requires their preservation'] as true orders of God" (*BC* 38.5). The confessors do not use words like "requires," "intends," and "approves" in the sense that the gospel adds additional legal binding. That would contradict the very reason why the confessors articulate the gospel as God's unconditional promise in Christ Jesus. God's law embodies sufficient binding authority just because it is God's. Rather, "requires," "intends," and "approves" are employed because these are grammatically emphatic words, particularly in Latin. Properly interpreted, the confessors are noting that the gospel fiercely acknowledges as appropriate, true, and binding what God's law already requires and approves, namely, that political authority, the state, marriage, and so on, be kept and cultivated as true orders of God's creative agency rather than institutions of Satan's agency.[16] It is precisely at this point, at the gospel's emphatic acknowledgment of the triune God's wide creational agency, including political rule, that the ELCA's formulation of "functional interaction" finds its initial justification as a Christian, evangelical predilection rather than as a sinful or demonic deviation from evangelical identity and integrity.[17] The Lutheran practice of testifying to this biblical imagination is itself an ongoing "delight in the law of the Lord."

The final aspect of *CA* XVI's theological strategy now emerges. These civil-political *bona opera Dei* are suitable, eminently suitable, as Christian vocational terrain. The confessors eagerly acknowledge all God's creational orders and any corresponding station in life as locations and agencies in which the triune God calls Christians in each one's own unique particularity and individuality—"according to each person's calling" (*BC* 50.5)—to love publicly and privately the neighbor with genuine good works. This is the justification for the confessors' strenuous critique of medieval monastic perfectionism. No wonder that contemporary philosopher Charles Taylor extols the confessors' theological reflections on Christian vocation as a "new radical reevaluation of ordinary life."[18] This fresh retrieval of public love instituted in Christian vocation stands among the most prominent Lutheran contributions to the general "delight in the law of the Lord" since the sixteenth century.

This culmination of *CA* XVI's theological strategy in the doctrine of vocation permits us to view *CA* XXIII and XXVII as well as Articles VI and XX as companion articles of 16. In light of these companion articles, the confessors' doctrine of Christian vocation means not only that creational terrain is sacred terrain and thus the location for true love, both public and private, but also that, in the gospel, God in Christ through the Spirit both constitutes our eternal righteousness in faith alone and quickens our temporal righteousness, our time-bound loving of the created world.[19] It is with the confessors' doctrine and practice of Christian vocation that the highly dynamic and dialectical interface between the triune God's Word of law and gospel, God's two basic modes of divine agency, surfaces most energetically.

Another aspect of *CA* XVI's vocational strategy merits notice. Only after locating Christian vocation within the triune God's creational orders as the ordinary apex of love does *CA* XVI take up the twin notions of subjection to political authority and obedience to its commands and laws. That is, such subjection and obedience are a derivative subset of public love and not the other way around. The fullest range of love, a manifold of good works, has an integrity of its own, because the broad range of loving good works issues first of all from God's own creating, preserving, and governing activities. Like God's own legislative-governing agency, political rule, and thus obedience, always and only rightly serves a more encompassing, primordial purpose, that is, God's gifting of temporal life.

Luther's Catechisms

Luther builds into the very structure of his catechisms the hermeneutical distinction between law and gospel that we saw embodied in *CA* XVI. That is, he begins his catechisms with the Ten Commandments as a brief epitome of the law and follows them with the Apostles' Creed as the story of the persons of the triune God of both law and gospel. For our purposes the Fourth Commandment is crucial, because here Luther locates political authority. None of the Ten Commandments explicitly thematizes political authority. Luther, of course, knows this. Still, because he is addressing sixteenth-century children and lay adults with little theological wisdom, he employs the Ten Commandments as a ready, theological shorthand to survey the whole compass of everyday temporal life as it relates to God's law.

In Luther's mind the sweep of the Fourth Commandment comes closest to the lived reality of political authority. The forms of political authority in Luther's day—at least as perceived from the popular, nonjuristic point of view that Luther adopts in the catechisms—seem to reflect the hierarchical nature of parental authority, "this [parental] sort of inequality" (BC 405.141). Luther claims, therefore: "For all other authority is derived and developed out of the authority of parents" (BC 384.141). This notion, of course, colors his 1520s understanding of the character and shape of political authority. In this sense he is, during the 1520s, quite conventional and conservative with regard to the hierarchical nature of political authority. This 1520s viewpoint, then, is one of the notable factors for why Luther places political authority within the orbit of the Fourth Commandment.

Now we can specify a second, less obvious but in fact more noteworthy reason for placing political authority within the field of the Fourth Commandment. Luther sees a special *theological* weightiness in the Fourth Commandment's demand of "honor." The Fourth Commandment is not first of all about children's "obedience" to their parents, especially in Luther's treatment in the Large Catechism. Obedience certainly has its place. However, the Fourth Commandment is principally about the "estate," the institution and office, of "parenthood." In the demand of "honor," Luther recognizes that God creates an office of parenthood possessing a "special position of honor" (BC 400.105). Parenthood resides "above all estates." That is, parenthood exists "next to" God. Honor, as Luther notes, is the subject matter of the first table of the Decalogue dealing with the relationship of humanity with God. In this way the Fourth Commandment's "honor demand" directs our attention toward a divine "majesty concealed within" parenthood. Parenthood functions preeminently, therefore, as God's "mask" through which God's ongoing creating of the social world takes place.[20] This is why, in Luther's words, we can consider parenthood "the most precious treasure on earth" (BC 401.109). People in the office of parenthood serve as "God's representatives . . . however lowly, poor, feeble, and eccentric they may be" (BC 379.108). The "honor demand" is the Fourth Commandment's way to identify parenthood as the first office through which God continually creates human society. Further, the "honor demand" testifies to God's general "agential immanence"—to say it in a clumsy way—in social time and space. Finally, the "honor demand" also bears witness to God's dependable and sustaining faithfulness to the office of parenthood and thus contributes to a durable "delight in the law of the Lord."

Already in his exposition of the First Commandment, Luther notes a crucial characteristic of the true God's creational agency. God ordinarily works in the world to create temporal, social life and to continue to create, preserve, and govern that life not immediately—that is, not without sociohistorical and natural media—but rather mediately. God's preferred mode of working is to employ ordinary, everyday, concrete, social and natural means in order to "lavish . . . richly" God's creational treasury and banquet upon all creation (*BC* 388.15).

> Although much that is good comes to us from human beings, nevertheless, anything received according to his command and ordinance in fact comes from God. Our parents and all authorities—as well as everyone who is a neighbor—have received the command to do us all kinds of good. So we receive our blessings not from them, but from God through them. Creatures are only the hands, channels, and means through which God bestows all blessings. For example, he gives to the mother breasts and milk for her infant or gives grain and all sorts of fruits from the earth for sustenance—things that no creature could produce by itself. No one, therefore, should presume to take or give anything unless God has commanded it. This forces us to recognize God's gifts and give him thanks, as this commandment requires. Therefore, we should not spurn even this way of receiving such things through God's creatures, nor are we through arrogance to seek other methods and ways than those God has commanded. For that would not be receiving them from God, but seeking them from ourselves. (*BC* 389.26–27)

In the Fourth Commandment's "honor demand" Luther discerns the Decalogue's way to recognize, elevate, and extend "this way of receiving through God's creatures." This applies to parenthood, to neighborhood, and to political authority, indeed, to all God's creational orders, institutions, and offices. The triune God employs these with the precise purpose that temporal life might thrive, and, therefore, rewards the honoring of "this way of receiving through God's creatures" with such thriving. Note the joy that Luther cites.

> Here you have the fruit and the reward, that whoever keeps this commandment will enjoy good days, happiness, and prosperity. On the other hand, the penalty for those who disobey it is that they will die earlier and will not be happy in life. For, in the Scriptures, to have a long life means not merely to grow old but to have everything that belongs to life—for example, health, spouse and children, sustenance, peace, good government, etc., without which this life cannot be enjoyed nor will it long endure. (*BC* 404–5.5.134)

While "honor" means first of all discerning "the majesty concealed within," it also means supporting and caring quite materially for these offices and for those serving in these offices. Because these orders, institutions, and offices are not easily expendable, they embody a considerable enduring quality about them. With reference to parenthood, for instance, Luther observes that if we did not have biological parents, then we would have to petition God for some sort of surrogate, even if of "wood" or "stone" (*BC* 403.125). Granted that important benefits emerge from the durability of these orders, institutions, and offices of God's creational agency, we must also inquire into Luther's reflections about the accountability and reformability of them and even about the possibility of quite revolutionary change. I take up this line of inquiry below.

Luther's theological discernment of the "majesty concealed within" parenthood leads, then, to an ethical corollary. Because parenthood is the triune God's own office, those who fill the office do so always with reference to "God, who holds you accountable for it" (*BC* 409.169). People ought never to exercise this divine office merely in whatever way they wish. Knavery and tyranny clearly contradict God's concurring creational agency. The parental office—and political authority by extension—is not principally about "homage" for parents or about conveniently putting children "to work like cows or donkeys," or about the "pleasure," "whim," or "amusement" of parents (*BC* 409.167–70). Rather, the parental office must "devote serious attention" toward the children and household servants, toward "what they learn or how they live" along three dimensions: material, civil, and spiritual (*BC* 388.171-175). This all pertains equally to the office of political authority, for the civil dimension needs "good, capable citizens" (*BC* 389.175).[21] I will now explore more deeply Luther's critical theological reflections on the character of the office of political authority. In doing so, I attend to show how in Luther's developing reflection the triune God holds political officeholders and, indeed, the office itself, accountable.

Luther's Critical Theology of Political Authority, Accountability, and Resistance

Like *CA* XVI, Luther's theology of political authority stands as a critical alternative both to the medieval heritage of papal political theology with its correlate of monastic perfectionism and to the emerging sectarian proposal of some Anabaptists. I will investigate (1) three basic themes of Luther's critical theology of political authority and (2) the development of Luther's thought on the question of resistance to the emperor. The three basic themes are (a) the divine constitution and agency of political authority and the specific question of the sword, (b) a critical "limit" and criterion of political authority, and (c) the conundrum of the accountability of political authority.

The Basics of Luther's Critical Theology of Temporal Authority

Constitution, Agency, and the "Sword"

Luther's critical theology of political authority emerges over the full course of his life. Many, though not all, of its basic features are already in place in his 1523 well-known treatise "Temporal Authority: To What Extent It Should Be Obeyed." Often interpreters of Luther, however, portray his account of law and political authority too reductionistically, taking account only of Luther's Augustinian accent on political authority as a remedy and dike against sin *(remedium peccati)*. They tend to interpret this 1523 treatise too abstractly, as if the 1523 context for his theological reflection about law and political authority did not exist. They succumbed to this temptation because Luther does indeed employ his comprehensive, remarkably enduring, and fruitful distinction between the triune God's two ways of ruling the world—often referred to as Luther's two-kingdoms teaching. Nevertheless, readers will gain better insights into Luther's understanding of political authority as well as the fruitfulness of his two-kingdoms teaching if they enter the "situated" door through which Luther invites them.[22]

Luther prefaces his treatise with a letter addressed to his soon-to-be prince, John the Steadfast. John had inquired of Luther whether he could exercise the full range of powers of the princely office with a good Christian conscience now that he had become an ardent defender of the evangelical cause. John was concerned about the power of "the sword," that particular, coercive power of last resort belonging in an exceptional way to political authority. "Temporal Authority" is Luther's theological reply to this situated request.[23] Some Anabaptist sectarians were perturbing John with certain Bible passages from Jesus' Sermon on the Mount, like "do not resist an evildoer"; from Paul's Epistle to the Romans, like "never avenge yourselves . . . vengeance is mine, I will repay, says the Lord"; and from Peter's epistle, like "do not repay evil for evil." These texts, claimed the sectarians, preclude without exception any true Christian, including those Christians occupying the office of prince, from bearing "the sword" (*LW* 45:81; also *LW* 45:87).

Luther must also deal with the normative medieval interpretation of passages like those from the Sermon on the Mount. According to that interpretation, a prince could bear "the sword" and remain a Christian in good conscience because these Sermon on the Mount passages were Jesus' "counsels" spoken only to those who were specially dedicated to "Christian perfection," a perfection that could be pursued only within the "religious vocation" of the monastery or sacerdotal priesthood. Accordingly, princes need not be held accountable to such high "counsels of perfection" since they, being lay Christians, remained "common" Christians. Luther will have nothing of such scholastic interpretive "wantonness and caprice." Among Christians there exists no external "class" distinction between perfect and common based on status markers like "outwardly male or female, prince or peasant, monk or layman" (*LW* 45:88). Here, Luther's doctrine of vocation comes into play. Passages like those from the Sermon on the Mount "apply to everyone alike" (*LW* 45:88). Part one of "Temporal Authority" represents Luther's critical theological reflection on the power of the sword of political authority in relation to the Christian life.

A second historical factor situates Luther's reflections. In Luther's earlier 1520 treatise, "To the Christian Nobility of the German Nation," he had appealed to the Christian nobility as lay people of the church to take the reform of the church into their own hands since the bishops had not. Luther noted that the political authority of rulers was not delegated to them hierarchically from the church and its bishops, as the dominant heritage of papal political theology often held. His provocative assessment of political authority left many wondering whether, by so emancipating political authority from the church, he had ascribed unlimited, totalitarian powers to political authority. Could princes, with legitimate authority, command as God's will "whatever they please"? And correspondingly, are the princes' subjects "bound to obey their rulers in everything" as they would be so bound to obey God's will (*LW* 45:83)? Luther addresses this situated question in part two of "Temporal Authority." In "the main part of this treatise," he stakes out the extent and limits of political authority and its power of the sword, which he considers (*LW* 45:104). In this way the treatise's subtitle remains significant: "To What Extent It Should Be Obeyed!" In part three Luther offers his own practical advice concerning the use of the prince's office in a Christian manner. Luther's remarks here bear the stamp of a layperson's political imagination, as he himself acknowledges, though, even here, we might meet some surprises.

Luther initiates his inquiry in part one by citing Rom. 13:1-2 and 1 Pet. 2:13-14. These texts clearly authenticate the constitution of political authority's obligation of "the sword" as "a godly estate" (*LW* 45:87) and thereby testify that God's agency accompanies "the law of this temporal sword" (*LW* 45:86). Luther argues that Gen. 4:14-15 and Gen. 9:6 strengthen the first two texts by emphasizing that the law of the political sword has "existed from the beginning of the world," of course after the Fall. God has found ways to inscribe this law into human community from the beginning of time, even though, Luther notes, communities have also found ways to have this divine work of the sword "not carried out." Exodus 21:14 and 21:23-25—the famous *lex talionis*—certify that Moses "confirmed" this inscribed-from-the-beginning law of the political sword. Matthew 26:52 and Luke 3:14 attest that Jesus and John the Baptist both "confirm" this inscribed-from-the-beginning law. Luther's conclusion: "Hence, it is certain and clear enough that it is God's will that the temporal sword and law be used for the punishment of the wicked and the protection of the upright" (*LW* 45:87). First Peter 2:14 (*LW* 45:86) and Rom. 13:3 (*LW* 45:91) warrant preventing wickedness and promoting uprightness as the twofold criterion of God's constituting will regarding the full range of political authority including its power of "the sword."

Luther perceives that God could and has employed a variety of possible forms of government for the purpose of preventing and punishing wickedness and protecting and promoting uprightness. He does not, in this treatise or anywhere, compare and contrast the possible forms of government with the aim of assessing which form might better conform to and thus participate in God's will and constitution of political authority against wickedness and for uprightness.[24] However, as I clarify below, a totalitarianism over the religious conscience lies outside the definitional bounds of divinely constituted political authority. Political authority stands among the orders, institutions, and offices of the triune God's creative work of bestowing and contesting for temporal life. This means that God wills to place the everyday temporal needs of subjects or citizens as the particular burden of every possible form and office of political authority.

Luther argues that God constitutes the full horizon of the first use of the law in general, and political authority with its coercive sword in the situated case before him, because of the circumstances of humanity. Humanity is composed of both righteous Christians and the unrighteous. Righteous Christians hear and trust the voice of Christ and, thus, the Holy Spirit of Christ himself works through their agency, directing it for the doing of right and bearing of wrong. By the Spirit, therefore, righteous Christians "do of their own accord much more than all laws and teachings can demand, just as Paul says in 1 Tim. 1[:9], 'The law is not laid down for the just but for the lawless'" (*LW* 45:89). Throughout Luther's career, 1 Timothy 1 is a hermeneutically significant text.[25] Accordingly, God constitutes the law not with such righteous Christians in view. Of course, Luther always keenly recognizes that many baptized Christians are so in name only and thus waste the Holy Spirit's agency for lives of vocationally loving their neighbors. "Christians are few and far between (as the saying is)" (*LW* 45:91). Luther numbers such false Christians among the unrighteous. The unrighteous, readily in the majority by Luther's calculus, live without the Spirit of Christ as the core agent of their lives and, thus, "need the law to instruct, constrain, and compel them to do good" (*LW* 45:89).[26] Indeed, these are key reasons why God constitutes the law in its first, political or civil, use. God institutes this first use of the law in order both to generate and to preserve a basic floor of justice (see below) as well as to promote and nurture the continued flourishing of temporal, creational life.[27]

At times, Luther summarizes this broadly construed understanding of the law's civil use, especially when he is situationally focusing on political authority with its coercive element of "the sword," as the placing of the "sinful and wicked" "under restraint so they dare not willfully implement their wickedness in actual deeds" (*LW* 45:90). Nevertheless, summaries like this do not imply that he maintains *only* a restraining conceptualization of the full horizon of the law's civil use or of political authority. We are reminded again of Luther's symbol of the "bread loaf" with its more socially generative connotations. That interpreters misconstrue him on this point is detrimental to the ongoing, lively use of his heritage of interpretation on this important matter. Still, make no mistake about it, Luther does strenuously highlight the restraining element of "the sword" within the total panorama of the triune God's civil use of the law because, quite frankly, there exist "few true believers and still fewer who live a Christian life" (*LW* 45:90). He remains a wide-eyed realist about sin and evil. Equally he remains a wide-eyed realist about the triune God's creational resolve to contest against sin and evil for the sake of creation! "For this reason God has provided them [the unrighteous] a different government beyond the Christian estate and kingdom of God. He has subjected them to the sword so that, even though they would like to, they are unable to practice their wickedness, and if they do practice it they cannot do so without fear or with success and impunity" (*LW* 45:90).

Luther's realism about sin and evil leads him to reflect on possible relationships of power wherein the "wolves, lions, [and] eagles"—the hoarders and inhibitors of God's temporal, creational banquet—would simply "devour" (*LW* 45:91, 92) the "sheep"—the most vulnerable among us and all of us in our vulnerabilities. If such a lax situation, devoid of boundaries, would persist, temporal life and flourishing would eventually be "reduced to chaos" (*LW* 45:91).[28] Because God is always mindful of oppressive and violent wickedness, argues Luther, the triune God constitutes two modes of governing the world, each with its own integrity with regard to divine purpose and power: "the spiritual, by which the Holy Spirit produces Christians and righteous people under Christ; and the temporal, which restrains the un-Christian and wicked so that—no thanks to them—they are obliged to keep still and to maintain an outward peace" (*LW* 45:91).

Luther's view of the integrity that political authority has, because of its constituting origin and ongoing basis in God's creation and law, critically distinguishes his theological reflection from the then dominant papal theology of political authority. Furthermore, given the divinely constituted integrity of both governments, "it is out of the question" that Christians should attempt to govern the whole world or even a single country by the kind of non-coercive, free and freeing spiritual governance of the gospel (*LW* 45:91, 93, 107–8). For this reason he recognizes a special Christian vocation to "carefully distinguish between these two governments. Both must be permitted to remain; the one to produce righteousness, the other to bring about external peace and prevent evil deeds. Neither one is sufficient in the world without the other" (*LW* 45:92).

Readied with this "both" kingdoms hermeneutic, Luther turns to the significance of Jesus' Sermon on the Mount injunctions. Christians are to have no recourse to the law or to political authority's sword in two types of circumstances: "among themselves" (*LW* 45:92, 94) and "by and for themselves" (*LW* 45:94). First, within the Christian community, we are not to seek recourse in the law or political authority's coercive sword. Second, Christians have no need for political authority's sword if what is at stake is only their own well-being (*LW* 45:95). The second circumstance flows from another basic distinction in Luther's construal of the relationship of Christians to the sword as well as to the full horizon of political authority: the distinction between the self and the neighbor or the other.

> Since a true Christian lives and labors on earth not for himself alone but for his neighbor, he does by the very nature of his spirit even what he himself has no need of, but is needful and useful to his neighbor. Because the sword is most beneficial and necessary for the whole world in order to preserve peace, punish sin, and restrain the wicked, the Christian submits most willingly to the rule of the sword, pays his taxes, honors those in authority, serves, helps, and does all he can to assist governing authority, that it may continue to function and be held in honor and fear. Although he has no need of these things for himself—to him they are not essential—nevertheless, he concerns himself about what is serviceable and of benefit to others, as Paul teaches in Ephesians 5. (*LW* 45:94)[29]

Luther argues that these three sets of distinctions—between the triune God's two kingdoms, between within and without the Christian community, and between self and neighbor—bring "into harmony" the two sets of biblical texts that on the surface might appear contradictory. On the one hand, as Christians we do not with the sword resist evil either among ourselves or for our own survival or gain. On the other hand, as Christians we are authorized and, indeed, are "under obligation to serve and assist the sword by whatever means [we] can, with body, goods, honor, and soul" in order to resist evil when oppressors afflict our neighbors. "For it [the sword] is something which you do not need, but which is very beneficial and essential for the whole world and for your neighbor" and, indeed, "[t]he world cannot and dare not dispense with it" (*LW* 45:95). By so serving and assisting even the sword, argues Luther, "in what concerns the person or property of others, you govern yourself according to love and tolerate no injustice toward your neighbor" (*LW* 45:96).

Christians participate in the whole panoply of the civil use of the law as well as more narrowly in political authority, including its coercive and restraining sword, because these exist as God's own "work and creation" (*LW* 45:99). They exist as God's masks for creating and sustaining the temporal life of the world (*LW* 45:96–100). Because the triune God is the one who constitutes political authority as one crucial component of the civil use of the law, therefore God's very own continuing creational agency resides effectively in and through political authority.[30] By serving and assisting the sword, Christians participate in

God's creative agency. Luther often articulates this sense of ardent participation by commending "obedience" to temporal authority. Participatory "obedience" appropriately exists within God's overall constitution of political authority to be "for the neighbors' good." This constitution extends the great variety of offices that "arrest, prosecute, execute, and destroy the wicked and [that] protect, acquit, defend, and save the good" (*LW* 45:103). Finally, because political authority exists to serve the neighbors' good, Christians can even "use their office like anybody else would his trade, as a means of livelihood" (*LW* 45:103). With these basics, Luther set in motion a Christian participationist predilection in political authority. I turn now to his contention for the critical dynamics within this heritage, rooted in a specific limit and a crucial criterion.

A Limit and a Criterion of Justice
In part two of "Temporal Authority" Luther takes up the question of a "limit" of political authority. The limit that he examines is divinely circumscribed and therefore is indispensable. As divinely constituted, does political authority extend into the area of eternal life and salvation, of "the soul" (*LW* 45:105)? Does the triune God institute political authority in such a way that the authorities may "coerce the people with their laws and commandments into believing this or that"? Note, on the one hand, that in this treatise Luther does not inquire in any kind of disciplined manner whether there might be other kinds of limitations regarding political authority, limits that represent the distinctive marks of different forms of government. Such questions become the hallmarks of classic political liberalism during the modern era. On the other hand, he is addressing a situation with some similarity to what we today have come to call "religious liberty."[31]

Luther argues that the triune God constitutes political authority with "no power over souls" because "in matters which concern the salvation of souls nothing but God's word shall be taught and accepted" (*LW* 45:106). Furthermore, God does not endow political authority as such with competencies for God's word (*LW* 45:106-7). Matthew 16:18 and John 10:27 are decisive in this regard. Appropriate competencies are crucial. For example, a court of law must have competencies concerning arenas about which it renders judgment. "But the thoughts and inclinations of the soul can be known to no one but God. Therefore, it is futile and impossible to command or compel anyone by force to believe this or that. The matter must be approached in a different way. Force will not accomplish it" (*LW* 45:107). Because political authority does not possess competencies regarding "souls," it is counterproductive to employ the divinely endowed competencies that it does possess, among which is "the sword," in reference to belief in God. "For faith is a free act, to which no one can be forced. Indeed, it is a work of God in the spirit, not something which outward authority should compel or create. Hence arises the common saying, found also in Augustine, 'No one can or ought to be forced to believe'" (*LW*

45:108). God institutes political authority with competencies, including "the sword," delimited to the Second Table of the Decalogue, the "outward compliance of the mouth and the hand," but not with competencies and thus not with authority regarding the conscience, which has its moorings in the First Commandment.[32] He argues for this limit on political authority by expositing the words of Paul (Rom. 13:3, 7), Peter (1 Pet. 2:13), Jesus (Matt. 22:21), David (Ps. 115:16), and Moses (Gen. 1:26) and finds this biblical consensus poignantly consummated in the *clausula Petri* (Acts 5:29) (*LW* 45:110–11).

The most that political authority could accomplish, even if it would utilize contrary to God's will the law's full resources, would be "only [to] compel weak consciences to lie, to disavow, and to utter what is not in their hearts" (*LW* 45:108). But, compelling consciences to lie is "even worse" than allowing them to remain in the error of unbelief (*LW* 45:109). He notes therefore that the *clausula Petri*, by sanctioning a limit on obedience to political authority, also sanctions a limit on political authority itself. Christians should not obey the political authorities when these authorities trespass on "faith." "For I tell you, if you fail to withstand him, if you give in to him and let him take away your faith and your books, you have truly denied God" (*LW* 45:112). In other places Luther invokes the *clausula Petri* when a governing authority orders subjects clearly to contradict the second table of the Decalogue.[33] Still, justifiably disobeying a specific order does not imply a justification for the total disobedience of political authority. Violation of the bounds of temporal authority at one point, even a crucial one, does not necessarily abrogate the totality of political authority that a government can still exercise.[34]

Luther then takes up the objection of those who say that political rulers are not so much compelling faith as they are "simply seeing to it externally that no one deceives the people by false doctrine" (*LW* 45:114). He does not concede any competencies to political authority on this issue as Calvin would later on. Rather, Luther extends his argument regarding the constitutional incompatibility of force and faith to pertain to force and heresy. "Heresy can never be restrained by force. One will have to tackle the problem in some other way, for heresy must be opposed and dealt with otherwise than with the sword. Here God's word must do the fighting" (*LW* 45:114).[35] From the point of view of texts like 2 Cor. 10:4-5 and Isa. 11:4, contesting heresy remains a prerogative of the argumentative persuasiveness of God's word. Furthermore, notes Luther, the triune God entrusts these persuasive competencies of God's word especially to the office of bishop, not prince.

For Luther the utmost criterion for the exercise of political authority is justice. When considering the contents of justice, he regularly turns to the Second Table of the Decalogue as a ready, everyday template of moral matters. Even as he finds the Second Table of the Decalogue to be an enduring template of moral matters, he also finds these issues discussed and explicated frequently throughout Scripture, and often far beyond the precise construal the Decalogue itself gives. Furthermore, both the Decalogue and the Scripture's discussions and elaborations of the Decalogue's template of moral justice are instances of particular, contextually connected, natural law reasoning. That is, Luther argues—most often on the basis of Scripture itself—that the natural law of justice precedes and, therefore, grounds both the Decalogue as recorded in Scripture and the scriptural explications of the Decalogue's template of topics. For this reason he regularly appeals to the natural law of justice, often as inscribed in the Decalogue or the Golden Rule or the second great commandment, as the crucial criterion for the functioning, positive law of a political region. For instance, in the closing section of "Temporal Authority," he points out, though without detailed analysis, the intrinsic connections between justice, natural law, the Golden Rule, and the injunction to love your neighbor as yourself. Finally, he discusses the role that prudence and untrammeled practical reason have in the discernment and administration of justice and law.[36]

In Luther's "Commentary on Psalm 82" (1530), which reads like an essay on the virtuous prince, he notes that second only to the princely vocation to secure the free opportunity for the church to teach God's word is the princely vocation "to help the poor, the orphans, and the widows to justice and to further their cause" (*LW* 13:53). Hear the rhapsody in his words:

> In a word, after the Gospel or the ministry, there is on earth no better jewel, no greater treasure, nor richer alms, no fairer endowment, no finer possession than a ruler who makes and preserves just laws. Such men are rightly called gods [by the psalmist]. These are the virtues, the profit, the fruits, and the good works that God has appointed to this rank in life. It is not for nothing that He has called them gods; and it is not His will that it shall be a lazy, empty, idle estate, in which men seek only honor, power, luxury, selfish profit, and self-will. He would have them full of great, innumerable, unspeakable good works, so that they may be partakers of His divine majesty and help Him to do divine and superhuman works. (LW 13:53ff.)

The third of his three chief, princely virtues is "peacemaking." A more extensive discussion of his thinking on these issues lies beyond the scope of this inquiry.

The Conundrum of Accountability

Luther harbors no illusions about the willingness of political rulers to remain within the divinely constituted bounds of political authority regarding "faith." They often desire and "actually think they can do—and order their subjects to do—whatever they please" (*LW* 45:83; also *LW* 13:43). Luther argues that God remains "a Judge over all" political rulers when they exceed the constituted circumference of their authority in matters of faith. While "faith" remains beyond the boundary of political authority, basic "justice," as we have seen, remains a divinely willed criterion for the functioning of political authority. Consequently, God also holds political governance accountable for ruling according to justice. Divine accountability applies to violations of both the circumference and the criterion of political authority.

In "Temporal Authority" Luther notes that God is pouring out divine "contempt" on those rulers of his day who violate the "faith" limit of temporal authority. Here Luther invokes Ps. 107:40. Furthermore he points to "the common man" as the instrument of God's displeasure (*LW* 45:116). That common people are "learning to think" impresses him mightily. He depicts the type of thinking that they are acquiring as moral reflection about the public world of political rule. These newly acquired capacities of common people involve public moral reflection about "wantonness," that is, about the excesses that signal the difference between vice and virtue. Beyond this, however, these new capacities involve discerning "tyranny," quite specifically a politically oriented moral capacity. "Men will not, men cannot, men refuse to endure your tyranny and wantonness much longer. Dear princes and lords be wise and guide yourselves accordingly. God will no longer tolerate it. The world is no longer what it once was, when you hunted and drove the people like game" (*LW* 45:116). Still, to be sure, in the 1520s and into the 1530s, Luther never counseled rebellion either by the princes toward the emperor or by the masses toward the princes. "Nevertheless it is not His will to allow the rabble to raise their fist against the rulers or to seize the sword, as if to punish and judge the rulers. No, they must leave that alone! It is not God's will, and He has not committed this to them" (*LW* 13:45).

When in 1530 Luther inquires, "Where, then, is God?" in reference to the divine accountability of political authority, he argues that God establishes the "office" of "a preacher by whom God rebukes" political rulers. They are to exercise this "very wide admonitory power" of the preaching office "uprightly and honestly," "openly and boldly" (*LW* 13:49).[37] This admonitory duty of the preaching office is "not seditious," but is "on the contrary a praiseworthy, noble, and rare virtue, and a particularly great service to God" (*LW* 13:50). By publishing a treatise like "Temporal Authority," Luther is himself self-consciously exercising this admonitory power of divine accountability.

Luther perceives that on a world-historical scope the triune God on occasion employs other means for exercising divine accountability. These he calls "God's extraordinary leaders" (*LW* 13:154–75).[38] Sometimes these "extraordinary leaders" are themselves political rulers; often they are not. They have "a special star before God" and are not so much trained or made as "created" and taught directly by God. They possess a special endowment of "natural law and natural reason." God raises up "such jewels, when, where, and to whom He pleases" "not only among His own people but also among the godless and the heathen; and not only in the ranks of the nobility but also among the middle classes, farmers, and laborers."[39]

Luther sometimes identifies external enemies, who themselves do not necessarily practice a politics of justice, as a type of political accountability of last resort. The aggressive Turkish army under Suleiman the Magnificent was a contemporary instance. Because the Holy Roman Empire, including the German people, practiced injustice and persecuted the gospel, "the Turk . . . is God's rod and the devil's servant [Isa. 10:5]; there is no doubt about that" (*LW* 46:170; also *LW* 31:92). This seems to be a political equivalent to what Luther often observes: "God will, as is usual in these situations, use one rascal to punish the other" (*LW* 46:32, 41; also *BC* 398.245). Luther identifies these four ways in particular—the common people who are learning to think, the admonitory obligation of the office of preaching, extraordinary leaders, and external political enemies—by which God holds political authority accountable, thereby actualizing a critical dynamic within God's continuing creational agency of temporal, social life. There is therefore initial reason to perceive "the functional interaction" of church and state in Luther's thinking along the lines of a critical participationist predilection.

The social world of Luther's day was changing, most significantly, in that the common people's "regard" for political authority mattered—something of which he himself took note (*LW* 45:116). Such "regard," as we will see in section four below, would eventually become the crucial dynamic in the matter of political accountability and, in fact, would come to matter so focally and forcefully that the basic form of political authority would itself become quite new—a *novus ordo seclorum*, as the great seal of the United States of America puts it. Certainly this eventuality lay well beyond Luther's own political imagination.[40]

The Question of Armed Resistance

One remarkable step toward this coming new form of political accountability and authority took place during a controversy that began within Luther's lifetime and continued in the years shortly following his death in 1546. This controversy centered on the question of the right and duty of armed resistance to the emperor.[41] After the Edict of Worms in 1521, the Lutheran reformers continually faced the possibility that Emperor Charles V would intervene militarily to put a stop to the Reformation. Was it right for princes and imperial cities to form a military league to resist the emperor in defense of the gospel? Of course, there always existed different dimensions to the question: Was it *politically* wise? Was it *legally* constitutional? Was it *morally* and *theologically* right? Luther reflected on all three dimensions, although I will concentrate on the latter. Shortly after Luther's death, military intervention did in fact occur with the Schmalkald War of 1546.

Luther's thinking developed and his mind changed "slowly but radically," in three stages.[42] The period of 1515–1530 we might call "nonviolent, publicly rhetorical resistance." Typical is the following:

A prince should not go to war against his overlord-king, emperor, or other
liege lord—but let him who takes, take. For the governing authority must
not be resisted by force, but *only by confession of the truth*. If it is influenced
by this, well and good; if not, you are excused, you suffer wrong for God's
sake. If, however, the antagonist is your equal, your inferior, or of a foreign
government, you should first offer him justice and peace, as Moses taught
the children of Israel. If he refuses, then—mindful of what is best for
you—defend yourself against force by force, as Moses so well describes it
in Deuteronomy 20 [:10-12]. But in doing this you must not consider your
personal interests and how you may remain lord, but those of your subjects to whom you owe help and protection, that such action may proceed
in love. (*LW* 45:124–25; author's emphasis)

During this period Luther would evenhandedly apply this principle—
inferiors ought not wage war against their superiors—to princes, cities, and
peasants.

After the failure of the Diet of Augsburg of 1530 to recognize confessional
unity and thereby promote political unity within the empire, Luther's thinking shifted, though ever so slightly. The shift appears in the "Torgau Declaration" of October 1530, penned by Luther and joined in by Melanchthon and
others. As he always had in the past, Luther again firmly rejected any armed
resistance to the emperor on the basis of the natural law right of self-defense.
Now, however, he was convinced by Gregory Brück and other Saxon jurists
that the "governing authority's law itself grants" the right of armed resistance
under certain circumstances. This law should be obeyed if the extreme circumstances warranted in the law—atrocious injury *[atrox iniuria]* or notorious
injury *[notoria iniuria]*—come about.[43] With the "Torgau Declaration" the
practical issue of armed resistance became for Reformation theologians more
a matter of constitutional, positive law than of theological-moral reflection.
We could refer to this stage of reflection as "constitutionally delimited armed
resistance."

A clear break in the collective reflection of the Wittenberg theologians
appears on December 6, 1536. Elector John Frederick had asked Luther and
the Wittenberg theologians to give him an official opinion, first, about how
the Protestants should respond to the summons by Pope Paul III for a general
church council, and, second, given the possibility of an accompanying political crisis, about whether armed resistance was justifiable. They begin their theological reflections, penned by Melanchthon and joined in "unanimously" by
Luther and others, in their familiar way, by confessing that the gospel is a spiritual teaching that does not dictate laws regarding temporal government but
rather confirms just laws and values them highly. But then the Wittenberg theologians immediately follow up their familiar beginning with an innovative
conclusion: "Therefore it follows that the Gospel permits all natural and equitable protection and defense that is authorized by natural laws or else by tem-

poral government."[44] In the "Torgau Declaration" they had recognized the possibility of armed resistance on the basis of positive law. Now they acknowledge the validity of a natural law justification for armed resistance—*vim vi repellere licet*—which the "Torgau Declaration" had rejected. While Luther endorsed the natural law argument for armed resistance several times during these years, he never explicitly made use of this argument in his own writings.[45] Rather, he developed his own argument for resisting the emperor by claiming that the emperor was a "soldier of the pope" *[miles papae]* and that the pope was an agent of the devil who must always be resisted. By the end of Luther's life, a Lutheran consensus existed regarding armed resistance to the emperor rooted in the combination of a constitutionally delimited justification together with a natural law theory of resistance.

Our inquiry points to the nuanced development of a Lutheran theory of armed resistance attained by the end of Luther's life. This inquiry stands at odds with a popular strand of interpretation of Luther's thinking gathered together "authoritatively" by Ernst Troeltsch and popularized in the United States, again "authoritatively," by Reinhold Niebuhr and William Shirer. This one-sided, reductive trajectory of interpretation disregards the significance of Luther's development of thought regarding resistance and instead portrays Luther's thinking as essentially completed in the 1520s. Furthermore, this interpretive trajectory implies that Luther's theological thinking on political authority invariably steered subsequent Lutherans in an unbroken line to "unconditional obedience towards the authorities which have come into being in the course of the historical process," to the "glorification of power," to political "absolutism," to "Machiavelli,"[46] to an "anti-democratic" spirit in which "the business of government is to maintain order by repression,"[47] and to every Nazi "ferocious believer in absolute obedience to political authority."[48] Thankfully, many North American Lutheran interpreters of Luther have worked to overturn this influential Troeltschian-Niebuhrian trajectory and have thereby indulged in a Lutheran "delight in the law of the Lord."[49]

The Nascent Heritage
of Lutheran Resistance Today

The continuing development of Lutheran resistance theory made an important contribution to the emergence of democratic political thought and practice in the West. Shortly after Luther's death, nascent Lutheran resistance theory found a home and flourished among a group of Augsburg Confession loyalists in the city of Magdeburg. In 1550 nine Lutheran pastors issued their "Confession, Instruction, and Admonition of the Pastors and Preachers of the Christian Church at Magdeburg" (The Magdeburg Confession) as their confessional response to the Augsburg Interim of 1548. Part one, "Confession," deals with crucial doctrinal issues like sin, justification, and good works that had been severely compromised in the Augsburg Interim.

In part two, "Instruction," these Magdeburg confessors take up the question of armed resistance to the emperor. Quite deliberately they summarize what Lutheran resistance theory had already established in various documents and writings. Following Luther, they begin by affirming the divine constitution of political authority and thereby the general duty under ordinary circumstances to obey such authority. They eventually raise the question of what happens when those who have an authority higher than city magistrates seek to destroy true Christian doctrine within the province of a city.

The argument of the Magdeburg confessors regarding "the duty of lesser magistrates to resist," as their notion has come to be called, proceeds on the basis of Rom. 13:3. The triune God constitutes political authority to be a terror to evil not to good. Rulers who habitually are a terror to the good, however, violate the norm within the divine constitution of political authority and thereby collaborate with the devil. Such rulers persistently and systematically erode the public recognition of and regard for God's institution of political authority. This damages the honor and worship due to God for the gift of political authority. How does God exercise divine accountability under such circumstances?

At this point the Magdeburg confessors initiate an innovative line of inquiry. "[W]henever a superior magistrate persecutes his subjects, then, by the law of nature, by divine law and by the true religion and worship of God, the inferior magistrate ought by God's mandate to resist him."[50] Here the Magdeburg Lutherans, based on a penetrating interpretation of Matt. 22:21, focus on the integrity before God of each jurisdictional level of political authority. For instance, because the office of a city magistrate possesses a direct—rather than a hierarchically mediated—integrity and accountability before God for the welfare of a city and its subjects, when a ruler higher than the city magistrate persecutes the city's subjects, the lesser city magistrate has by virtue of office the duty before God to hold the higher authority accountable and, if persuasive means fail, to resist the persecution perpetrated by that higher authority. The subsequent history of political theory and practice in the West bears out the significance of this original and innovative line of argument by the Magdeburg Lutherans.[51]

The Magdeburg confessors distinguish four gradations of persecution, injustice, and injury and the corresponding modes of justifiable resistance. The least offensive injustice is one rooted in a ruler's human weakness that causes some injustice in small matters. The appropriate response to grade one injury is admonition and, if unresolved, bearing the injustice. A second level of offense comes when a superior uses armed violence on an inferior magistrate contrary to a positive law. Such grade two injury permits resistance, but vindication is usually better left directly in the hands of God, especially if the offense is only toward the magistrate. Third grade injustice occurs when a superior ruler causes a lesser magistrate to sin violently against one's own subjects—for instance, when Pharaoh ordered the Egyptian midwives to kill all newborn Hebrews. The lesser magistrate's obligation regarding a grade three offense is to disobey or even resist as long as other worse calamities would not be probable. The Magdeburg confessors regard rulers who commit grade two or three offenses as tyrants.

The most egregious persecution, injustice, and injury occur with the deliberate and systematic undermining of "the highest and most essential law." Such grade four offenses—for instance, establishing a law that abolishes marriage or that makes incest legal—systematically and severely injure not only persons but the very integrity of another fundamental order, institution, or office of God's ongoing creational agency. Lesser magistrates are obligated to resist with armed force if necessary. "Thus a pious inferior magistrate can and ought to protect and uphold as best he can, both himself and those over whom he has been placed, against such unjust force [by the higher authority], in order to protect the true doctrine and worship of God, body and life, property and honor."[52] Importantly, the Magdeburg confessors recognize that grade four offenses systematically cloak the honor due God and subvert the very worship of God, thereby precipitating blasphemy, paganism, unfaith, and atheism among the general population of a political jurisdiction. According to the biblical imagination, such circumstances disclose the very wrath of God.

Lutheran resistance theory put forth in the 1550 Magdeburg Confession found its way already in 1554 into the widely influential thinking of Theodore Beza, who would become Calvin's successor in Geneva and a source of Huguenot political theory in France.[53] Eventually Beza would make the Magdeburg Lutherans' insight regarding the resistance duty of lesser magistrates one key for his *Right of Magistrates* of 1574. In the 1560s John Knox would also take the Magdeburg Confession as the point of departure for his doctrine of the lesser magistrate and then expand that in a populist direction. For Knox, as previously for Luther and Beza, the basic question is the relation between ruler and ruled. Rulers exist to serve the ruled, not the ruled to serve the rulers.[54] The populist expansion of the doctrine of lesser magistrates would explode on the Western world in Huguenot political theory after the Bartholomew's Day Massacre of 1572. In this populist expansion the ruled would no longer be merely the subjects of the ruler; they would become citizens. At the core of such citizenship lies the critical, reflective "regard" that citizens train on the exercise of political rule. Correspondingly, citizenship fixes the attentiveness of political officeholders precisely on the critical "regard" that citizens direct toward the exercise of political authority accountable to criteria of justice and law. In this way the integrity of citizenship would become a prominent component of political authority itself.[55] This conceptual

transformation from subjects to citizens was accompanied by a social transformation of immense proportions, eventually giving rise to the nascent ethos of
deliberative democracy. In the concluding section, I explore how a Lutheran
critical participationist predilection might transpire within the particular contexts of contemporary life.

The State, Civil Society, and Congregations as Public Companions

The Emergence of Civil Society as "Order of Creation"[56]

I begin by exploring how we might theologically discern the emergence of
"civil society" in the West, and perhaps globally as well, as a new form of the
orders of creation brought about by the triune God's continual activity of creating a thriving world. The transformation of the nature of the relationship
between ruler and ruled and the subsequent emergence of an innovative
ethos of citizenship became tied up in the West with a transformation in the
very form, structure, and procedure of that "public space" that had bound
ruler and ruled together for centuries. Despite numerous sociological and historical differences in the structure and ethos of the "public spheres" of
medieval Europe, of the Renaissance, of the Reformation, and of the absolutist monarchies of the seventeenth and eighteenth centuries, one common
feature still united these eras: "representative publicness." We can describe
the structural transformation of public space in the West as a movement from
a "representative" form of the public sphere to a "civil society" form of the
public sphere.[57]

In the various European public spheres structured according to "representative publicness," representation does not refer to an assembly of delegates
who represent the wider population. Rather, "representation" refers to the
ethos and capacity of the few, elite people of status—those who inherit,
embody, and cultivate some sort of higher power or excellence or dignity or
courtly virtue or "manner"—to *present* themselves *in public*. That is, they display themselves with their "highness"—whether riches, authority, culture,
manner, education, or birth—*before* the ordinary people in order to accentu-
ate the great gulf in status between themselves and the common people. As
commoners recognize, through various modes of acclamation and applause,
the honor due to such grandeur, they also recognize and acknowledge the
shame that accompanies their own low status. Such representative publicness
remains the normative template overlaying a host of events such as corona-
tions, balls, high holy days, jousts, hunts, and festivals.

The weakening of representative publicness began as the forms of display
became more and more enclosed within the royal courtyard and thus perpet-

ually off limits to commoners. Emergent forms of capitalism added to the pro-
gressive enclosure of representative publicness. The capitalist traffic in goods
set off the "unique explosive power" of the press that heralded these new
goods.[58] Soon the nation-states of the seventeenth and eighteenth centuries
began employing the press in order to promulgate new ordinances targeted
both toward private economic enterprises and toward the consuming choices
of private households. In this way the press was systematically made to serve
the interests of the nation-state. An unintended consequence of great import
also happened, however. Through the press the nation-state administrations
addressed a new audience of people and thereby called into existence a new
public, the "bourgeois" class. Over time this new class became "the real carrier
of the public" and began to see itself as a public other than the public of the
nation-state. This "other" public is the "emerging *public sphere of civil society*."[59]

The emergence of this new "bourgeois" public sphere was accompanied by
a plurality of other parallel and competing public spheres. These emerged in
various social and historical settings and with different and unique dynamics,
which remain well beyond the bounds of our considerations here.[60] It is
important to bear in mind that this great plurality of public spheres is a structural phenomenon different from "the state" or from "the economy" or from
"the family" and private friendship. It is this great plurality of public spheres
that has now come to be known as "civil society."[61] That is, civil society is that
great plurality of different kinds of associations, affiliations, movements, and
institutions for the prevention and promotion of this, that, and the other
thing.[62] It is precisely such prevention and promotion that leads this teeming
plurality in the direction of moral formation and critical moral reflection.
Generally speaking, civil society is a public arena highly charged with moral
and ethical sensibilities, commitments, and undertakings. The emergence
and growth of a flourishing moral sphere of civil society will contribute in a
remarkable way to the development of more democratic forms of political
authority. With a flourishing civil society, which is in no way automatic,[63] citizens commonly imagine their citizenship spanning the overlapping spaces of
civil society and the political state. Indeed, it is this constellation of factors that
contributes most significantly, though not exclusively, to the formation of constitutional states of deliberative democracy.

At the time of the Reformation, the Lutheran confessors recognized
"church," "state," and "family" (with "work" emerging as a distinguishable
fourth) as the three great "orders of creation" or estates through which God
continually acts to create, preserve, and govern the social world. Can we in our
era discern a new creational order of the triune God arising with the historical emergence in the Western world of "civil society"? Spurred on by Luther's
theological reflections regarding the exercise of political accountability
through the preaching office and extraordinary heroes, can we in our own era
think—and act—imaginatively and reconstructively about the relationship of

civil society with political accountability and authority? Finally, how might such an emerging creational order also be globally salutary? Such imagining and acting surely counts as "delight in the law of the Lord" in our day.

In our own era the godly task and vocation of political accountability occurs most effectively in and through the public sphere of civil society in its overlapping configurations with democratically constituted states. Rather than political accountability being circumscribed solely by the office of preaching or merely by individual extraordinary heroes, now the whole public sphere of civil society exercises political accountability together with democratically constituted states. Indeed, have we not since 1989 come more fully to recognize civil society's rather heroic office, so to speak, on behalf of constitutional states of deliberative democracy? Of course, much more specificity is needed than I can provide here.[64]

By identifying "civil society" as a creational order with its own integrity, we can begin to think imaginatively beyond the constraints imposed whenever our theme is reduced simply to "church and state." The ELCA's formulation of "institutional separation" and "functional interaction" remains a significant step beyond theocracy or quietism or the separationism of a "wall" between church and state. Still, the samples of "functional interaction" in the ELCA constitution fail to be cognizant of "civil society" and thus thematize the political accountability function of "church" as inevitably only a straightforward, one on one, "interaction" with the "state." That is, we incur an imaginative liability when we accede too readily to the metaphor of "the intersection of church and state."[65] Such an "intersection of church and state" even gets inscribed visually by that well-known poster of the city street sign at the corner of "church" and "state" streets, which adorns the walls of seemingly every mainline denomination's church in society division, including the ELCA's.[66] By identifying the political accountability task of civil society—though civil society cannot in any way be reduced to only this single moral task—we can imagine civil society as a broad sluice whereby the "church"[67] joins together with a host of agents with moral interests and capacities responsible for political accountability. The appropriate poster—if it is to be of a street intersection—would have to feature something more like a traffic circle. I return to this question below ("The Vocation of Congregations").

The Public Use of Communicative Reason as "Delight in the Law of the Lord"

The Lutheran confessors recognized that human reason was among the triune God's great good gifts for the purpose—among others—of discerning God's justice and of the making and amending of God-pleasing law and political government, even as that same faculty of reason is tainted by sin and the temptations of the old evil foe. I now explore the emergence of public reasoning as an additional significant feature facilitating a public "delight in the law of the Lord."[68] The emergence of civil society brought along with it a "momentous shift" toward the development of "public reason."

Prior to the late eighteenth century, critical public reasoning concerning the political coordination of society made its way into the press by first passing through burgeoning gathering places, like coffee houses in Britain, salons in France, and table societies in Germany. These gathering places, in conjunction with the press, became the nurseries both for "civil society" and for "public reason."

> The bourgeois public sphere may be conceived above all as the sphere of private people come together as a public; they soon claimed the public sphere, [traditionally] regulated from above, against the authorities themselves, to engage them in debate over the general rules governing relations in the basically privatized but publicly relevant sphere of commodity exchange and social labor. The medium of this political confrontation was peculiar and without historical precedent: people's public use of their reason.[69]

Can churches in our day and place nurture a theological imagination in a distinctive direction? Can we discern in the public use of moral reasoning within the sphere of civil society, particularly in its quest for political accountability within a constitutional state of deliberative democracy, a contemporary vocation to "delight in the law of the Lord"?[70] Pursuing this prospect in an adequate manner means developing a *communicative* model of civil society.[71] A communicative civil society welcomes and indeed accentuates questions of moral truth that have practical import for everyday life. The hallmark of the communicative shape of civil society is that claims to practical moral truth must be redeemed critically through participatory practices and public communicative reasoning. This communicative shape eschews elitist moral display and purist moral trumping that often accompany the pursuit of moral truth. Instead, participatory procedures and practices of public communicative reason empower traditions and institutions that are affected by a moral claim to have a say in the formulation, stipulation, and adoption of moral norms. Boldly stated, communicative civil society "comes into existence whenever and wherever all affected by general social and political norms of action engage in a practical discourse, evaluating their validity."[72] In this way the communicative mode of public reasoning and civil society does not succumb to the extremes either of totalizing and colonizing moralism or moral neutrality and relativism.[73] A communicative civil society also does not subscribe to overly rigid boundaries between public and private but rather allows for overlapping terrains of public and private life.[74]

A communicative civil society recognizes that a plurality of differing cultural traditions harbors moral wisdom. On the one hand, a communicative civil society extols the capacity for creative moral possibilities embodied within the practices of public, communicative reason. On the other hand, it also focuses on the systematic distortions that accompany the self-interested monologue of any single moral tradition. In this way the communicative conceptuality of civil society concurs, though at an evident distance, with an insight that we met in Luther's critical theology. With his two-fold reason, Luther highlighted both God's resolve to incorporate the natural law's moral wisdom within the creational orders of global everyday life and the morally distorting determination brought by human sin and demonic wickedness.[75] Might a Lutheran confessional, critical participationist predilection in our time and place imagine "delight in the law of the Lord" as the public use of reason within a communicative civil society flexed toward the moral mooring of political authority?

I have investigated the theological development of a Lutheran critical participationist heritage of "church and state" and have positioned that heritage within an emerging and, hopefully, ascending communicative civil society context. I conclude by offering an apt metaphor to the congregations of the church—*congregations as civil society companions*—for the real life of congregations desiring a public vocation of "delight in the law of the Lord."

The Vocation of Congregations as Civil Society Companions

Vocations are the places and ways that anyone and everyone, knowingly or not, participate in the triune God's ongoing creative work to bring, nurture, and sustain temporal life in the world. In trusting the gospel of Jesus Christ, we acknowledge these places and ways as the triune God's creative work on behalf of our neighbors, and we recognize ourselves as this God's creative companions in this work. Like individuals, congregations have a variety of vocations in which to bring God's ongoing creative agency to bear on the life of our neighbors and our neighborhoods. Today the building up of the moral milieus that make life in our public and political communities possible commends itself as just such a calling. Civil society is the location for this vocation of public moral companion, and communicative moral practice is the best model for nurturing the contemporary moral milieu and for the political accountability that political authority needs and is called for by a constitutional state of deliberative democracy.

Congregations participate in the moral life of the community in at least two ways at once, one more internal and the other more external. Internally, congregations have often assisted families in the task of the moral formation of its members, in particular of the young, and this will continue as a prime moral vocation of congregations. As they engage in this vocation of moral formation, congregations sometimes fall prey to the temptation to view themselves as private Christian enclaves, alienated, isolated, and protected from the truth claims of other moral traditions.[76] In our ever more pluralistic public environment, however, innumerable traditions make claims on congregations that bid congregations to offer justification, in the sense of public moral reasoning and ethical grounding, for the truth character of the moral formation imparted in congregational life. In this way, among other even more important ways, congregations exist as a meeting place of private and public life.[77]

As the meeting of private and public life, congregations respond with integrity to their more external public moral vocation as civil society companions.[78] Today an increasing number and variety of the associations, affiliations, movements, and institutions of civil society need public moral companions who will encounter with them the moral meanings latent in the problems of contemporary life. This is a risky vocation, because Christian congregations do not have a corner on the moral wisdom needed in many conflicted situations. As civil society companions congregations become encumbered communities, shouldering the moral predicaments of the other institutions of civil society and bearing the citizenship that accompanies constitutional states of deliberative democracy. Beyond that, Christian congregations can expect to grow in moral wisdom due to their companionship within civil society.[79] Such dynamics contribute positively to civil society's vocation of keeping the constitutional state of deliberative democracy politically accountable. Christian congregations, however, are no stranger to an encumbered life, to a life of the cross of the triune God.[80] Herein lies the redemptive moment characterizing every vocation when encumbered companionship puts a congregation's enclosed centrality to death.[81] As civil society companions, congregations have the best opportunity to answer God's call to an ethos of deliberative democratic citizenship and in this way, among others, to participate in the triune God's creative agency of political authority in our era. Lutheran congregations in North America have frequently nurtured a lively ethos as civil society companions and have regularly done so by drawing from those ecclesial practices that have roots deep in Christian conciliar traditions.[82]

Finally, certain marks characterize the congregational vocation of civil society companion. As civil society companions, congregations acknowledge a *conviction* that they participate in the triune God's ongoing creative activity in and for the temporal world. In a communicative civil society congregational companions exhibit a *compassionate commitment* to other institutions and their moral predicaments. The commitment of civil society companions always yields a *critical* and *self-critical,* and thus fully *communicative,* procedure and practice of moral engagement and public reason. Finally, as civil society companions, congregations participate with other institutions of communicative civil society to *create* and *strengthen* the moral fabrics that fashion a life-giving and life-accountable contemporary society and political state.

Epilogue

The emergent reality of civil society as an encompassing milieu, or traffic circle, for the creational vocations of both "church" and "state," coupled with our "companionship" metaphor and its marks, can prompt further creative thinking. For instance, is the ELCA's "institutional separation and functional interaction" formulation terminologically apt. Among many possible expressions might be "constitutional integrity and creative, critical companionship." The term "integrity" evokes the intent of a distinct identity sought after by "institutional separation" but without the separationist baggage that invariably comes within the United States context of a "wall of separation." The qualifier "constitutional" denotes that the integrity being ratified resides at the elemental level of incorporating precepts. The advantage of "companionship" over "interaction" lies in its proficiency as a metaphor and, thus, in its potential to shape the imaginative outlook of actually existing congregations. Perhaps denominational constitutions are not intended to serve such a purpose; still, that is what is most often needed. "Creative" imparts a theological fitness to our formulation that "functional" just does not possess. "Critical" is the qualifier that best gets at the ethical and criteriological orientation of our heritage's critical participationist predilection.

Blessed are those whose delight is in the law of the Lord!

3

A Lutheran Tradition
on Church and State

John R. Stumme

The Evangelical Lutheran Church in America (ELCA) summarizes its approach to church and state relations in its constitution's pledge to "work with civil authorities in areas of mutual endeavor, maintaining institutional separation of church and state in a relation of functional interaction."[1] This affirmation identifies a distinctive approach to church and state relations in a pluralistic society, one that emerges out of the experience of Lutheran churches in the United States. It offers a perspective in and for a contemporary context of religious freedom that depends on Martin Luther and the Lutheran Confessions. The affirmation voices a positive attitude toward government and sets forth a two-pronged principle—institutional separation and functional interaction—to govern this relationship.

To understand the ELCA's position, we need to recall the tradition of reflection and definition of which it is a part. A 1963 study first used the phrase "institutional separation and functional interaction,"[2] and in subsequent social statements the phrase came to characterize an official Lutheran approach to church and state relations.[3] In what follows I describe and interpret what these social statements say about institutional separation, functional interaction, and religious freedom. In order to see what gave rise to this tradition, I begin by placing it within a broader historical context. I conclude by drawing out what it might mean for the church's continuing public witness at the intersection of church and state.

Beyond Separationism

Historians of Lutheranism in the United States in the twentieth century tell the story of a quietistic tradition that developed a growing sense of social responsibility, especially after World War II.[4] World-shattering events—particularly

51

the Great Depression and World War II—the changing sociological status of Lutheran churches (more and more a part of the mainstream of American life), the ecumenical movement, and theological creativity were factors that influenced this increasing attention to the many dimensions of society's welfare.

Part of this development was a change in attitude toward the relation of church and state. Throughout the century—and before—Lutherans in the United States consistently looked with favor on the constitutional guarantee that "Congress shall make no law respecting an establishment of religion, or prohibiting the free exercise thereof. . . ." They insisted that the state should not control the church nor should the church control the state. Within this continuity there has been a significant shift in Lutheran attitudes, which I want to illustrate by reference to three writings.

At the beginning of the twentieth century, Lutherans in the United States were, for the most part, strong separationists. They tended "to draw a strict line of separation between the sphere of the state and the sphere of the church."[5] An article on "Church and State" in the important *The Lutheran Cyclopedia* of a century ago demonstrates this separationism.[6] As Lutherans do today, author Frederick W. Stellhorn appeals to the New Testament and the Augsburg Confession to assert that church and state are ordinances of God, that they differ, and that the two are not to be confounded. The Lutheran church, however, came to confer on kings and princes in their secular dignity "the authority of governing the Church also." After quoting theologians from Lutheran orthodoxy that support his reading of history, Stellhorn concludes: "It needs no proof that this is doing what the Augsburg Confession warns against, confounding the civil and the ecclesiastical powers. But such in substance for centuries was the arrangement in the state churches and in Germany and Scandinavia."

While he discredits the experience of Lutheran churches in Europe, Stellhorn enthusiastically endorses the form of church and state relations in the United States. He calls it "*total separation* of Church and State," which he describes as "neither demanding or exercising any direct influence upon the government of the other, as was the case in the first centuries of the Church and now is in our United States." Since the ideal of a true Christian state is not realizable, total separation "is the only arrangement that is just and fair to all citizens."[7] Moreover, "Luther entirely agreed with this principle," although in his circumstances he allowed civil government to take hold of the church's government hoping that "the time would come when the correct principle could be carried out fully."

For Stellhorn, that time had arrived in the founding of the United States. His message is clear: Lutheran doctrine and the pattern of church and state relations in the United States are fully compatible. Significantly, he describes the proper relation of church and state with language that is found neither in the Lutheran Confessions nor the United States Constitution: total separation. His view parallels Thomas Jefferson's metaphor of "a wall of separation between Church and State," which the Supreme Court had evoked for the first time in 1879.[8]

Lutherans supported "total separation" because it meant that they could practice their faith without government interference. It showed their willingness to be American: to accept a situation in which the state did not support their churches and institutions and to rely on "'do-it-yourself' volunteerism."[9] It expressed their sociological status as a marginal "enclave of enclaves"[10] in a time when government was much smaller and less intrusive than it is today, and when the Supreme Court had made only a few rulings on the religion clauses of the First Amendment.

By mid-century voices arose that questioned the adequacy of separationism, which had become deeply entrenched in the piety of American Lutherans. One such voice was Conrad Bergendoff, who in a 1946 article called for a "re-thinking of the relationship of the Lutheran Church to the community and state."[11] It is "unrealistic," he argues, when Lutherans "contend for a complete separation of church and state in America," since "there never was a Lutheran country where state and church were altogether divorced, and in our Lutheran thinking we have unconsciously, or subconsciously, continued to think in patterns of one influencing the other." In reading European theology, which assumes a very close connection between government and church, we transferred it "without much discrimination" to our country, "and consequently thought of government as Christian government, unaware of the fallacy of our thinking."

> We have taken for granted that somehow, somebody, would see to it that government would not be antagonistic to the Church, but we have ourselves done practically nothing to shape that government. What is worse we have, unintentionally, I hope, given our people the impression that we need do nothing to influence the government. The authorities, we have gone on repeating, are of God, and God will take care of them. Our duty is to obey, and if things get too bad, even to endure persecution.

Bergendoff further observes that Lutheran thinking has not recognized the special character of "the political constitution of America" in which sovereignty rests "in the people themselves." "If God has permitted this change in the source of authority, how can we speak of a state which is entirely separate from the Church?"

> [A] government which is of, and by, and for the people, stands in a different relationship to the Church than a government which is despotic or oligarchic. But we in America still speak as if the State were an impersonal entity deriving authority from God, regardless of who makes up that State.

In effect we tend to put the State out of the Christian sphere of thought
and action, and the non-Christian element of society are happy enough to
have it so. They agree readily enough that government is not the business
of the Church—they go on to claim that it is their business. . . . So the
Church stands helpless in the face of corrupt government, having
defaulted on its responsibility. In theory at least the Lutheran Church in
America has no political philosophy, a part of the reason being that it has
believed it should have none. . . . We have yet to discover how the heritage
of Lutheranism can be brought to bear on life in America, where the people have the responsibility of ruling and where consequently Christian
people have political responsibilities.

Bergendoff perceives that in separationism the church willingly vacates the
political arena. "Why should the State listen, when the Church says it has no
right to talk!" For Bergendoff, abandoning the public square on the basis of
theological principle runs counter to both Lutheranism and democracy. He
challenges Lutherans to find an alternative to total or complete separation.

George W. Forell, Herman A. Preus, and Jaroslav J. Pelikan set out to do that
in a 1953 article, "Toward a Lutheran View of Church and State."[12] In drawing
on law-and-gospel and two-kingdom thinking, the authors anticipate the theological approach that would shape later Lutheran social statements. Their theological critique of separationism complements Bergendoff's historical
critique. In discussing the alternatives, they devote an entire section to the concept of "absolute separation": "a division of human life into two neatly separated spheres, one the sphere of the state, where the church dare not trespass,
and the other the sphere of the church, where the state does not trespass."[13]

Forell, Preus, and Pelikan claim that absolute separation "was usually the
result of utter despair over the sinful world and of the eager hope that the
impending return of the Lord would put an end to the abominations of the
state." They recall examples of it in the history of the church, including
"Pietistic Lutherans [who] feel that the Christian should tolerate the state as a
necessary evil, pay his taxes, and serve in the army, but otherwise should have
as little as possible to do with the affairs of the state." They see another form
in nineteenth-century German theology that developed the notion of the
"autonomy" of various areas of life, whereby the laws in one realm could not
be transferred to another. They observe that totalitarian states welcome
absolute separation since "it leaves almost all areas of life to the state's complete and exclusive control."

The authors criticize the concept of absolute separation as "a counsel of
despair," since "it ultimately surrenders too much of life to the powers of darkness." It "tends to give up the doctrine of creation, that God is Creator and
Lord of both church and state and that his will is law in both realms. Luther
felt that Christians were under an obligation to do everything in their power
to strengthen the state as an ordinance of God." The authors also appeal to

the doctrine of the church. The function of the Christian community to be "the salt of the earth" and "the light shining in darkness" assumes an interaction between the church and state and other areas of life "for which the concept of absolute separation has not made adequate provision." As an alternative to absolute separation, as well as to the church's rule of the state or the state's rule of the church—two views they also criticize—the authors propose "the interpenetration of church and state."[14]

We can trace in these three writings a major shift in twentieth-century American Lutheran thinking on the relation of church and state. The concept of total, complete, or absolute separation so eagerly embraced at the century's beginning had become by mid-century the target of strong attack by leading theologians. The criticism by Bergendoff, Forell, Preus, Pelikan, and many others was persuasive enough to lead at least a part of Lutheranism to break with separationism. The social statements of the American Lutheran Church (ALC) and the Lutheran Church in America (LCA) represent the attempt to move beyond separationism and to set forth a constructive alternative.

The social statements view their own proposal as a distinctive alternative within a fourfold typology: "Most often the relationship of church and state has been seen in static thought patterns: namely state rule of the church, church rule of the state, or the 'wall of separation' doctrine. No static or absolutist interpretation is adequate today."[15] While the first two types or models have been very important in church history, they have not been serious options in twentieth-century United States; the latter model, however, has exerted considerable influence among Lutherans and in the general society. "We advocate the institutional separation and functional interaction of church and state. This position rejects both the absolute separation of church and state and the domination of either one by the other. . . ."[16] The change as well as the continuity in Lutheran attitudes on the relation of church and state are evident in the way the statements position themselves among the alternatives.

Let me underscore two reasons for this movement beyond separationism in post–World War II Lutheranism. One reason was practical: the expanding role of government, especially of the federal government. One statement speaks of "the extension of governmental influence into nearly every phase of life" as well as "the difficulties for the churches in meeting the growing demands and complexities of their programs of health, education, and welfare."[17] Another notes that with changes in the role of the federal government in education and welfare, religious agencies "are being invited to participate more fully than ever before in publicly sponsored programs and in the acceptance of public financing." Church and state were not in fact sealed off into separate spheres but interacting on a practical basis, and ecclesial reflection needed to account for that reality.

A second reason was theological: Lutherans were revising their understanding of the two kingdoms or God's twofold rule of the world. They were rejecting a dualistic interpretation in favor of one that called for critical participation in society.[18] It was "a transition from a *negative* to an *affirmative* interpretation of the doctrine . . . from a *restrictive* to a *constructive/critical* interpretation." Instead of functioning primarily "to tell the church what it cannot do and must not do (namely, to interfere in the realm that is the responsibility of the secular authorities)," it takes on a positive function: "It serves to tell the church what it can and must do (namely, to call those authorities to account as to how they carry out those responsibilities, under the sovereignty of God)." In stressing that both kingdoms are God's, "Lutheranism . . . has become aware that its total message, comprising Law and Gospel, includes a word to be spoken to public as well as private life."[19] Revised two-kingdom thinking provides the theological framework for the social statements' approach to the relation of church and state.

The Integrity of Church and State

"Institutional separation and functional interaction" is a two-pronged principle or guideline that is theologically rooted and contextually shaped. It grows out of the Lutheran church's understanding of God's activity, relying on Scripture and the Lutheran Confessions. It is influenced by and addresses the structures and dynamics of a twentieth-century context of religious freedom and pluralism. It is intended primarily to offer direction to a church for how it should relate to government and for how this church should view government's relation with it and other religious bodies. The principle of a minority religious tradition (as all are) in a larger pluralistic society, it is also meant to contribute to public discussion of the relation of religion and law. Bearing the distinctive marks of the Lutheran tradition, it shares characteristics with other religious and secular traditions.

By "church" the social statements mean the universal "community of believers" created by the Holy Spirit through the word of God that "also takes on institutional form and exists as a legal entity."[20] It is "both a divine organism related to Christ and a human organization related to society."[21] The focus on church accentuates the corporate dimensions of Christian faith and the institutional aspects of religious freedom. In defining "church" and the discussion in specifically Christian terms, Lutherans are not asking for special constitutional privileges for Christianity but exercising their religious freedom in a way that other traditions do and should do. They are addressing the relation of law and religion in a pluralistic society out of their own doctrinal convictions. Because the statements see churches as part of "the institutionalized religious order of society" as well as in Christian terms, what they say about "church" as institution may often be extended to all religious bodies.[22]

By "state" the social statements mean "the institutions of government and law,"[23] "all units of government which exercise political authority, whether at the local, state, or national levels,"[24] or "civil authority" that operates through the "sword" or the law of the whole society and its enforcement.[25] Lutherans reject the idea that "state" and "society" are synonymous, and thereby affirm a limited, nontotalitarian government and allow "for the proper roles of various nonpolitical associations in dealing with public affairs."[26] Government as well as the churches are part of a more encompassing society. "State" refers concretely to the constitutional, federal, and democratic form of government in the United States, where citizenship and public office are not restricted by a religious test. Although the statements recognize that "state" is a complex network of institutions, they do not develop views on the proper roles of the levels and branches of government. They say nothing, for example, of the role of the judiciary.

Despite rejecting separationism, Lutherans use the word *separation* in their summary principle. One may question if that was the wisest choice.[27] Perhaps it was used because "the phrase 'separation of church and state' has become the symbol of the American approach" to the relationship of the two,[28] perhaps because churches and government are in fact separate institutions in the United States, and perhaps because Lutherans understand church and state to be two distinct authorities that are not to be confused. Whatever the reasons, the social statements speak of "separation" but refine its meaning.

Clearly the "functional interaction" prong of the Lutheran principle qualifies separation (see the next section). So does the adjective "institutional." This adjective, so different from the qualifier "absolute," locates the place where separation should exist: in the organization and governance of the two institutions. Neither the one nor the other should be an institutional part of the other nor be subordinated institutionally to the other. "In affirming the principle of separation of church and state, Lutherans in the United States respectfully acknowledge and support the tradition that the churches and the government should be *separate in structure.*"[29] Lutherans are not advocating the separation of "religion" and "politics," nor are they confining "religion" to a private sphere divorced from a public sphere. By limiting the scope of separation, they maintain the public character of religious faith and hold public life open to religious influence.

The church therefore does not violate any barrier of separation when, for example, it carries out its mandate to address government in light of its understanding of God's will. The belief that "the state is to be respected and obeyed as an expression of the sovereign will of the Creator . . . forbids any state from deifying itself, for its power is not inherent but is delegated to it by God to be employed responsibly for the attainment of beneficial secular goals." The social statement continues with a striking passage: "The *constant need of the state,* therefore, is not for the church's uncritical loyalty and unquestioning obedience but for the prophetic guidance and judgment of the law of God

which the church is called to proclaim, in order to be reminded of both its secular limits and potentialities."[30] This understanding of Christian faith dis-
tances itself not only from quietism but also from any notion of separation
that reduces religion to a private affair "between God and me."

The statements also significantly qualify the term by the meaning they give
to "institutional separation." Their concern is not severing all ties or erecting
a wall between church and state as if one were from God and the other from
the devil; their driving interest is maintaining the integrity and freedom of two
divine ordinances. "Our concern is that the church be free to be the church,
the state to be the state, each true to its own God-ordained functions."[31] Institutional separation means "that church and state must each be free to perform its essential task under God."[32]

What this position rejects are "those theories of relationship which seek the
dominance either of church over state or of state over church."[33] To guard
against the dominance of one over the other and maintain the integrity of
both, Lutherans oppose the confusing of word and sword. The church may
only propose, proclaim, and persuade, while the state may compel in earthly
matters. The church has no divine authority to take up the sword to carry out
its mission, and the state has no divine authority to preach the gospel or any
other religious message. The church lives under the divine mandate not to
invoke the state's coercive power to compel faith in God, and the state lives
under the divine mandate not to coerce faith or disbelief. Institutional separation serves to keep the church reliant on God's word and to keep governmental coercion out of what the church believes, practices, and communicates
about God's relation with humans. In resisting the confusion of word and
sword, it protects religious liberty for all (see below).

The integrity of church and state comes from God (and not from the other
institution), who confers on both their distinctive calling and authority and
holds both accountable. Both are "instruments for accomplishing God's purposes" in a sinful world;[34] both "are subject to the will and rule of God, who is
sovereign over all things."[35] The calling and the limits of each depend on distinguishing the two modes of the one God's rule in law and gospel, creation
and redemption, this age and the age to come, civil righteousness and the
righteousness of faith. "Lutherans acknowledge the twofold reign of God,
under which Christians live simultaneously. God is ruler of both the world and
the church. The church is primarily the agency of the Gospel in the new age
of Christ, while the state is primarily the agency of the Law in the old age of
Adam."[36]

Lutherans affirm that the state's calling belongs to the secular realm. Their
understanding of secular, however, differs profoundly from the view that "secular" is a world or arena without God, that "secular" is the opposite of "religious" or "sacred." Secular refers to "this age," to temporal, earthly life. "The
secular realm, though not redemptive, is still a sacred reality of God's cre-

ation. It provides many of the 'masks' through which God graciously preserves the world from its sinful self-destruction."[37] While free from the church's domination, the state, called to be a servant of God, is not outside God's rule and blessing; it is a part of a "sacred secularity."[38]

In light of this understanding of God's sovereign activity, the statements outline the church's mission and the government's role. They describe the church's calling in ways that reveal a clear sense of identity in the Christian faith, and they view the state's task in both negative (to curb evil) and positive (to support good) terms. A characteristic summary reads as follows:

> [The church's] distinctive mission as an ecclesiastical institution is to proclaim the Word of God in preaching and sacraments, worship and evangelism, Christian education and social ministry.
>
> The distinctive mission of the state is to establish civil justice through the maintenance of law and order, the protection of constitutional rights, and the promotion of the general welfare of the total citizenry.[39]

"The Nature of the Church and Its Relationship with Government" offers the most extensive description of the calling of the two authorities.[40] Written in response to "instances in which laws, rulings, and regulatory procedures on the part of government appear to infringe upon the churches and their agencies and institutions," the statement forcefully reasserts the church's freedom to define its own mission, which the statement does comprehensively. It speaks of the church in terms of the gospel, as a fellowship, and with authority to determine and educate its leadership. Noteworthy is what it says about the church's ministry in the world and its internal governance:

> God also calls the church to be a creative critic of the social order, an advocate for the needy and distressed, a pioneer in developing and improving services through which care is offered and human dignity is enhanced, and a supportive voice for the establishment and maintenance of good order, justice, and concord. Another mark of the presence of the church in the world is in its ministries involving activities, agencies, and institutions through which the church and society seek to fulfill their goals in mutual respect and cooperation.
>
> On the basis of their commitment to him who is both Lord of the church and Lord of the world, Lutheran churches establish, support, operate, and hold accountable their congregations, agencies, institutions, schools, organizations and other appropriate bodies.

The statement reaffirms "the civil government's distinctive calling by God . . . to maintain peace, to establish justice, to protect and advance human rights, and to promote the general welfare of all persons." It insists that "government has the authority and power in the secular dimensions of life to ensure that individuals and groups, including religious communities and

their agencies, adhere to the civil law." Most tellingly, the statement underscores the limits of the government's authority:

> Government exceeds its authority when it defines, determines or other-
> wise influences the churches' decisions concerning their nature, mission,
> and ministries, doctrines, worship and other responses to God, except
> when such decisions by the churches would violate the laws of morality
> and property or infringe on human rights.[41]

Interestingly, this social statement does not contain a parallel passage describing when the church exceeds its authority. The notion of "institutional separation" speaks also to the limits of the church's authority: The church as
church does not wield the sword, nor is it to control the state. But in the context, Lutherans perceived the threat to the freedom of church and state to
come from the state. This perception is especially important for a time when
laws and governmental regulations affect all of areas of life. It shows one side
of the critical edge in this Lutheran tradition on church and state.[42]

While the term is not used, the attitude of institutional separation is present in Lutheran social statements on prayer and Bible reading in public
schools.[43] The statements support the Supreme Court's ban on officially prescribed religious practices in public school rooms, largely because these practices are seen as confusing the callings of church and state. Because public
schools are government schools, and government involves coercion, these
practices are seen as another case where government exceeds its authority
and threatens the church's integrity. They appropriate a function of church
and family, they use governmental power to promote religious ends, and they
"open the door . . . to governmental prescription of an official faith."[44] They
also are detrimental to the church, since such practices result in a distortion
of the Bible, a dilution of its religious message, and the promotion of "a
vague or syncretistic religion that conveys none of the substance, the depth,
and cutting edge of the historic Christian witness."[45] Yet, cautions one statement, "it is as wrong for the public schools to become agents for atheism,
godless secularism, scoffing irreligion, or a vague 'religion in general' as it
is for them to make religious rites and ceremonies an integral part of their
programs."[46]

With institutional separation Lutherans affirm the freedom of church and
state to live out their divine calling, set limits on both, and oppose their confusion. With functional interaction they affirm cooperation between church
and state. This two-pronged principle grows out of an understanding of God's
sovereign rule. "We dare never forget that the same God is Lord of the nations
as well as Head of the church. By clearly distinguishing God's law of creation
from his gospel of redemption, the Reformers found a way by which church
and state could interact without being united and yet remain distinct without
being divorced."[47] I turn now to this interaction.

The Interaction of Church and State

As well as resting on Lutheran theology, the "both/and" attitude of "institutional separation" *and* "functional interaction" reflects what people experience daily in American society. Those who are both citizens and baptized belong to overlapping communities. Church and government are actors in the same society, have responsibilities for the other, and share a commitment to the common good. In speaking of functional interaction, Lutherans acknowledge that there are areas in which both are "legitimately engaged"[48] and affirm that they may and should cooperate without undercutting their institutional separation. Both church and state "serve genuine needs of human beings," and they "complement one another as they devote themselves to the best interests and well-being of persons."[49] Their practical interaction "in areas of mutual endeavor" is intended to assist "in the maintenance of good order, the protection of and extension of civil rights, the establishment of social justice and equality of opportunity, the promotion of the general welfare, and the advancement of the dignity of all persons."[50]

The statements sketch out how church and government act in "responsible cooperation" with the other:

The church relates to the interests of the state by
- offering intercessory prayers on its behalf
- encouraging responsible citizenship and government service
- holding it accountable to the sovereign law of God
- contributing to the civil consensus which supports it
- championing the human and civil rights of all its citizens
- volunteer[ing] its resources as a channel for meeting the needs of society through cooperation with government

The state relates to the interests of the church by
- ensuring religious liberty for all
- acknowledging that human rights are not the creation of the state
- maintaining an attitude of "wholesome neutrality" toward church bodies in the context of the religious pluralism of our culture
- providing incidental benefits [police and fire protection, for example] on a nonpreferential basis in recognition of the church's civil services which are also of secular benefit to the community
- providing funding on a nonpreferential basis to church agencies in the performance of educational or social services which are also of secular benefit to the community[51]

Aspects of functional interaction go back to the New Testament, when the church prayed for governing authorities and the Roman Empire provided order for the church to gather and to evangelize. An early social statement

(1966) claims that "in its practical operation the American heritage generally has embodied a flexible pattern of cooperation between church and state in providing persons such services as are deemed to be in the public interest and for the good of the community." This "flexible friendly cooperation . . . has been especially true in the areas of education, welfare services, and ministries to persons in institutions and the armed forces."[52] This claim overstates the cooperation—especially in the area of education—and overlooks instances of the government's hostile attitude toward some religious bodies; yet in the broad context of the antagonism, oppression, and even persecution that has frequently marked the state's relation with the church through the centuries, the statement rightly acknowledges noteworthy cooperation in the history of the United States.[53]

An example of this history is the place and support government gives "to the chaplaincy ministry in the armed forces, in correctional institutions, and in governmental hospitals," which is seen as "both a valid exercise of governmental interest in the whole person and an example of the religious neutrality of the state." Lutherans affirm that "the state properly should exercise reasonable administrative controls over those who provide this spiritual ministry, while protecting their right to minister according to the dogma and practices of their ecclesiastical tradition."[54]

New demands and opportunities for cooperation came with the growth of the welfare state during the 1960s and later. Lutherans (and other religious bodies) had to decide what attitude they should adopt toward receiving government funds for social welfare as well as for higher education. Functional interaction represents the Lutheran response: "The government may conclude that efforts and programs of the churches provide services of broad social benefit. In such instances and within the limits of the law, the government may offer and the churches may accept various forms of assistance to furnish the services." Education and social services are seen "as the tasks of society as a whole," as "public services." When churches contribute to their fulfillment, "they may accept a measure of public support and a concomitant degree of monitoring by government on behalf of the public," and "government may provide assistance on a nonpreferential basis in recognition of the public services provided."[55]

For Lutherans, institutional separation and the non-establishment of religion do not mean that the government cannot provide any financial assistance to religious organizations. Government aid is permissible provided two conditions are met: (1) it is given for "public" services or those of "broad social benefit," in distinction from those activities that are the exclusive prerogative of the religious body; and (2) it is given nonpreferentially, that is, it does not discriminate for or against particular religious organizations or agencies. Functional interaction depends, it should be noted once again, on viewing "society" and "public" as more all-embracing than government.

The statements generally speak of governmental aid for religious service providers with the rubric "may." At one place, however, they speak "should" language. "Benefits to which the person is entitled through statute by reason of citizenship, residence, need, special service, or unusual ability should not be denied or limited because he chooses to use the services of agencies and institutions of the church rather than those of government."[56] Persons should not be burdened or penalized because they exercise their religious freedom to be served by a religious agency. If government provides a benefit, then it should give equal treatment to all who meet the requirement and not discriminate on the basis of religion.

There is, interestingly, one strong note of caution about governmental aid for church-related organizations. It points to the "danger" of "too-close an identification" between the two. While such aid "may enable the church the more effectively to serve the needs of an expanding society," it may also "compromise the religious character of the institution and jeopardize its essential integrity." Aid also may give an unfair advantage to some religious groups who then may influence government to their temporal advantage.[57] These warnings provide Lutherans with criteria for the continuing task of evaluating the impact of government funding on their social ministry organizations. Because Lutherans recognize the importance of religious service providers maintaining their religious identity, they have reason to support laws and regulations that allow that to occur while respecting other constitutional values.[58]

One area where an early social statement takes a firm stand against functional interaction is governmental support for K–12 educational institutions sponsored by religious bodies. "Any form of direct public support" for such institutions "jeopardizes the religious freedom of persons who are not members of that religious body" since "it compels them to support the indoctrination of religious views which they do not share." Providing bus transportation or school textbooks at public expense to parochial schools "is fraught with decisive consequences." The statement does not explain why its reasoning for a "no aid" policy for these educational institutions does not also apply to religious social welfare agencies. Nor does it speak of religious educational institutions providing "public" services or "broad social benefit."[59] The same statement does, however, encourage further exploration of "released time, dismissed time, and shared time," programs "that would require rejection of the dogmatic and inflexible approach fostered by the slogan 'separation of church and state.'"[60]

A later social statement, however, in recommending study of new proposals on governmental funding for church-related education and social services, frames the discussion differently. The purpose of such aid, contends the statement, should be to increase citizen access to services they choose. "That in order to maximize the access of citizens in our pluralistic society to education and social services from agencies and institutions of their choice," the recommendation "encourage[s] the further exploration and assessment of all constitutional means of government support for a variety of social and educational services at all levels, whether public, private, or church-related."[61] By framing the discussion in terms of this purpose, the statement opens up the possibility of supporting governmental aid to citizens who choose to send their children to religiously sponsored K–12 educational institutions. It expresses a new willingness on the part of Lutherans to explore and assess such specific proposals. In speaking of "functional interaction," Lutherans come to view citizen access to services of their choice a social good and seek to promote it.

As Lutherans have developed it in the United States, the two-pronged principle of institutional separation and functional interaction of church and state is intertwined with religious freedom. The category changes, but the perspective is the same. In supporting religious freedom, Lutherans acknowledge that religious bodies in their sociological organization are voluntary associations, not governmental agencies. They endorse religious freedom for all members of society and believe that government is in some sense to be neutral toward all religious bodies and relate to them on a nonpreferential basis. "As the U.S. Constitution provides, government neither establishes nor favors any religion. It also safeguards the rights of all persons and groups in society to the free exercise of their religious beliefs, worship, practices, and organizational arrangements within the laws of morality, human rights, and property."[62] Lutherans affirm that religious freedom is a vital area of mutual endeavor: The church cooperates with the state "by championing the human and civil rights of all its citizens," and the state cooperates with the church "by ensuring religious liberty for all." While the concept permeates the social statements on church and state, Lutherans also made religious freedom the topic of a separate social statement. I turn now to this Lutheran account of religious freedom.

Religious Freedom for All

A theological and an ethical thread run through the social statement "Religious Liberty."[63] Lutherans give a theological account for why they support religious freedom, and they focus on what makes for the effective protection of religious freedom, so that the neighbor might indeed be served.

"'Religious liberty' is to be distinguished from 'Christian freedom.'" This first sentence of the statement, in characteristic Lutheran fashion, distinguishes between law and gospel—in order to avoid their confusion, affirm both, and relate them. Christian freedom is a gift of God received by faith, and religious liberty is "a political term describing one major aspect of civil liberty." In rejecting notions that would equate the two freedoms, this distinction reminds Christians that their freedom and that of the church given in Christ do not finally depend on any one political arrangement. It also makes religious freedom a political good for the whole society whose general validity may be recognized through "the moral knowledge of all persons, which enables them to perform good deeds and pursue truth and justice."[64] Any confusion of the two would be detrimental to both Christian faith and political order.

While distinguishing Christian freedom from religious liberty, the statement nonetheless views religious freedom in light of God's relation to humans. Its theological account of religious liberty states:

> Christian faith asserts that religious liberty is rooted in our creation in the image of God and in God's continuing activity in the created world. . . . [W]e are creatures to whom God speaks and from whom God expects a response. This is essential to our humanity. To deny religious liberty and other civil liberties, therefore, threatens to dehumanize us all.
>
> Christian faith asserts that God will not force anyone into communion with God. If then, God refuses to impose divine will on humanity, then persons exceed their prerogatives if they try to use coercion of any kind on one another to obtain religious conformity. Religious liberty for all is thus not only a demand of civil justice but also an aid to our response to the Christian gospel.[65]

Lutherans ground religious freedom in God's creative activity. At this crucial point, the statement does not take a "secular move": It does not, for example, attempt first to define "religion" in a supposedly neutral and comprehensive way and then construct a theory of why this human phenomenon should receive special constitutional protection. It begins instead from within a particular religious tradition and states what that tradition believes to be true universally: "Christian faith asserts. . . ." Faith, it is believed, illumines human reality in a unique way whose truth holds for all: To be human is to be addressed by God. Political orders ought always to protect religious freedom because humans are creatures created for communion with God. Lutherans welcome and offer other reasons for religious freedom, but their most fundamental account is theological. Lutherans are among those who believe that the ultimate basis of religious freedom is found in God's relation to human creatures.

This relational view of humans is significant for a concept of religious freedom. The statement does not view the human being as an "unencumbered self"—"who is installed as sovereign, cast as the author of the only obligations that constrain"—where religious freedom is seen as one aspect of autonomous choice.[66] It understands instead that humans are creatures who are embedded in patterns of preexistent relationships and who are addressed by God, who expects them to respond. A rationale for religious freedom that assumes each person creates his or her own meaning and obligations stands in sharp contrast to one that asserts God is the giver of meaning and obligation. In the former case, religious freedom is important, because the individual's sovereign choice is the ultimate value; in the latter case, religious freedom is essential, because the creator speaks and humans are called to listen, receive, and obey. While the former may have difficulty explaining why religion should have special legal protection, the latter considers the reason clear and paramount: "We must obey God rather than any human authority" (Acts 5:29).

Lutherans also ground religious freedom in God's saving activity, specifically in the way God redeems and makes Christians free. God speaks and calls humans "into communion with God" through the living word, the Holy Spirit, and faith, that is, without coercion. Government cannot establish this communion and therefore is under divine obligation to keep its coercive power out of this relationship. While not the same as Christian freedom, religious liberty is "an aid to our response to the Christian Gospel" and, one might add, called for by that gospel.

The argument echoes Martin Luther, expressing one of the deepest strains of a Lutheran approach to religious freedom. While his role in the history of religious freedom is ambiguous, [67] Luther in his first and most important essay on "Temporal Authority" defined its limits with the same argument. God "desires that our faith be based simply and entirely on the divine word alone. . . . Therefore in matters which concern the salvation of souls nothing but God's word shall be taught and accepted."[68] "For faith is a free act, to which no one can be forced. Indeed, it is a work of God in the spirit, not something which outward authority should compel or create. Hence arises the common saying, found also in Augustine, 'No one can or ought to be forced to believe.'"[69]

Accordingly, the statement speaks of religious liberty as "the right of a person, whether a believer in God or a nonbeliever . . . to be immune from coercion to participate in religious acts or affirmations" and as "the right of a church or religious organization as a corporate body . . . to conduct its internal affairs without interference by government or any other person or group. . . ."[70] For Lutherans, noncoercion and noninterference, both for the individual and the corporate religious body, belong to the core of religious freedom. Consequently, Lutherans have strong reason to view government persecution and oppression of religious persons and groups wherever they may occur as fundamental violations of human dignity and to give high priority to combating such situations.[71]

While affirming that all persons are free to be religious or not to be, Lutherans also hold to the principle that religious status, belief, practices, and conduct require special protection from government. "The religious liberty of a person or group may be limited by government only on the basis of an important and compelling public interest. Nothing less than a serious and immediate threatened violation of other basic human rights should warrant restrictions on religious liberty."[72] As I have suggested, the reason for this stance is that religious believers in their relation with God are bound to a loyalty beyond all created realities: "You shall have no other gods before me." In carrying out its legitimate functions, government has an obligation to act in ways that do not require (or minimize the impact on) citizen believers to be disobedient or disloyal to that transcendent reality with whom they are in relationship. For Lutherans religious liberty requires that government accommodate religion.[73]

Lutherans do not call upon government to endorse a specifically Christian basis for religious freedom, but they do expect government to disavow a pretension that contradicts the Christian faith. Government should "acknowledge" that religious freedom and other human rights "are not the creation of the state."[74] The 1963 study on church and state views the "long-standing tradition" illustrated in the Declaration of Independence that all are "endowed by their Creator with certain inalienable rights" as making this acknowledgment. While admitting such affirmations are often ceremonial and "theologically minimal," the study does not dismiss them, since "they may still serve as restraints upon the introduction of a godless secularism as the unofficially 'established' religion of the land."[75]

The theological thread in "Religious Liberty" asserts that this liberty is a substantive right and a universal good. Religious liberty should be accompanied by other civil liberties, but it is not reducible to them. The ethical thread sets forth conditions for the effective protection and promotion of this human good. In combining practical concern for the welfare of people with a sober realism, the statement opens up the broad horizon where care for the whole political order and for the civility of society are obligations for those who support and promote religious freedom.

The importance of considering religious liberty as a civil liberty—like the freedoms of press, speech, and assembly—becomes evident here. As a political term, religious liberty refers to a way of ordering the political life of a society that restrains government (not citizens or religious bodies) from acting in religious matters (as does the Constitution in prohibiting Congress from making any law "respecting an establishment of religion, or prohibiting the free exercise therefore"). Religious liberty "is implemented by legislative enactments, which require for their effectiveness an organized civil community which is willing and able to enforce them impartially." Therefore "the way in which the civil community and its laws operate is of crucial importance to the actualization of religious and other liberties." The obligation of Christians is to "strengthen and uphold government when it maintains in fact the freedom and welfare of all people in a just and equitable manner." The statement warns that "the weakening of civil authority in a democratic society is more likely to undermine liberties than to produce them." Democratic participation that actively affirms the rights of all citizens is "a check against the ever-present tendency to abuse of authority by the state or other structures of power."[76]

Religious liberty depends on legal guarantees and the vitality of democratic institutions that "rest on and find their strength in a broad-based appreciation of the need for mutual respect among divergent persons." This statement recognizes that, in the church and among individual Christians, "far too often professions of loyalty to the principle of religious liberty have been betrayed by actions or attitudes grounded in prejudice." Such prejudice "may not only threaten the exercise of religious liberty but subvert its constitutional guarantees." To maintain religious diversity, the public must recognize "not that all religions are equally valid, but that all enjoy equal status before the law." That "is possible only when persons and groups, without compromising their own convictions, respect the integrity of the convictions of others and avoid hostility when their efforts to win others to their positions are rejected." The church, admitting its own past failures, should act "to develop understanding among those with divergent points of view, to oppose prejudice and intolerance wherever they may be found, and to deal creatively with the real tensions which exist."[77] In welcoming religious diversity, the statement emphasizes the church's role in forming people's beliefs, feelings, and attitudes toward others who are different. In contrast to certain "periods of tragedy" when the church contributed to "vicious intolerance, suffering and death," the statement aims to foster "a climate of interreligious understanding."[78]

"Religious Liberty" gives depth and breadth to the concern for religious freedom. The depth is given in its theological thread whereby religious freedom finds a home in the Christian narrative. The Lutheran commitment to religious freedom for all arises out of what the church believes to be true about God's relation to humans, not from indifference to truth or a thoroughgoing skepticism that denies truth or considers it unknowable. The breadth is given in the statement's ethical thread whereby the focus on the conditions for a genuine exercise of religious freedom includes constitutional, legal, political, and cultural dimensions. In rejecting a one-dimensional approach, Lutherans recognize that each of the interrelated dimensions is complex and multifaceted. Protecting religious freedom is an area of mutual endeavor in which state, church, and the whole of society share responsibility.

A Public Witness

I have been recalling the tradition that gives meaning to the ELCA's pledge to "work with civil authorities in areas of mutual endeavor, maintaining institutional separation of church and state in a relation of functional interaction." I have described and interpreted this tradition of discourse with the hope that persons within and without the ELCA may better understand how Lutherans have sought to make sense of the church's relation to government in pluralistic United States.

As an "insider-participant" (rather than an "outsider-observer") in the tradition, I care for its future as well as its past. With this exercise in remembering, I hope to encourage ELCA Lutherans to draw on and build on what we have received in facing the challenges of a new century. We should learn from and argue with our tradition, not forget or abandon it. It would be arrogant and foolish for us to assume that our reflection on church and state begins from zero or that the tradition resolves all our quandaries. We do better by gratefully acknowledging our dependence on tradition to give us context and direction, by humbly recognizing its limits and unfinished character, and by faithfully accepting responsibility for its future.

In this spirit I offer some personal thoughts on what we might learn from this tradition for our church's public witness to God at the intersection of church and state. By "public" witness I mean both that it is made in the "open" and deals with concerns of the "whole" society. I will pick up and all-too-briefly comment on some aspects of this living tradition that should be prominent in deliberation on its future.

Lutherans in the last half-century have moved "Beyond Separationism,"[79] and it is not likely that we will go back to 1900. We have gone from believing that the church should not influence government to thinking that it is part of our mission to do so. The social statement "Religious Liberty" voices clearly a major thrust of the tradition: The church "declares its right and duty to address government and the general community, both though its members and through its corporate forms, not only in its own interest but especially in the interest of the welfare of all people."[80] Because this change came about on Lutheran premises, it is likely to have lasting significance for Lutherans. This right and duty to speak appears to have wide support among Lutherans, at least in principle, although we will continue to debate the forms this speaking should take, the priority it should have, the issues it should address, and the positions it should adopt.[81]

The social statements we have examined represent the most important and sustained official Lutheran reflection on our topic in the United States. What emerges from this tradition is a comprehensive understanding of church and state relations. Lutherans are committed to the integrity of church and state, to their practical interaction, indeed, cooperation for the common good in a constitutional order that guarantees religious freedom for all. This threefold commitment, grounded theologically and shaped contextually, summarizes the basic trajectory of our tradition. This trajectory opens us up to the complexity of church and state relations in an increasingly pluralistic society. It does not lock us into a one-sided and unfruitful metaphor ("wall of separation"), expect us to work for a "Christian state" or theocracy, or allow us to acquiesce to however government or society might define the relationship. When the question arises about what is at stake in church and state relations—whether as general stance or in relation to specific issues—we come with not one but three sets of considerations: those relating to integrity, interaction, and religious freedom for all.

What is most pervasive and fundamental in our tradition might be called its Trinitarian theocentrism. It is centered in God, that is, it carries out the church's mandate and gift to see God in relation to all. It views church and state in light of God's story with creation as revealed in Scripture, confessed in the church's creeds, and taught in the Lutheran Confessions. The calling, authority, and norm for church and state, it asserts, come ultimately from the triune God, whose sovereign and gracious governance embraces the past, present, and future of each person, every nation, and the entire cosmos. Our approach to church and state rests on knowledge given in faith in God. Trinitarian theocentrism is public witness to God that makes claims about what is true. God's true story with creation is essential, we believe, for protecting human life and dignity, affirming and limiting the state, and giving the church its mission.

Our public witness to the triune God takes place in a culture that is "past the place where underlying Christian culture and beliefs are assumed in its life."[82] This is not to underestimate the continuing imprint of the biblical heritage in our culture or to forget the vitality of churches in our time. Yet we cannot simply expect that our culture's ethos and institutions will support or reinforce the church's teachings; indeed, frequently they undercut them. In part this reflects the "disestablishment" of a once-dominant Protestantism and the increase in religious diversity. More than that, it points to the power of the mass media and other culture-forming institutions to create a world whose presuppositions and values often run counter to the Christian vision. And when we also remember that for many the demands and promises of economic life become their "gods," we can recognize that deep strains in our culture are ignorant of, indifferent to, or hostile toward Christian faith.

Such a culture "heightens the need of the church for strength to stand alone, lofty and unshaken, in American society. It calls for greater depth of conviction in all Christian men and women."[83] Above all, the church needs to keep its own counsel, remember God's commandments and gospel, and center its own life in God. A vibrant public witness to the triune God comes first of all through living communities of faith and the lives of Christians in their vocations.[84]

For the church to keep its own counsel is not, however, a call for the church to turn its back on our culture, even if that were possible. Because God also works through human culture and institutions and holds them accountable, we have responsibility to take part in and influence them. If this is the case, then the ongoing debate about the public role of religion has importance for the church. Religion is not about to disappear, in spite of predictions for two centuries of its coming demise. Most people in the United States believe in God, and Christian and other religious groups (in the United States and around the world) have shown that religion remains a powerful personal and public reality. The once widely accepted secularization theory that claimed that a "de-religionifying" of society inevitably accompanied modernization has lost much of its plausibility.[85] Some commentators argue that our culture marginalizes, trivializes, and excludes religion from the public square; their belief that society should ensure a public role for religion is congenial to the church's public witness.[86]

Because God's care and call embrace all of life, we will "naturally" draw upon our faith and its knowledge when we contend for the common good. We cannot accept the notion that what we say on the basis of our faith about culture and the ordering of society is out-of-bounds in the public arena because it is religious. We cannot be true to our deepest beliefs and accept a rule of public discourse that says only nonreligiously based knowledge and argument count. Guided by the Golden Rule, we should insist that all religious groups have the freedom to bring their religiously based insights, claims, and values into the public discussion, while also insisting that religiously grounded appeals and arguments should be subject to the same messy democratic debate as are other appeals and arguments. My point is not that what the church or other religious groups say is always correct and proper; they too are composed of sinners and can be as wrong-headed and nasty as other groups. It is rather that our understanding of who the triune God is does not permit us to box our faith in God out of public life.

Our church's public witness to God is structured by God's twofold governance of the world through law and gospel. The distinction between God's (continuing) creating and preserving governance through human action and institutions and God's redeeming and sanctifying governance through word and sacrament permeates and shapes our tradition. If we take our cue from this discourse, we will not collapse God's activity into the singular. This happens, for example, when Christians make the American experience a part of salvation history, when they identify a political movement with the Christian faith, when they reduce the gospel to inspiration for a moral cause, or when they confine God's activity either to the church or to the world. Nor will we look for salvation outside of Jesus Christ. Family or civil society or government or the economy are not salvific or redemptive; they are arenas of responsibility that we affirm with thanksgiving, for in and through them God acts to resist sin and to protect and bless human life.

The belief that state and church belong to distinctive ways God governs a fallen world is formative for Lutherans. Note that I am not equating God's rule through the (civil use of) law with the state, as Lutherans have too often done. When we understand the state to be part (not the whole) of God's care for the world through the law, we are perhaps more apt to appreciate government's complex interrelationship with civil society and the economy. From there we may speak of the uniqueness of government: It is the one institution that claims authority to act on behalf of the whole of society and possesses the right to make laws and enforce them for the sake of peaceful order. In a democratic order government is to be subject to the agreement and control of citizens.

Government's calling and authority are secular; they belong to this age that will pass away (see pp. 58–59). The church's public witness fulfills one of its most important tasks in reminding government that its significance is temporal not eternal. Government is not the divine agent to bring in God's kingdom; it is the divine agent—God's mask—to bring relative peace and justice to secular society. Within the secular order, it is accountable to God for making judgments that favor what is good and oppose what is wrong. Lutheran thinking differs from political philosophies that argue that government should remain "neutral" in relation to competing understanding of the good life and leave all judgments about them to individual choice.[87] When considering public policy on difficult and divisive issues in our society—economic activity, environmental regulations, abortion, divorce, homosexual unions, assisted suicide, gambling, cloning—Lutheran thinking does not presume that personal autonomy trumps other considerations of what is good and right. Instead of dismissing all conceptions of what is good and right as speculative, subjective, and therefore irrelevant to public policy, we should recognize that conflict about such conceptions belongs to secular life and encourage vigorous public discussion about them. The church's public witness includes the task to contribute to defining what government sees as pertinent to its responsibility for a good secular society.

The belief that government's authority is secular, that its reach is restricted to temporal life, supports Lutheran commitment to religious freedom. For centuries Lutherans have gratefully acknowledged that in this country we "enjoy the free exercise of religion."[88] The overwhelming attitude has been that "we cherish the freedom and responsibility the First Amendment assures us," coupled with the belief that "the guarantees of religious liberty . . . have served this nation well."[89] The experience of Lutheranism in the United States offers a historical example of how a religious tradition can draw on its own theological heritage formed in a situation that assumed religious monopoly to be the norm to embrace religious freedom.

Our church's public witness contributes to the ethos that sustains religious freedom when we preach and teach God's twofold governance of the world. While government has authority to coerce in secular matters, we teach, the church has authority only to proclaim and persuade. An effective order of religious freedom presupposes a general consensus that religious bodies renounce the use of coercion to advance their specific beliefs. Not all religious bodies or traditions accept this premise; some teach that government force should be at the service of their beliefs. The issue is in large part theological. Do we not have responsibility to seek out dialogue with such religious traditions? Especially when we think of religious freedom and persecution on a global scale, we can understand the need for interreligious contact and conversation.

Because of our own generally positive experience, Lutherans may overlook the fact that the promise of religious freedom has been denied or truncated for many in our country's history: American Indians, African American slaves, Roman Catholics, Mormons, Jehovah's Witnesses, and others. As in the past, threats to religious freedom are likely to appear in relation to smaller, unpopular, marginalized or new religious groups that lack political connections to protect their freedom. Our commitment to religious freedom leads us to support their legitimate claims and to be vigilant in countering threats to the free exercise of religion by all citizens. This includes careful monitoring of Supreme Court decisions.

The Lutheran theological approach to church and state relations takes into account and incorporates constitutional and legal considerations. It employs key legal concepts—such as wholesome neutrality, nonpreference, compelling interest, and accommodation—found in Supreme Court decisions, and it addresses specific areas of conflict. This approach invites us to continue to work at the crossroads of theology and law. The interaction of religion and government touches every aspect of life and is dynamic and ever-changing; the proper distinctions between them are often difficult to draw in a religiously diverse society; new religious expressions, new legislative proposals, and new Supreme Court decisions change the terms of their relation; and the disruptive power of sin constantly makes itself felt. To sustain a credible and competent public witness at the intersection of church and state, we will need to take up this never finished task of our tradition with renewed vigor.[89]

The Lutheran tradition on church and state presented in this chapter illustrates the church's public witness as well as calls for and offers direction for this witness to the triune God. In arguing for the institutional integrity of both church and state and their practical interaction in areas of mutual endeavor, it charts a course beyond church domination, state domination, and absolute separation.[90] In contrast to the beginning of the last century, Lutherans at the beginning of this century are recipients of a lively tradition that challenges us to witness in the public square of a pluralistic society to the one God, Father, Son, and Holy Spirit.

4

Promoting the General Welfare: Lutheran Social Ministry

Susan Kosche Vallem

Lutheranism, through its social ministry endeavors, exemplifies a long history of response to God's call for service. Lutheran churches have often cooperated with government—and government with churches—in addressing human need and promoting the general welfare. Today in the United States the responsibilities of church and government and their relationship are in a state of flux. The passage of the 1996 Personal Responsibility and Work Opportunities Reconciliation Act, more commonly referred to as federal welfare reform, marks a dramatic change in how government responds to human need. Lutheran social ministry organizations along with other faith-based organizations are finding their way in this new situation.

The welfare reform legislation offers increased opportunity for faith-based service organizations to receive government funding. This policy poses important constitutional issues related to religious freedom and the non-establishment of religion. It also compels Lutheran social ministry organizations to consider anew whether we can retain our Christian identity and integrity while meeting federal requirements for funding. It calls citizens to evaluate the effects of the legislation on poor people and to ask whether the federal government is abdicating its unique role and responsibility to provide for the general welfare of all of its citizens.

The work of Lutheran social ministry organizations is both sacred and secular; that is, it is embedded in Christian faith, and it addresses social needs that are also the responsibility of government and others in society. It is an area of "functional interaction" between church and state. How the church will respond today is influenced by welfare reform, but it is finally rooted in who we are and what we believe. I begin therefore by reviewing the scriptural, theological, and historical foundations of social ministry. I will then consider church and state relations and conclude by outlining a Lutheran response to the present situation.

Faith and Care for Poor People

Jesus declared, "The time is fulfilled; the kingdom of God is at hand" (Mark 1:14). He taught that the reign of God includes community, care of others, and love toward all. Jesus' words and actions—indeed his entire ministry— demonstrate what community is like.[1]

God's vision for the world is recounted in Genesis 1 and 2. Human beings are created in the image of God, and when God breathes into the human, the creature becomes a living soul. All humans have this identity and deserve to be treated with dignity. Living out this God-given human identity means that humans are to have

1. Food: God gives humans every green plant in the garden
2. Living space: God creates a universe and a place to live
3. Community: God creates male and female to live and work together
4. Occupation: Humans have work to do, to nurture and protect the earth
5. Health: God provides well-being for humans.[2]

The Old Testament speaks of divinely given laws and obligations for the care of people. A merciful and compassionate God commands the Israelites to care for widows and for people who are poor, and to extend hospitality to strangers as well.[3] Landowners are instructed to leave the corners of their fields and vineyards at harvest time for poor people and strangers to glean (Lev. 19:9-10). God expects a righteous Israelite to give freely and warns those who oppress the poor: "Those who oppress the poor insult their Maker, but those who are kind to the needy honor him" (Prov. 14:31). Caring for the poor is seen as an act of justice.[4]

Israel's concern for the welfare of the most vulnerable became an integral tenet of the Christian tradition. Jesus admonished his disciples to care for one another, poor people, and children; to give alms freely; and to love their neighbors as themselves. When an expert in the law asked Jesus who was his neighbor, Jesus responded with the parable of the Good Samaritan (Luke 10:25-37). He encouraged the rich young ruler to sell all that he had and to give it to the poor (Mark 10:17-22). In the Beatitudes Jesus admonished his hearers to give to all who asked and not turn them away (Matt. 6:42). Jesus also spoke about where he was to be found (Matt. 25:35-36):

> For I was hungry and you gave me food, I was thirsty and you gave me
> something to drink; I was a stranger and you welcomed me, I was naked
> and you gave me clothing, I was sick and you took care of me, I was in
> prison and you visited me. . . .

When challenged to say when he was given food, drink, clothes, and care,
Jesus identified with every hungry and homeless person: "Just as you did it to
the least of these who are members of my family, you did it to me."

Scripture is replete with stories of Jesus' acts of care for the well-being of
others. One such account is his feeding the five thousand: Jesus took a young
boy's gift of a few fish and loaves of bread and fed a multitude of hungry people (Mark 6:30-44). One lesson is that small gifts, when blessed by Jesus, can
multiply. A more subtle lesson is that Jesus did not discriminate between those
who were worthy or unworthy to receive food. Jesus simply instructed that all
were to be fed without restriction. Martin Luther reiterated Jesus' perspective
when he noted that Christ fed not only the pious and good but also those who
followed him for their own good.

In the fourth century, Christianity reached a turning point that affected
church-provided care for poor people. After Constantine declared Christianity to be a legal religion in 313, Christian membership multiplied, and with
the increased membership came increased demands for charity. Early Christian almsgiving had been based "on the conception of giving as an expression
of loving-kindness and activity necessary to the carrying out of God's will."[5] As
some Christians prospered, the church had to deal with the matter of private
property and the accompanying disparity between rich and poor. In response,
the church shifted its perspective on charity and promulgated the doctrine
that "good works" and charitable acts could contribute to personal salvation as
well as be responsive to God's will. The views of fourth-century Christian writers can be summarized as follows:

> Chrysostom praises the presence of beggars at the church door as giving an
> opportunity to those entering to cleanse their consciences from minor fault
> by almsgiving. Augustine also teaches . . . the belief that almsgiving could
> atone for the sins of the departed as well as for those of the living. . . . He is
> careful to limit the efficacy of charity to those whose lives were acceptable to
> God. It availed nothing for living or dead who were of evil reputation.[6]

The church reaffirmed acts of charity by describing the benefits to both the
givers and receivers. By the thirteenth century, the church declared that welfare was not optional: The rich had a legal and moral obligation to support
the poor, and the poor had the right to expect such support. In the Middle
Ages, the poor were viewed with benign tolerance and charity was, doctrinally
at least, an entitlement.

> The doctrine that the poor man had a right to the help he received . . . col-
> ored the whole relationship between benefactor and beneficiary in the
> Middle Ages, tending to discourage both sentimental self-esteem on the
> part of the donor and excessive humiliation in the recipient.[7]

Monasteries and convents put aside a portion of the harvest for the poorest
people as a commitment to Jesus' teachings. This perspective changed when
the Black Death of 1348–49 devastated the populations of Europe. Laborers
were scarce, and English legislation forbade the giving of alms to so-called
able-bodied beggars. By 1536 churches were encouraged to take up regular
collections for the poor and to provide employment for the able-bodied.[8]

Care for Poor People in the Lutheran Tradition

In the sixteenth century, the church cared for the poor, but solicitation for
funds also included a vested self-interest. Charity could be generous when
used to maintain religious influence but became increasingly ineffective in
meeting the needs of the growing numbers of poor people.[9] Church solicitation for building projects as well as charity reached a pinnacle in 1517 with the
sale of indulgences, a method of solicitation that prompted Martin Luther to
write his "Ninety-five Theses." Luther reflected Scripture when he stated in
Thesis 43: "Christians are to be taught that he who gives to the poor or lends
to the needy does a better deed than he who buys indulgences." Luther further stated in Thesis 45: "Christians are to be taught that he who sees a needy
man and passes him by, yet gives his money for indulgences, does not buy
papal indulgences but God's wrath."[10]

The Reformation brought with it other changes in social welfare. In the
Middle Ages, the church, principally priests and nuns, administered charitable programs. With the closing of the religious orders, Protestant churches
and communities had to reorganize hospitals, schools, and charities. As a
result, much of the welfare work was taken over by laity in congregations in
conjunction with civil governments.[11]

Luther developed his social teaching through his doctrine of the "two kingdoms," the "temporal" that was ruled by the sword and the "spiritual" that was
ruled by grace and forgiveness.[12] While Luther distinguished the two kingdoms (or governments), he insisted that they overlap in Christian life and
ministry. Christians reside in both kingdoms and are to care for all God's people. Through baptism, Christians receive a vocation to do God's work by serving God in community: to love our neighbors and to work toward a just and
equitable world.

Scholars debate how much influence Luther's teachings had on European social thought and practice. One scholar, however, points to the importance of Luther's teaching on love that freely flows from faith in Jesus Christ:

> In his sermons, Biblical commentaries, and devotional writings, Luther transmitted to his descendants a profound sense of this bleak world's need for love. Love could not save the world, no more than could the law, but it could soften the harshness and cruelty of life in the Three Estates.[13]

In his commentary on the Sermon on the Mount, Luther wrote, "Every city should store away as much as possible for the common need, and in addition every parish should have a common treasury for the poor."[14] For Luther, the sharing of possessions was not viewed as compulsory but as a work of Christian love freely given.[15]

Luther understood social welfare activity as a work of the people flowing from worship. Worship thrusts the Christian into the world to serve the neighbor. Indeed, Luther can characterize the daily life of the Christian as worship, because to serve the neighbor and thus obey God's commandment is worship.[16]

In Luther's Germany both church and local government provided social welfare. Parish and governmental functions and responsibilities overlapped. Luther took an active role in developing social welfare as a means of enhancing social order. He called on the city council of Wittenberg, for instance, to establish a community chest, the Wittenberg *Beutelordnung*, to gather donations for the poor. An actual wooden chest was placed in the parish church and locked with three keys. The mayor had one key, and the stewards of the chest, who were appointed by the church, had the other keys. The stewards met with the poor of the community, determined their need, and allocated the charity accordingly. The stewards were held accountable to the mayor of Wittenberg, to the city councilors, and to the parish pastor.[17]

Another ingredient in the Lutheran development of social ministries was the diaconate ministry. Luther recognized differences in the ministries of clergy—who were to preach and administer the sacraments—and the lay diaconate who were to administer charity. Luther described their role in "The Babylonian Captivity of the Church":

> The diaconate is the ministry, not of reading the Gospel and the Epistle, as is the present practice, but of distributing the church's aid to the poor, so that the priests may be relieved of the burden of temporal matters and may give themselves more freely to prayer and the word.[18]

The diaconate ministry in Lutheranism developed in the early and mid-nineteenth century in response to the increased need for care of poor and needy people and a search for a role to be played by congregations. The title of deacon came to designate a person in the congregation responsible for the collection and distribution of charity care for the needy. Women began to take a more prominent role in charity care as diaconate programs for women, similar to Roman Catholic convents, were established by Lutheran and other Protestant churches. Deaconesses served as teachers, social workers, and nurses.

Wilhelm Loehe, a Lutheran pastor in the 1850s, established an early diaconate program when he came to the small rural village of Neuendettelsau, Germany, and was struck by the misery of its peasant citizenry. Loehe saw Christian ministry as holistic, involving worship and sacraments, witnessing and mission, and service and charity; he wanted these three foci to determine the mission of congregations.[19]

Loehe trained 350 men and sent them abroad as missionaries, but he was also concerned for the unmarried women of the village who had no means to obtain an education or specialized training and thus became economically dependent. So Loehe began a diaconate program, personally training five young women for two years and returning them to their congregations to provide service work. The congregations, however, forced the young women back to the homes of their brothers. Against his hopes of establishing congregations as the center of service through diaconate ministry, Loehe was compelled to provide the deaconesses with special uniforms and a motherhouse from where they could safely work and effectively serve Lutheran congregations.[20] Since the German secular system frequently did little for poor people in the nineteenth century, the church continued with a system of both preaching the gospel and meeting the physical and social needs of the community.

Another prominent Lutheran, William Passavant (1821–1894), established social service agencies and began the diaconate program in the United States. Passavant founded more orphanages, hospitals, homes for the aged, and other social service institutions than any other Lutheran in America. He began the first Protestant hospital in America in 1849 in Pittsburgh, another in Milwaukee in 1863, and one in Chicago in 1865. Passavant is credited with establishing the first Protestant orphanage in America in Pittsburgh in 1852 and others throughout New England, and he developed the diaconate movement in America to staff the increasing number of Lutheran social services institutions. Many of the nurses, social workers, and teachers in the Lutheran institutions came from the diaconate ministry. Other Lutherans followed Passavant's lead and established social service institutions throughout the country. Deaconess work among the Swedish Lutherans in the Midwest began in 1879 with the establishment of a Lutheran hospital in Omaha, Nebraska. The Norwegians also established deaconess programs during the nineteenth century, primarily for hospital work.[21]

Development of Social Welfare
in the United States

Lutheran social ministry work and public welfare services developed along separate but sometimes intersecting tracks. Lutheranism had little influence on the early development of the American public social welfare system even though Lutherans established a vast network of social ministries throughout America. Public social welfare began in colonial times and was influenced by the English system and later to some extent by Social Darwinism. In the late nineteenth century, the Social Gospel movement helped spur renewed interest in social welfare in America. Lutheranism continued to develop its own social welfare system sometimes in cooperation with the public system but without substantial influence from the Social Gospel movement.

The foundation of the American public welfare system is based on the English system with its roots in the Elizabethan Poor Law of 1601. The Poor Law codified the English government's responsibility to provide charity care. This law provided for

- public, tax-supported aid to the destitute
- locally financed and locally administered relief, with a publicly appointed overseer of the poor as administrator
- a system that included direct aid for those unable to work and work for the able-bodied. Thus the law began a system of classification and differential treatment of the poor.
- responsibility for the care of needy relatives
- apprenticeship of children as a way of both caring for and educating them[22]

In institutionalizing the categorization of the poor, the Poor Laws were based on two unfortunate assumptions: "that there were clearly distinct categories of dependency which are reflective of people themselves, and that the government must therefore means-test those who seek public welfare to assess their worthiness."[23] This attitude toward the poor was carried to the colonies and directly influenced the attitudes of many early policymakers. The American public social welfare system adopted similar poor laws and codified the concept of governmental responsibility for the care of the poor based on a system of classification and differential treatment of categories of poor people.

In the late nineteenth century, a new social philosophy, Social Darwinism, arose in America and England to strengthen the legal categorization of the poor and support the limitations on the public social welfare system. Social Darwinism, which traces its roots to well before Charles Darwin, was a social version of "the survival of the fittest," and received its clearest exposition in the work of the English philosopher, Herbert Spencer. Spencer's view held that

> Nature had decreed that some people were fit to advance the cause of life and should survive, but that others were unfit and that the misfortune of poverty for the unfit was to be expected. Meddling by the state in regulation of industry, subsidies to the poor, public education and even the improvement of sanitation was a conspiracy against the natural order. Such actions not only deprived people of their inherent right to fulfill themselves but were contrary to the laws of nature and a crime against the gradual advancement of the human race.[24]

Social Darwinism gave scientific approval to rapid industrialization and the burgeoning capitalistic, laissez-faire beliefs already prevalent in American society.

Not wanting to hinder the "advancement of the human race," as warned by Spencer, the American government operated on the belief that a hands-off, laissez-faire policy was appropriate for business and for poor people (although it did recognize that government had a minimal responsibility to some classifications of poor). Only minimal assistance should be given the poor lest they become dependent; if left alone, the poor would surely find greater incentive to work. Little governmental provision was made for those whose circumstances prohibited them from becoming self-sufficient.

American public welfare policies assumed that poverty was the fault of the victim not the economy: Aside from the special categories identified in the Poor Law, most people should be able to work. Those who worked hard enough would be directly rewarded with wealth and well-being. Poor people had to be coerced to work and thereby deterred from pauperism.

From 1870 through the early 1900s the Social Gospel movement challenged Social Darwinism and its laissez-faire policy. It reacted to "the pietistic individualism that had been so largely responsible for the churches' removal from the field of social action."[25] One Social Gospel leader proclaimed, "The 'let alone theory of society' . . . bears the mark of Cain. Its theological definition is hell." Another called laissez-faire "the science of extortion, the gentle act of grinding the faces of the poor."[26]

Through the Social Gospel some American Protestants sought solutions to the new and growing problems that resulted from the Industrial Revolution. They argued that laissez-faire principles were incompatible with Christian principles of reaching out and extending assistance to the poor.[27] Social Gospel devotees sought to apply Christian teachings of charity to social and economic problems and to conform the public social realm to Jesus' teachings. The Social Gospel movement, although it later lost momentum, helped make the American public more acutely aware of the growing problem of urban poverty in America.

American Lutheranism was minimally influenced by the Social Gospel movement. The majority of Lutherans in the late nineteenth century were German and Scandinavian immigrants in rural areas who focused on their own survival. Lutherans generally exhibited sociopolitical quietism. Yet the increased awareness of social problems emphasized by the Social Gospel was not entirely lost on the Lutherans. For example, by 1900 the *Lutheran Observer* (published by the General Synod) began to give more attention to the church's social mission, "sensing the foolishness of preaching abstract righteousness while society was dominated by corruption." The *Observer* encouraged preachers to address the need for economic and social reform from their pulpits.[28]

Most Lutherans were social and theological conservatives who saw their greatest calling to uphold the faithful preaching of the gospel and bring the saving grace of Jesus Christ to a sinful world. Social Gospel theologian Walter Rauschenbusch wrote of Lutherans in 1912:

> They hold that the Church should preach the Gospel, administer the sacraments, and leave it to the individual to do his duty in society and the State. . . . In theory this position leaves individuals free for christianizing activity in society; in practice it leaves them unstimulated, uninstructed, and even sterilized against social enthusiasm.[29]

Historian E. Clifford Nelson wrote of the Lutheran response to the Social Gospel:

> Lutherans' pessimistic view of unconverted (and sometimes of converted) man, of society, and of history coupled with its fear of invading the domain of the state would still have determined how they responded. Failure to probe Luther's positive theology of "civil righteousness" (justice) only compounded the negative views of social action.[30]

In spite of their minimal involvement in the Social Gospel movement and social action, Lutherans were actively engaged in social welfare as an extension of their mission effort. They called it "inner mission," a term that meant the care of the physical and social as well as the spiritual needs of God's people. Inner mission work led to the Lutheran network of social ministry organizations.

Church and State Cooperation

Major social changes in the twentieth century have affected Lutherans' responses to social needs. As a result of the Great Depression and the ensuing New Deal legislation, the federal government became more directly involved in the delivery of social welfare. Even though this era is marked by the rapid development of public social welfare institutions, the federal government also relied on private, faith-based agencies to provide services. This reliance was not new: the government had already established a system of assistance to private educational institutions, and state and local taxes supported orphanages and hospitals.[31] In 1901 Frank Fetter, a sociologist from Cornell University, wrote, "Except for possibly two territories and four western states, there is probably not a state in the union where some aid [to private charities] is not given by the state or by counties and cities."[32] Especially after the 1950s, government contracting with faith-based agencies increased dramatically in providing a wide range of services, "including day care, homeless shelters, child protection, counseling, home health, legal aid, family planning, respite care, and community living."[33]

Lutheran social ministry agencies have a history of contracting and partnership with government. Bremwood in Waverly, Iowa, is one example of this church and state cooperation. Bremwood (then called the Lutheran Children's Home) opened as an orphanage in 1864; it began as a local congregational project to care for children orphaned as a result of the Civil War. By 1872, after incurring considerable debt, the Children's Home requested and obtained a $5,000 loan from the State of Iowa. The debt was later forgiven. The episode illustrates how more than a century ago public monies along with congregational support flowed into a religious institution to meet a public need. As social needs changed in the 1930s, the Children's Home increased its services to include residential treatment for children with emotional problems and added a foster home program. By the 1960s the home, now renamed Bremwood, was no longer an orphanage but focused completely on residential treatment for youth. The greatest percentage of services were paid by the Iowa State Department of Social Services from monies passed to the state from the federal government. In return for payment Bremwood had to meet state and federal professional standards. Currently Bremwood provides residential treatment services and contracts with state agencies to offer in-home and other family and counseling services. Although it receives a majority of its funding from state and federal programs, Bremwood retains it affiliation with the Evangelical Lutheran Church in America (ELCA). This affiliation is expressed through Bremwood's membership in Lutheran Services in America, the participation of Lutheran churches on its board of directors, and more recently, through its appeal to Lutheran churches for greater financial support to offset recent federal and state funding cuts.[34]

Constitutional Questions

The increasing reliance of government on faith-based agencies to provide social welfare services has raised significant questions of constitutional law for the courts to decide. Government aid must conform to the Supreme Court's interpretation of the First Amendment of the United States Constitution, which stipulates that "Congress shall make no law respecting an establishment of religion, or prohibiting the free exercise thereof. . . ." The Supreme Court has dealt frequently with government aid for religious educational institutions but less so with social ministry agencies. While primary and secondary religious schools have usually been denied aid, faith-based agencies have been able to accept public funding and with less scrutiny than faith-based educational institutions. The Supreme Court has ruled that government funding for faith-based social welfare agencies does not violate the First Amendment's Establishment Clause.

> It has done so on the basis of the sacred-secular distinction and the pervasively sectarian standard. The sacred-secular distinction says that a religiously-based organization has both secular and sacred functions and activities, and that government may fund the secular ones but not the sacred ones.
>
> Closely related to the sacred-secular distinction is the pervasively sectarian standard. The Court held in one of these cases (Hunt v. McNair): "Aid normally may be thought to have a primary effect of advancing religion when it flows to an institution in which religion is so pervasive that a substantial portion of its functions are subsumed in the religious mission. . . ."[35]

The Supreme Court has decided two cases that specifically involved the practice of public funding for faith-based social ministry organizations, *Bradfield v. Roberts* (1899) and *Bowen v. Kendrick* (1988). "In each case the Supreme Court upheld the program of financial cooperation between government and nonprofit organizations within the context of its no-aid-to-religion strain of judicial interpretation."[36]

Bradfield v. Roberts dealt with government funding of a Roman Catholic hospital. The court determined that the funding was constitutional because of the secular nature of the hospital's activities. The court saw it as "simply the case of a secular corporation being managed by people who hold to the doctrines of the Roman Catholic Church."[37] The more recent case, *Bowen v. Kendrick*, establishes the contours of contemporary law in this area. In *Bowen*, the Supreme Court considered the constitutionality of federal funding through the Adolescent Family Life Act (AFLA) to nonprofit organizations, including religious organizations, for services relating to teenage sexuality and pregnancies. The challenge claimed that AFLA's funding for education programs encouraging sexual abstinence was in fact providing federal funds to teach religious doctrine. The Supreme Court ruled that the act on its face did not violate the Establishment Clause and remanded the case to the lower courts to determine whether or not it did so as actually administered. The majority opinion concluded that the act had a secular purpose: "As we see it, it is clear from the face of the statute that the AFLA was motivated primarily, if not entirely, by a legitimate secular purpose." The Supreme Court wrote, "Only in the context of aid to pervasively sectarian institutions have we invalidated an aid program on the grounds that there was a substantial risk that aid to these religious institutions would, knowingly or unknowingly, result in indoctrination."[38]

Courts have relied on several elements to classify aid recipients as "pervasively sectarian":

1. location near a house of worship
2. an abundance of religious symbols on the premises
3. religious discrimination in the institution's hiring practices
4. the presence of religious activities
5. the purposeful articulation of a religious mission[39]

Although the presence of any one of these factors would not necessarily disqualify a faith-based agency from receiving public funds, courts are much more reticent about upholding aid to such agencies.

Welfare Reform

Lutheran churches and their social ministry organizations are directly affected by the welfare reform movement of the 1990s, sometimes referred to as "new federalism" or "devolution." "New federalism" describes the changing relationship between the national and state governments as they sort out their roles and responsibilities within the federal system. "Devolution" entails passing policy responsibilities from the federal government to state and local governments. This process may include any combination of block grants to states, reduced grants-in-aid from the federal government, and increased flexibility for states in complying with federal requirements. Because many social services programs are funded by federal block grants, states control the extent to which those funds are used at the state level or passed through to localities. States may fund additional services and determine for those services the level of program administration. Under the law, faith-based organizations must be allowed to compete equally for block grant monies.

The welfare reform legislation, specifically entitled, The Personal Responsibility and Work Opportunity Reconciliation Act (P.L. 104–193), dramatically changed the nation's welfare system by requiring work in exchange for time-limited assistance. Temporary Assistance to Needy Families (TANF) replaced Aid to Families with Dependent Children (AFDC) program. The law gave states specific options and mandates to provide welfare-to-work programs and welfare-related services to the poor through block grant monies and through contracts with charitable, religious, and private organizations.

In response to the pending welfare reform legislation, the board of the Division for Church in Society of the ELCA published a guide, *Working Principles for Welfare Reform*.[40] The guide affirms that the public welfare system is in need of significant reform, and it advocates for such reforms based on the ethical implications of the church's theological affirmations and social statements. The working principles cited are: the obligations of government; dependence on God; interdependence with mutual responsibilities; human dignity and basic needs; freedom and initiative; human work; investment in families; nurturing and support of children; caring for the stranger; and the uniqueness of the individual.

In a preliminary study of the impact of welfare reform, the Rev. Paul Wee, then of the Lutheran Church of the Reformation in Washington, D.C., stated:

> On the eve of the decision to terminate the welfare system the major Christian social service providers in the country, Catholic Charities, Lutheran Services in America, the Salvation Army, and the YWCA, issued a joint statement predicting that "The proposed policy changes will increase hunger, homelessness, and abuse and neglect within families." The statement expressed deep concern "that the partnership between government and religious institutions, which has worked so well in the past, is now being broken." Following the prophets and the reformers of the church, [we] will continue to remind the government that it, the government, not the church, has been entrusted by God with the responsibility for, "establishing justice, protecting and advancing human rights, and providing for the general welfare of all."[41]

Results of research studies on the impact of welfare reform have been mixed. Initial data showed a decrease in the number of people on welfare throughout the country. Nonetheless, uncertainty abounds about the long-term benefits and harms of this reform and also about the possible impact of an economic recession on welfare reform. Some evidence also suggests that people are not necessarily better off; they may be off welfare but are still poor.

While some benefits lost in the initial welfare reform legislation have been restored, Lutheran agencies have felt the impact of welfare reform legislation in increased requests for food and shelter. They are not alone. An early twenty-nine-city survey conducted by the U.S. Conference of Mayors, for example, addressed the extent of hunger and homelessness in these communities. The study found that

> overall demand for both emergency food and shelter grew during 1997 for most of the surveyed cities. Demand for food increased at a higher rate, and in more cities, than has been reported in recent years, and demand for shelter increased at a lower rate, and in fewer cites, than in past years although more of the shelter demand remained unmet, and shelters in more cities have had to turn people away.[42]

Research conducted by the Lutheran Office for Governmental Affairs of the Division for Church in Society of the ELCA on "The Impact of Welfare Reform on Lutheran Social Ministry Agencies and Congregations" found similar results. Agencies and congregations indicated an increased need (in descending order) for food, housing assistance, transportation, and job assistance. Reasons cited most often for the need for emergency services were unemployment or wages too low to meet family needs, lack of available affordable housing, high medical costs, substance abuse problems, and domestic violence. Agencies and congregations have had to turn people away because of insufficient food or resources.[43] Congregations have not historically sought government funding for service provision and have left that role for the social ministry organizations. Time will tell if congregations can or will seek government contracts for service provision.

The federal government recognized its long relationship with private welfare providers and the successful history of religious organizations in meeting human need by including faith-based service organizations and religious congregations in Section 104 of the welfare law, called "Charitable Choice." This provision allows states to contract directly with "charitable, religious or private organizations" and provides specific language regarding the participation of religious organizations in delivering welfare services. States must consider religious organizations on an equal, nondiscriminatory basis with other groups when deciding to contract with private institutions.[44]

Charitable Choice allows faith-based organizations greater independent control over employment practices and definition, development, practice, and expression of their religious beliefs. In return faith-based organizations must provide the same fiscal audits as all other service providers and are prohibited from using federal funds for religious worship, instruction, or proselytizing. In addition faith-based organizations may not discriminate against a beneficiary on the basis of religion, religious belief, or refusal to participate actively in a religious practice.

The 1996 welfare reform legislation presents a paradigm shift in the provision of services to people in need and has the potential to impact the complementarity of the church and state relationship. If the government itself provides fewer direct services for the welfare of its citizens, then what is the government's role in financing and regulating the provision of services by faith-based entities? Should the church, through its social ministry organization and congregations, directly accept increased federal and state funding and, along with the dollars, a greater responsibility for the safety net? Can the church accept the increased funding and responsibility and still maintain the integrity of its prophetic role in criticizing the state? If the state shifts its role of primary responsibility to the least of its citizens to the faith-based agencies, will the church have difficulty calling the state to its responsibility? Will the church be afraid of biting the hand that feeds it?

An additional issue concerns federal regulation of agencies that receive federal funds. One view is that if the government wants increased provision of services from the religious sector, then it must provide greater religious freedom for faith-based agencies. This perspective is implied in the Charitable Choice provision. The opposing position argues that increased federal monies should require increased federal oversight and regulation. While the Supreme Court (in *Bowen v. Kendrick*) has upheld some aspects of government funding of religious social ministry organizations, the fate of Charitable Choice is less clear. The Center for Public Justice and the Christian Legal Society argue that Charitable Choice is constitutional and offer guidance to both government agencies and congregations on how to comply with the law. On the other hand, Americans United for Separation of Church and State expresses some doubt as to the constitutionality of the provision.[45] The debate is likely to be decided through the courts.

A Lutheran Response

In the *Constitution, Bylaws, and Continuing Resolutions of the Evangelical Lutheran Church in America,* the church affirms its commitment to social ministry: "caring for the sick and the aged, advocating dignity and justice for all people, working for peace and reconciliation among nations, and standing with the poor and powerless and committing itself to their needs" (Chapter 4: Statement of Purpose, 4.02.c). The ELCA recognizes a partnership between government and the church in caring for the earth and for God's people. It also recognizes and affirms the U.S. Constitution and the "institutional" separation of church and state. In this partnership of separate institutions, the church retains its integrity by distinguishing between the church's service role—provided in significant part through its social ministry organizations—and its prophetic role to hold the government accountable for its obligations to all citizens.

The history of social welfare provision by Lutheran churches in the United States exemplifies God's command to care for people who are poor and to be actively involved in God's vision for community. Clearly the church has a role in providing direct services and in developing social policy. How the current welfare reform will affect the continued provision of services by Lutheran agencies and the level of governmental involvement in those services remains to be seen. To deal with this unknown, the church needs to have a clear and strong identity, a commitment to direct service to poor people, and involvement with legislatures in the development of just social policy.

Through a series of social statements, Lutheran churches have addressed the need for social welfare services, church and state interdependence, and church and state separation. The social statements affirm the Lutheran com-

mitment to social ministry service provision and active involvement in advocating for just social policy.[46]

The church can build on Luther's belief that God rules over both kingdoms and that Christians live in both kingdoms simultaneously. Church and
state are inextricably linked. Luther outlined the responsibility of the civil government when he wrote:

> So too the civil government should rule people as to insure that body,
> goods, wife, children, and all professions remain in peace and safety for
> earthly happiness. God would have civil government become a prefigura-
> tion of the true blessedness of His heavenly kingdom.[47]

This vision of civil government finds echoes in Lutheran social statements,
such as "The Nature of the Church and Its Relationship with Government"
(American Lutheran Church, 1979):

> The government's obligation under God includes establishing justice, pro-
> tecting, and advancing human rights, and promoting the general welfare
> of all persons. . . . The church relates to the interests of the state by cham-
> pioning the human and civil rights of all its citizens. Christians believe that
> under God the state exists for the people, not people for the state.

The following, from the 1991 ELCA social statement "The Church in Society: A Lutheran Perspective," speaks of the Lutheran response to social needs
and the church's relationship with the state:

> The Gospel liberates from sin, death, and evil and motivates the Church
> to care for neighbor and the earth. . . . Through the divine activity of the
> Law, God preserves creation, orders society, and promotes justice in a bro-
> ken world. . . . God works through the family, education, the economy, the
> state, and other structures necessary for life in the present age. God insti-
> tutes governing authorities, for example, to serve the good of society.

The ELCA social statement on economic life "Sufficient, Sustainable Livelihood for All" (1999) calls for

- government to provide adequate income assistance and related
  services for citizens, documented immigrants, and refugees who are
  unable to provide for their livelihood through employment
- adequate, consistent public funding for the various low-income
  services nonprofit organizations provide for the common good of all
- scrutiny to ensure that new ways of providing low-income people
  with assistance and services (such as through the private sector) do
  not sacrifice the most vulnerable for the sake of economic efficiency
  and profit

- correction of regressive tax systems, so that people are taxed progressively in relation to their ability to pay
- opposition to lotteries and other state-sponsored gambling because of how these regressive means of raising state revenues adversely affect those who are poor

Christians may serve the common good by participating in the political process, advocating for the protection of civil rights, and promoting social and economic justice. The Division for Church in Society of the ELCA supports an extensive advocacy network that includes Corporate Social Responsibility, Lutheran Office for World Community, Lutheran Office for Governmental Affairs, and a number of state public policy offices. Lutherans put their faith into practice through monitoring governmental policies and through the coordination of grassroots efforts.

Along with advocacy, God calls the church to be directly involved with service to people who are poor. Direct service is provided in many forms including the large network of Lutheran social ministry organizations and Lutheran Services in America. Lutheran social ministry agencies are in the forefront of social change. In his book on the history of Lutheran social services in Iowa, *Hope for all Generations,* George Hanusa shares several suggestions for response to change by social ministry organizations. He suggests a "many faceted response" to today's world:

- It means finding and keeping competent staff members who can be committed to the agency's mission and remain with LSS for fewer dollars than they could earn elsewhere.
- It means building and enabling a cadre of volunteers from church and community who invest themselves in the care of others.
- It means continual reaffirmation of this ministry as a ministry of the church, and making all of the connections on national, state, synod and local levels.
- It means asking for money and being able to tell why.
- It means communicating with, and sometimes confronting, elected and appointed officials of government.
- It means insisting that investment in the least and the poorest, in the earliest time possible, will really bode better for everyone.[48]

Congregations can become directly involved in working for and with these agencies. They can provide financial support and volunteer support or provide facilities or space. Congregations also have options to become involved in welfare reform, ranging from informal collaborations with community agencies to government contracts for specific service provision. The following examples of partnerships between faith-based social welfare agencies and the government are provided by the Welfare Information Network:

- San Diego County, California, Department of Social Services established a resource desk in the lobby of the local welfare office. The desk is staffed by faith community volunteers who provide information to people in crisis and help refer them to appropriate public and private resources.
- Ottawa County, Michigan, contracted with Good Samaritan Ministries to recruit, train, and monitor congregations that adopt families on welfare. Good Samaritan has also been approached about using congregational resources for local welfare reform efforts.
- The Anne Arundel County, Maryland, Department of Social Services began a pilot project offering welfare recipients the option of forgoing their direct cash welfare benefits and instead getting assistance passed through a community organization, which spends the money on behalf of the recipient. So far all of the current participants are congregations. The congregations are directed to work closely with the family for at least six months in providing supportive services, financial and job counseling, and related help.
- In other states, state and local agencies increasingly are establishing adopt-a-family and mentoring programs with congregations.

"This approach builds on traditions within the faith community of assisting individuals and families through personal guidance and support."[49]

Whether the welfare reform legislation is ultimately good public policy and socially just in meeting basic human needs is still an open question. If we believe that God created all people in God's image as living souls, then all people must be treated with dignity. From that perspective the church can play a variety of roles in alleviating human suffering. We are to nurture God's people and call upon the government to do likewise with equity and justice. Achieving a dignified, just, and caring world—God's vision for the world—necessitates the close working relationship of church and state. The church must work together with the state, continue to provide direct service, and advocate for social justice. In those ways we as the church fulfill Jesus' commission: "You shall love the Lord your God with all your heart and with all your soul and with all your mind; and you shall love your neighbor as yourself" (Matt. 22:37-39).

PART II

THE LEGAL CONTEXTS
OF CHURCH-STATE INTERACTION

5

Religious Liberty: A Constitutional Quest

Myles C. Stenshoel

S ince its inception the church has interacted with government and politics. The story of Jesus, from his birth in Bethlehem under imperial
decree to his suffering and death under Pontius Pilate, presaged a continuing question for believers: How are Christians to relate to the governments under which they live and with which the church coexists? What does it
mean to "render unto Caesar that which is Caesar's"? For two millennia and
under profoundly differing political systems, the answers have varied widely,
reflecting not only diverse theological perspectives of religious groups about
the proper role of government but also various philosophical and practical
understandings of governmental authorities about the role of religion in their
public policy decisions.

American Christians, simultaneously members of the body of Christ and
citizens in democratic political systems, illustrate the complexity. Citizens have
the authority and responsibility to influence the creation and application of
the legitimate civil laws that believers have been urged since apostolic times to
obey. That they live in a democracy imposes on them a share of the biblical
burden of the "emperor" to rule, and to do so in the context of myriad laws,
rules, and regulations of national, state, and local governments—a burden
complicated by constitutionally separated but constantly interacting legislative, executive, and judicial powers.

Thus an important task for United States citizens involves coping with complex relationships between civil government and religion: "church and state"
issues. Significantly, today we are part of a population in which religions are
increasingly diverse; all are now in some sense "minority" faiths. While
abstractly most Americans, including Lutherans and other Christians, appear

to affirm and support "freedom of religion," including a right to freedom *from* religion, no firm consensus defines that freedom or its precise derivation from the United States Constitution. That lack of consensus echoes, I shall argue, more than a half-century of contradictory decisions and opinions of the United States Supreme Court in cases involving parts of the Constitution that protect or otherwise impinge upon religion. If we as Christians and citizens are to act responsibly—in either role or both—we will do well to pay attention to the problems these provisions entail. The focus here is on governmental attitudes toward church/state issues rather than on theological or ecclesiastical concerns.[1] Because the Supreme Court is the nation's highest authority on the meaning of its Constitution, we emphasize its decisions applying the "religion clauses" of the First Amendment.

The Religion Clauses

"Congress," begins the First Amendment, "shall make no law respecting an establishment of religion, or prohibiting the free exercise thereof. . . ." Here is the prime constitutional locus of religious liberty, often called the "first freedom," in part because of its placement at the beginning of the Constitution's Bill of Rights. Some preliminary comments may clarify this task.

A major observation is historical; it involves the original function and purpose of the First Amendment. When the Philadelphia convention proposed a new Constitution forming a stronger national government to replace the powerless general government under the Articles of Confederation, many were uneasy about the changes. Some states would support the new Constitution only if a Bill of Rights, protective of individuals and the states, were part of the picture. A deal was soon struck, and the promised protection was added in the first ten amendments in 1791, two years after the Constitution was adopted. Thus the Bill of Rights was originally a limitation only upon the national government—upon *Congress*, as the First Amendment expresses it—in order to protect the rights of individuals and the states.

Only an understanding of this circumstance can adequately explain the strange wording of the First Amendment. While it is clear that "no law respecting an establishment of religion" effectively forbade Congress to *establish* a religion, what may be less obvious but was nevertheless equally implicit in these words was that Congress could not constitutionally interfere with—could not *disestablish*—religious establishments created by the states. Preferential treatments of various religious groups did exist, and vestigial preferences persisted in some states for many years.

Thus the original intent of the First Amendment religion clauses emphasized deference to the states concerning religious matters. The "more perfect union" envisaged by the Constitution would be possible only if the states, each free to determine the role of religion in its own domain, left such matters at home when working together in the new national government. And the First Amendment, far from assuring full religious liberty throughout the land, promised states' rights under the Establishment Clause and limited protection of individuals' "free exercise" of religion. Under both clauses, the guarantee was merely freedom from national interference—it was what "Congress" shall not do. States could, and did, make their own rules.

A second observation involves terminology. Although the distinction between "an establishment of religion" and "the free exercise thereof" does not really involve two clauses, I shall retain the traditional terminology, referring to the "Establishment Clause" and the "free exercise clause." How the two are related in addressing legal problems of church and state is a fundamental and divisive issue that continues to plague the Court and the nation in ways we shall consider.

Finally, while my emphasis is on the religion clauses and their relationship, other parts of the Constitution also involve religion either directly or indirectly. Article 6 specifies that all legislators and officeholders "shall be bound by Oath or Affirmation, to support this Constitution; but no religious Test shall ever be required as a Qualification to any Office or public Trust. . . ." This optional use of an "affirmation" as an alternative to an oath of support has traditionally exempted both the nonreligious and Quakers from the need to swear by a deity the former cannot honestly acknowledge and the latter revere too highly to invoke the divine name. The prohibition of any "religious test" for government officeholders underscores their right to be an adherent of any religion or of no religion. And Article 1, which gives the president ten days to sign or veto a bill passed by Congress, specifies "except Sundays," implicitly reserving that day for worship or rest. Moreover the First Amendment contains freedoms of speech and press; religious expression has sometimes been directly protected under this general rubric, as *expression* rather than specifically as religion.

For a century and a half, the religion clauses were little more than rhetoric. But their meaning and their impact would ultimately undergo major and revolutionary changes, beginning in the 1940s when the Supreme Court "incorporated" them into the Fourteenth Amendment.

The Fourteenth Amendment:
Liberty and Due Process

Three amendments were added to the Constitution after the Civil War to liberate and integrate the former slave population into the political and social life of the nation. These amendments—in sharp contrast to the Bill of Rights—were clearly intended to restrict the states. Thus the Fourteenth Amendment's special protections included this clause: "nor shall any State deprive any person of life, liberty, or property without due process of law. . . ."

While a person's "life" and "property" are relatively easy to recognize, the content of the "liberty" protected by that clause has been variously defined over time. More than seventy years passed before the Supreme Court decided in 1940 that the word "liberty" of the due process clause included the religious liberties of the First Amendment that the amendment had previously protected only against the national government. The case then decided, *Cantwell v. Connecticut*,[2] involved only the free-exercise clause, and many legal scholars understood the establishment issue to involve states' rights rather than personal liberties. Thus the inclusion of the Establishment Clause as part of that "due process" liberty was not clear until 1947; that year in *Everson v. Board of Education*,[3] the justices first allowed a taxpayer to challenge a law arguably involving a state "establishment" of religion—New Jersey's public funding of children's transportation to parochial schools.

Now for more than a half-century the due process "liberty" has been available to protect the religious liberties of individuals from all American governments—states, counties, cities, and villages, as well as school boards and other single-purpose governments. From this perspective, the Court's decision has universalized the protection of the religion clauses. In the process, of course, it has effectively changed their meaning, especially that of the Establishment Clause. If the original intent of that clause was to protect states' rights from the power of the national government, the opposite is now true: the Court as an organ of the national government now *requires* the very disestablishment the clause originally *forbade*. In that development the protection once assigned to the state now belongs to individuals. What does this mean? What are the implications of this change for relations between church and state?

Among the consequences of the judicial "incorporation" of the religion clauses into the liberty protected by the due process clause of the Fourteenth Amendment, several seem especially critical to an examination of what I characterize as the Court's quest for religious liberty:

- a major increase in church/state cases decided by the Supreme Court after 1940
- a new focus on personal religious liberty under both religion clauses
- conflicting judicial rationales of religious liberty under the two clauses

The Major Increase of Church/State Litigation

Prior to the inclusion of the First Amendment religious liberties in the Fourteenth Amendment, court cases involving religion were occasionally decided by the Supreme Court under other parts of the Constitution. Thus, for example, in 1925, *Pierce v. Society of Sisters*[4] invalidated an Oregon compulsory public school law. It did so, however, by treating a parochial school as a business: the sisters had a Fourteenth Amendment property right—as did a private military academy—to operate the *business* of education.[5] In 1930, *Cochran v. Louisiana*[6] upheld as a proper public use of tax funds the provision of free textbooks for children attending public or nonpublic schools. The Court used a "child benefit" theory to reject the argument that purchasing such books for children attending church-related schools was an illegal private use of public funds to aid such schools.

In 1940, Jehovah's Witnesses, whose theology interprets a salute to the flag as a violation of the First Commandment's prohibition of worship of other gods, had failed to win an exemption from a compulsory school flag salute for their children in *Minersville v. Gobitis*.[7] But three years later, in the *Barnette*[8] case, they won a reversal of *Gobitis* when the Court, avoiding the specifically religious issue, found exemption unnecessary; the compulsory flag salute was itself now held to be unconstitutional regulation of *expression* broadly protected by the First Amendment.

With the absorption of the religion clauses into the due process liberty, the prior trickle of church/state cases became a relative deluge. (An appendix lists, categorizes, and summarizes many of these cases; see pp. 169–71.) Under the free-exercise liberty mediated by the Fourteenth Amendment, the Jehovah's Witnesses cases of the 1940s would be augmented by numerous others. Subsequent cases involved Russian Orthodox churches, orthodox Jews in business and in the military, Seventh Day Adventists, conscientious objector status for mainline Christians and for nonreligious pacifists, and—much later—the Santeria sacrifice of chickens.

If free-exercise claims opened the dam, the Establishment Clause cases that began with *Everson*[9] seven years later have since provided even more of the flood of church/state litigation. Especially numerous have been the conflicts involving education, public and private, with emphasis on the years from kindergarten through the senior year of high school. Important religion cases are decided almost every year.

Two other factors have likely contributed to the post–incorporation growth in church/state litigation. One is America's increasingly multicultural and religiously diverse population, providing new or differing concepts and practices that interact with government. Another is the concurrent growth of governmental functions at all levels and its increasing impact (despite the persistent rhetoric and occasional reality of deregulation) on the lives of the people. Whatever their past contribution to the problem of church/state relationships, these factors will have to be considered if we and our courts are to take seriously the goal of protecting religious liberty.

A New Focus on Personal Religious Liberty

When the Supreme Court read the religion clauses into the Fourteenth Amendment a half-century ago, it modified and implicitly strengthened the promise of constitutional protection of religious liberty in several ways. By forbidding states to prohibit "the free exercise" of religion, it broadened the protection many of the states had provided in their own constitutions; all states were included, and the justices' holdings now provided added protection for the religious exercise of minority groups.

We have already encountered the most obvious change. The apparent original intent of the Establishment Clause that allowed *states* to favor religions was repudiated when the Court included this clause in the "liberty" protecting persons from arbitrary state power under the Fourteenth Amendment's due process clause. The new function of the Establishment Clause, as part of the due process clause, was to provide individuals an implicit "establishment liberty"—a constitutional right allowing involved persons to challenge in the courts alleged state or local "establishments" of particular religions or religious perspectives. The focus was now on personal liberty—on freedom rather than federalism, under both clauses.

Thus the judicially imposed disestablishment presumptively added to the religious liberty of individuals a constitutional right to enjoy state and local governments that no longer favored, financially or otherwise, any other religious option over their own. If properly implemented—a big "if"—this requirement would add effective governmental "neutrality" to the substantial religious liberty (including the right to worship and to proselytize) that already existed in most American states. It would exceed the religious liberty in European nations still possessing the historic religious establishments in the twentieth century, for example, of the Anglican Church in Britain, and of the Lutheran Church in Nordic countries. Moreover—and of special importance—this comprehensive freedom of religion was recognized as a self-subsisting constitutional goal, not merely a subset of other protections.

How has the Supreme Court implemented the two clauses in practice? How closely has the protection of religious liberty approximated its implicit post–incorporation promise? With more than five decades of experience and scores of religion decisions, it is clear that the quest is unfinished; the Court's promise exceeds its performance.

The Court's Competing Rationales
of the Religion Clauses

Four principles have dominated the religion decisions of the Supreme Court: separation, accommodation, impact analysis, and secular intent. Two have undergirded the Court's major free exercise holdings, and three have focused the justices' arguments in various establishment cases. This survey begins with the rationales used to protect free exercise.

Free Exercise and Secular Intent

Two recent Supreme Court cases, *Employment Division v. Smith* (1990)[10] and *Church of Lukumi Babalu Aye v. Hialeah* (1993),[11] probably reflect part of the "original intent" of the clause forbidding Congress to make a law "prohibiting the free exercise" of religion. In the *Hialeah* case, the city's law regulating the religious slaughter—but not other killing—of chickens was held to violate the sect's free exercise and therefore the constitutional protection; it was, the Court concluded, an intentional prohibition of a worship practice of a particular religion. In *Smith,* on the other hand, the Court refused to provide government employees, members of the Native American Church, a claimed exemption from Oregon's drug laws for the sacramental use of peyote during worship. Here the state's intent to prohibit any religious exercise was not discernible; the law in question was viewed as a religiously neutral secular law controlling hallucinogens.

However closely *Smith* reflected the original intent of the free exercise clause,[12] it departed significantly from the traditional emphasis of the Court. Opposition to such a change had generated many "friend of the court" briefs supporting Smith's cause, brought by churches and other groups hoping to maintain judicial protection of religious differences. The impact of the change was confirmed by a major political reaction: In the Religious Freedom Restoration Act of 1993 (RFRA), Congress overwhelmingly instructed the Court to return to its precedents. Framed as "appropriate legislation" to enforce the Fourteenth Amendment, RFRA declared its purposes:

1. to restore the compelling interest test as set forth in *Sherbert v. Verner* . . . (1963) and *Wisconsin v. Yoder* . . . (1972) and to guarantee its application in all cases where free exercise of religion is substantially burdened; and
2. to provide a claim or defense to persons whose religious exercise is substantially burdened by government.[13]

In *Boerne v. Flores* (1997), the justices of the Supreme Court invalidated RFRA, deciding by a six-to-three vote that Congress lacked the power to tell them how to interpret the Constitution.[14] But the Court's vacillation concerning the requirements of the free exercise clause was clear. What was the rationale so many critics preferred to the *Smith* approach?

Free Exercise and Impact Analysis

If the "secular intent" approach of the *Hialeah* and *Smith* cases focuses on what legislatures may *not* do to *prohibit* free exercise, a quite different judicial approach found in the precedents emphasizes what courts *may* do to *protect* free exercise. I refer to this rationale as "impact analysis"; it assumes that an actual negative impact of government on a religious activity—effective prohibition—better measures governmental incursions on religious liberty than do the words of the law or the intent of the legislators or bureaucrats who created it.[15]

Under impact analysis the typical remedy of such an incursion has been judicial exemption from the offending law, not its repudiation. Thus in *Sherbert v. Verner*[16] a Seventh Day Adventist dismissed from her job because she refused to work Saturdays and later refusing other proffered employment for the same reason was held eligible for unemployment compensation. As written, the state law had declared ineligible for such benefits persons who turned down jobs for which they were qualified. The law did, however, permit a person to refuse Sunday work. Recognizing that religious liberty involves the right to follow different patterns of worship, the Supreme Court carved out a special comparable exemption for a religious Sabbatarian. Fairness, the Court concluded, was not possible if all faiths were treated alike in every respect; the goal was not identical treatment, but equitable treatment. In the 1972 *Yoder* case,[17] Amish parents were exempted from a Wisconsin compulsory education law and permitted to end their children's education after the eighth grade—earlier than the statute allowed—to fulfill their religious obligations.

Sherbert and *Yoder* were not anomalies; the Supreme Court had provided exemptions for religious exercise in its earlier post–incorporation cases. Jehovah's Witnesses, whose street-corner and front-door proclamations Justice Douglas once compared to Presbyterian preaching from the pulpit, had been exempted from minor breach of peace charges,[18] from the need to purchase a solicitor's license to sell religious literature,[19] and from a bookseller's tax.[20] Sincerity of religious belief had justified exemption from a particular rule of evidence in *U.S. v. Ballard*,[21] a criminal fraud case.

Occasionally impact analysis has provided other creative remedies. In *Kedroff v. St. Nicholas Cathedral* (1952),[22] a church property case involving establishment issues as well as free exercise, the Court recognized the right of churches to differ in their polity and governance and, even during the Cold War, upheld control of the cathedral by the patriarch of Moscow. Noting that the Russian Orthodox Church is hierarchical, it found no justifiable reason to allow local democratic dissidents—with or without the aid of the New York state legislature—to change its polity and wrest control from the mother church. *Kedroff* was not, however, the last word; a "neutral principles" secular law approach that ignores differences of polity among religious organizations has characterized subsequent church property cases.[23]

Nor has the Court's impact analysis approach always provided the exemptions sought by persons claiming that a law imposes a substantial burden on their religious exercise. The prima facie presumption that an exemption would enhance the religious liberty of the claimant has not resolved the issue. Such a claim has regularly been weighed against the needs of society; a "compelling" or "paramount" countervailing state interest could overcome the claim. Justice O'Connor, who disagreed with the majority in the *Smith* peyote case in their rejection of the impact analysis precedents, was nevertheless willing to refuse the claimed exemption on the ground that the nation's "war on drugs" provided just such a compelling and countervailing state interest.

While the Court has often exempted Jehovah's Witnesses from general laws interfering with their efforts to proselytize, it refused to exempt from child labor laws a youngster who, with her guardian, was on the street selling the Witnesses' literature.[24] More recently the justices refused an exemption from the Air Force dress code to permit an orthodox Jewish officer to wear his yarmulke indoors.[25]

Similarly, after broadening by interpretation the congressional exemption from military service of persons who "by reason of religious training and belief" were consistent pacifists to include nontheists[26] and the nonreligious,[27] the Supreme Court refused to exempt *selective* conscientious objectors from mainline Christian churches who in the tradition of St. Augustine and the Augsburg Confession were unwilling to serve as soldiers in what they concluded were "unjust" wars.[28] There was, the Court concluded, a compelling U.S. interest that did not permit such doubtful exemptions, so difficult to determine in time of war.

Thus the impact-analysis principle is by no means able to protect all kinds of religious activity in all sorts of circumstances. Yet it has in many situations significantly supported the right of persons to be religiously different, adding an important element of judicial balance to the resolution of legislatively unanticipated problems in the conflict of government with a citizenry of all faiths and of no faith. Whether the Supreme Court will revive its flagging interest in impact analysis, with or without congressional prodding, is unclear. Most current justices apparently prefer to avoid the rationale and the burden it imposes.

Establishment and Separation

Justice Hugo Black, writing for the Court in the 1947 *Everson* case that announced the incorporation of the Establishment Clause into the due process liberty of the Fourteenth Amendment, defined the impact of that clause grandly, broadly, and imprecisely (including free-exercise elements):

> The "establishment of religion" clause of the First Amendment means at least this: Neither a state nor the Federal Government can set up a church. Neither can pass laws which aid one religion, aid all religions, or prefer one religion over another. Neither can force nor influence a person to go to or to remain away from church against his will or force him to profess a belief or disbelief in any religion. No person can be punished for entertaining or professing religious beliefs or disbeliefs, for church attendance or non-attendance. No tax in any amount . . . can be levied to support any

religious activities or institutions, whatever they may be called, or whatever form they may adopt to teach or practice religion. Neither a state nor
the Federal Government can, openly or secretly, participate in the affairs
of any religious organizations or groups and vice versa. In the words of Jefferson, the clause against establishment of religion was intended to erect
"a wall of separation between church and state."[29]

Everson did not, in fact, apply the separation imperative the opinion proclaimed. Addressing the question whether a state law providing tax-derived
funds to bus pupils to and from nonprofit private schools as well as public
schools is an establishment of religion supporting parochial schools, the five-
justice majority found no violation. Black understood the busing to be religiously neutral:

> Of course, cutting off church schools from [general governmental serv-
> ices] would make it far more difficult for the schools to operate. But such
> is obviously not the purpose of the First Amendment. The Amendment
> requires the state to be neutral in its relations with groups of religious
> believers and nonbelievers. . . . State power is no more to be used so as to
> handicap religions than it is to favor them. . . . The State contributes no
> money to the schools. . . . Its legislation . . . does no more than provide a
> general program to help parents get their children, regardless of their
> religion, safely and expeditiously to and from accredited schools.[30]

Thus the Court introduced confusing and competing principles: What is the
nature of the "neutrality" required? Is it fair treatment of believers and non-
believers? Is nonestablishment, like free exercise, subject to impact analysis?
Does it require exemption or other relief from laws that negatively impinge
on particular religious bodies or faith systems? Or is neutrality satisfied by secular general laws, as the majority concluded in *Everson* and more recently in
another five-to-four decision, *Rosenberger v. University of Virginia*,[31] in which they
similarly approved a law they found to have a secular intent and rejected the
dissenters' pleas for strict separation of church and state? Or is nonestablishment dominant over free exercise and is separation its mandate, as the *Everson* dissenters implied when they acknowledged "the burden which our
constitutional separation puts on parents who desire religious instruction
mixed with secular for their children"?

One year after *Everson*, in *McCollum v. Board of Education*, the Court provided a paradigm of the strict separation *Everson* had announced, invalidating
a program of released time religious education classes taught in Illinois public schools during regular school hours by representatives of Protestant,
Catholic, and Jewish faiths. Mrs. Vashti McCollum, an atheist, had brought the
suit as a taxpayer and parent, arguing that the program set her son apart, caus-
ing him embarrassment and humiliation as he sat alone in the study hall while

his classmates attended religion classes. Now Justice Black drew upon his threefold *Everson* prohibition—"separation" meant no governmental practice of religion, tax support for religion, or cooperation with religion. The facts of the case, he said,

> show the use of tax-supported property for religious instruction and the close cooperation between the school authorities and the religious council in promoting religious education. . . . Pupils compelled by law to go to school for secular education are released in part from their legal duty upon the condition that they attend the religious classes. This is beyond all question a utilization of the tax-established and tax-supported public school system to aid religious groups to spread their faith. And it falls squarely under the ban of the First Amendment . . . as we interpreted it in Everson.[32]

The sole dissenter from the decision was Justice Stanley Reed, who asserted that "a rule of law should not be drawn from a figure of speech," adding that "for me, the history of past practices is determinative of the meaning of a constitutional clause. . . ."[33] The Court should, he argued, have drawn from American history and tradition; had it done so it would have permitted local authorities to continue a working relationship with the various religious groups. Reed's comments were suggestive of things to come. Despite the ease with which Americans generally equate the phrase "separation of church and state" with the First Amendment religion clauses, Jefferson's famous figure of speech would soon be replaced in most Supreme Court opinions by other terms; instead of *requiring separation* of church and state, it would later *forbid* their *fusion* or their *"excessive entanglement."*

Moreover, Reed's view of tradition unveiled a nascent conflict between the religion clauses. For him, and soon for others, this interpretation of an atheist mother's "establishment liberty" to protect her son from embarrassment seemed too costly: *McCollum* had effectively restricted the very worship and religious education that many perceived to be part of the "free exercise" of their religion.

Establishment and Accommodation

After four years and considerable criticism of *McCollum*, the Court decided another released time religious education case, this time from New York City. The state legislature had authorized the absence of children "for religious observance and education . . . under rules that the commissioner shall establish." The rules permitted absences of not more than one hour per week—the same hour for all religions—for religious instruction; parents would have to initiate the request, classes would be held off school property, and attendance reports would be sent to the school. By a six-to-three margin in *Zorach v.*

Clauson (1952), the Supreme Court upheld this governmental "accommodation" of religion.

Justice William O. Douglas, writing for the Court, explained that, unlike *McCollum,* the New York program "involves neither religious instruction in public school classrooms nor the expenditure of money." "We follow the *McCollum* Case," he wrote,

> but we cannot expand it to cover the present . . . program unless separation of Church and State means that public institutions can make no adjustments of their schedule to accommodate the religious needs of the people. We cannot read into the Bill of Rights such a philosophy of hostility to religion.[34]

Sounding rather like Justice Reed in his *McCollum* dissent, Douglas explained:

> We are a religious people whose institutions presuppose a Supreme Being. . . . We sponsor an attitude on the part of government that shows no partiality to any one group and that lets each flourish according to the zeal of its adherents and the appeal of its dogma. When the state encourages religious instruction or cooperates with religious authorities by adjusting the schedule of public events to sectarian needs, it follows the best of our traditions. For it then respects the religious nature of our people and accommodates the public service to their spiritual needs.[35]

The dissenters correctly categorized *Zorach* as a retreat from the separation mandate. The cooperation of government and religion forbidden by Justice Black was now welcomed, praised, and celebrated by Justice Douglas as helpful encouragement and accommodation following the "best of our traditions." Separation theory (for Douglas primarily an economic, tax-related touchstone of religious liberty) would never again command the almost universal support it had enjoyed in 1948. But if *McCollum* represented the zenith for separation, *Zorach* served that function for accommodation, although tradition-based accommodation has subsequently exempted churches from local property taxes[36] and approved use of chaplains by state legislatures.[37] Each theory limits the other. When the Court accommodates, it does not separate; when it separates, it does not accommodate. The more recent distinction between "excessive entanglement" and permissible nonexcessive church-state interaction suggests what remains of the competitive thrust of the two theories.

One of the anomalies of *Zorach* was that the Court that here protected an exercise of religion—religious education—from the "hostility" of invalidation should argue that it would take "obtuse reasoning to inject any issue of the 'free exercise' of religion into the present case."[38] The dissenters had urged the free-exercise clause as a basis for invalidating this program of "voluntary" religious instruction; they saw the New York program, as well as that in Illinois, as coercive. Was this a dilemma from which the only escape from official encouragement of religion was official discouragement? Critics of the *McCollum* separation decision had complained that it favored atheist and minority religious perspectives over those of mainstream majority religionists. For critics of the *Zorach* holding, the complaint was reversed: legislative accommodation of the majority viewpoint would, and in this case did, coerce religious minorities. This dilemma increasingly underscored another: the failure of the Supreme Court to provide an acceptable way to relate its decisions under the Establishment Clause to its decisions under free exercise. Was there a way to cut this Gordian knot?

Establishment and Secular Intent

Perhaps a third principle, secular intent, might provide the governmental religious "neutrality" needed to protect religious liberty. Could it do more than occasionally trump the separation principle as it had done in *McCollum?* Could it become a rationale to overcome the fundamental conflict between the separation and accommodation principles? And might it, in the process, provide a basis to reconcile the two religion clauses of the First Amendment? Increasingly during the final decade of the twentieth century, the Court appeared to be moving, under both clauses, toward that view.

An ardent early advocate of secular intent as *the* way to reconcile the two clauses was Philip Kurland, who had recognized the problem of the Court's contradictory holdings. In 1961 Professor Kurland defined his proposed theory, popularly referred to as a "religion blindness" approach:

> The principle tendered is a simple one. The [free exercise] and [establishment] clauses should be read as stating a single precept: that government cannot utilize religion as a standard for action or inaction because these clauses, read together as they should be, prohibit classification in terms of religion either to confer a benefit or to impose a burden.[39]

In affirmative terms such a proposal assumes that government is properly concerned only with secular matters, that it will be neutral if it ignores the impact of its secular programs upon religion. Church-related education, for example, could not be singled out for aid (as might be possible under accommodation theory), nor could it be excluded from aid (as has sometimes occurred under separation theory). Legislatures could not classify religious schools as beneficiaries of governmental subsidies; they could, however, as Kurland explained his theory, be classified as *nonpublic* schools, providing benefits to all schools in that nonreligious classification, including, of course, religious schools.

Kurland saw secular intent as the sole governmental imperative under the religion clauses. Neither separation of government from religion nor legislative accommodation of religion appeared possible in an era of welfare/warfare governments interacting with hundreds of contending systems of faith and spirituality. Nor should courts spend their time and energy doing impact analysis and creating special exemptions from the laws. Secular laws appeared sufficiently religiously neutral.

While the Supreme Court has never overtly adopted his religion-blindness theory, formally reading the two clauses together or officially repudiating the rationales that Kurland intended his theory to replace, its opinions and decisions have frequently reflected the secular-intent rationale. Thus in 1961 the Court upheld several Sunday Closing laws, rejecting the claim that they tended to "establish" the Christian day of worship; the justices found adequate secular motivation for the laws, sociological (family togetherness) and economic (labor and entrepreneurial) in character.[40] In one of these cases, *Braunfeld v. Brown*,[41] an orthodox Jewish merchant unsuccessfully brought suit under both clauses, seeking an exemption allowing him to open his store Sundays, while closing it Saturdays. Having to close his store the entire weekend, he had argued, not only favored other religions over his own; it also amounted to a major economic burden placed by government on the exercise of his Sabbatarian faith, coercion measured in hundreds of thousands of dollars. (Although unwilling to use impact analysis to provide an exemption here as it had in the earlier free-exercise cases, just two years later the Court, without repudiating *Braunfeld*, exempted the Sabbatarian Mrs. Sherbert.)

Judicial decisions focusing on the concept have recurred over the years, often interspersed among holdings based on other rationales. The secular intent approach has thus (1) upheld state provision of textbooks, computers, and instructional equipment used in parochial schools;[42] (2) resolved, as noted above, some church property cases;[43] (3) approved a tax-funded signing interpreter for a deaf student attending a Catholic high school;[44] and (4) in 1997 overturned a precedent that for twelve years forbade, as "excessive entanglement" of church and state in violation of the Establishment Clause, tax-funded remedial education teachers to enter parochial schools.[45] Under this 1997 decision, *Agostini v. Felton*, the teachers' remedial assistance was recharacterized as "secular," so they may, at a much lower cost to the taxpayers, assist the eligible parochial students in their own schools, rather than require the students to receive the assistance in ad hoc tax supported facilities away from the church school property.

Merging the Rationales of Religious Liberty

Chief Justice Warren Burger was appointed in 1969. Two years later, referring to the Establishment Clause in *Lemon v. Kurtzman*, he announced:

> Every analysis in this area must begin with consideration of the cumulative criteria developed by the Court over many years. Three such tests may be gleaned from our cases. First, the statute must have a secular legislative purpose; second, its principal or primary effect must be one that neither advances nor inhibits religion . . . ; finally, the statute must not foster "an excessive government entanglement with religion. . . ."[46]

The *Lemon* test, as these words are known, would dominate the Supreme Court's establishment cases through the 1970s and 1980s. With what result?

The three-part test does indeed involve the four major rationales used by the Court, but each in a significantly weakened version. Separation of church and state is required, but only when the justices determine that the church-state entanglement is "excessive." Accommodation is permitted, but only implicitly, when the entanglement—church/state interaction—is not excessive. Secular intent, while mandated, is only part of the process, not the final answer it had been in the religion blindness principle proffered by Kurland. And only a principal or primary effect of a law advancing or inhibiting religion is to be considered relevant; thus, under the *Lemon* test of establishment, "effect" is a mere verbal echo of the impact analysis protection found in the free exercise precedents.

What significance should be attached to this rather extraordinary fusion into a single test of what had been competing perspectives? It appeared to reflect judicial recognition of a theoretical impasse. No theory had become dominant, but none had been completely ruled out. All four found at least a toehold in *Lemon,* and each could live to fight another day. In this view the three-pronged test amounted to a judicial agreement to disagree, at least for a time, perhaps with a nod of deference to its author during his early years as chief justice.

The implications were several: First, so long as *Lemon* endured, the Court would be unable to achieve a coherent general theory of the religion clauses. Second, the need for an alleged establishment to surmount three separate hurdles would make any challenged law extraordinarily vulnerable to invalidation. Third, because the logic of each part of the test ran counter to the logic of the other parts, *Lemon* guaranteed continuing conflict and argument among the justices, who often preferred one principle over the others. Finally, for the same reason, vacillation, case by case, would continue.

The Court's recent emphasis on the imperative of secular legislative intent in its interpretation of both clauses, as well as criticism of the *Lemon* test by some justices since the retirement of Chief Justice Burger, suggests that his merger of competing religion rationales has again given way (or is now giving way) to overt competition among them. The question remains whether any of the rationales the Court has used has the potential to provide the additional protection of the First Amendment religious liberties implicitly promised when they were added to the liberties of the Fourteenth Amendment due process clause.

Criteria for an Acceptable Rationale
of Religious Liberty

Evaluation of the major contending principles is more complex than one might wish. All have strengths as well as weaknesses. Does any have the potential to become a general theory of the religion clauses?[47] Addressing this task, I have found a number of criteria helpful. In my judgment, an acceptable theory to apply the religion clauses now embedded in the Fourteenth Amendment will have to:

- define "religion" broadly so as to include alternatives to traditional theistic definitions of the term, and to do so consistently under both clauses
- be able to reconcile, in theory and practice, the establishment and free exercise clauses
- focus on the protection of religious liberty as such
- address problems of "balance": (1) accord the religious liberty protected by each clause a prima facie preference over secular governmental policy, rebuttable only by a countervailing sociopolitical necessity: a "paramount" state interest and (2) provide for an equitable balance among competing religious claims
- be cognizant of and consonant with the subtle realities of liberty in the positive state; be sensitive to those realities in analyzing problems and in supplying remedies.

Let me briefly explain my commitment to each of these criteria.

Defining "Religion" Broadly and Consistently

A constitutional principle to protect religious liberty cannot avoid the prior task of defining the "religion" involved in the issue. It is essential to justify a broad constitutional definition of religion and note some implications.

While the Supreme Court has self-consciously avoided defining true religion, it has explicitly and implicitly defined the religion the Constitution protects. In the 1961 *Torcaso* case,[48] Justice Black included in the "religious" category groups not affirming the existence of a god: "Buddhism, Taoism, Ethical Culture, Secular Humanism and others." This went beyond the concept of religion as "duty towards the Creator" enunciated by Madison and long accepted as the judicial standard. Subsequent cases accord the atheist and the agnostic the same religious rights as the Catholic and the Methodist.[49] By implication the Court has defined the atheist as a religionist and secularism as a religion—for purposes of the First Amendment—so long as, and insofar as, they pose alternative choices to those which have been, or normally are, viewed as "religious." The concept is that of a religious marketplace that government protects, but in which government is forbidden to take sides with any of the competing systems of "religious" belief and practice.

If religious liberty is thus understood as a self-subsisting liberty distinguishable from other constitutional protections, and the constitutional meaning of "religion" includes traditionally recognized religions and their competitors in a religious milieu, why does the Constitution provide this special protection? What such systems appear to share is their claim of ultimacy in the lives of their adherents, a point reminiscent of Madison's "Remonstrance," often quoted to support interpretations of the religion clauses; there he stressed both rights of individuals and the duty toward a deity:

> The Religion then of every man must be left to the conviction and conscience of every man; and it is the right of every man to exercise it as these may dictate. . . . It is unalienable also because what is here a right towards men, is a duty towards the Creator. . . . This duty is precedent both in order of time and degree of obligation, to the claims of Civil Society. . . .[50]

This view of protecting religious liberty is consistent with the social contract theory of John Locke, whose understanding of "natural rights" undergirded the Declaration of Independence and the due process clauses of the Constitution. Government is not itself the highest good; and the United States in the late twentieth century was still "one nation *under* God" (or other ultimate commitment).

In brief, religious liberty is acknowledged by the Constitution to involve the domain of the "highest good." The state may not favor theism over secularism or atheism. By the same token, the state may not favor secularism over affirmative religious belief. A principle to implement the religion clauses will somehow have to deal with this reciprocal imperative.

Reconciling the Establishment and Free Exercise Clauses

While individual justices have sometimes sought to reconcile the religion clauses, the Court's fifty-year failure to do so represents a major problem. This inability to bridge the clauses apparently stems in large part from an unwillingness to acknowledge and build on the "establishment liberty" the Court created by making the Establishment Clause part of the "liberty" of the Fourteenth Amendment. Since incorporation, an establishment liberty belonging to individuals implicitly parallels their Free-Exercise liberty; logically both are now protected against state infringement.

Thus understood, the two are not, as sometimes assumed, a "freedom" clause and a "separation" clause, each, pressed to the extreme, antithetical to the other.[51] Rather, the two clauses protect religious liberty in overlapping yet discernably different ways. The Free-Exercise liberty protects the right of individuals to practice the particulars of their faith, while their establishment liberty is a constitutionally protected right to have their religious entity (faith, denomination, congregation, synagogue, mosque, society of atheists or secular humanists, or other ultimate commitment) treated fairly and equitably by government relative to other such entities. Thus protected by their own establishment liberty, individuals such as Mrs. McCollum and Mr. Braunfeld effectively serve as surrogates for their faith. This should not be surprising; a governmental incursion on a particular religious exercise almost certainly simultaneously threatens or injures the religious entity or faith with which that practice is associated (and vice versa), a point unsuccessfully argued in Mr. Braunfeld's Sunday Closing case.

Until the Supreme Court bridges the chasm it has created between the clauses, the quest for constitutional protection of religious liberty will remain far short of its goal. Currently partisans of each clause tend to pit their cause against partisans of the other. Although both assert support for freedom of religion, Establishment Clause enthusiasts emphasize freedom *from* religion (traditionally defined), while Free Exercise advocates seek more freedom *for* traditional religion.

Protecting Religious Liberty as Such

Stressing protection of religious liberty as such addresses several concerns. First, this is a particular kind of liberty intentionally given a special constitutional status beyond whatever it may share with generally protected expression (speech, press, assembly, petition) and other due process rights. The incorporated religion clauses are properly perceived as an addition to the constitutional protections, not a subtraction from them.

Second, while religious liberty has often, and persuasively, been understood to contribute to political peace and stability, the religious freedoms protecting "persons" under the First and Fourteenth amendments remain the proper prior focus, the means to achieve the related goal of governmental harmony.[52]

And, third, it is the resultant religious liberty that must test the assumptions about any means employed to achieve that liberty. Focus on effective religious liberty as such provides a major proof of the juridical pudding.[53]

Addressing Problems of Balance

An acceptable theory will also have to resolve two problems involving the balance of constitutional concerns. The first, well recognized, is to compare the rights of individuals under either clause against governmental needs and the values of society. The second and more difficult is the need to balance the religious liberties of variously situated claimants, pitting right against right, a problem exacerbated by the history of dichotomously interpreted religion clauses.

Although no constitutional guarantee is absolute, the free exercise of religion has sometimes (and appropriately, in my judgment) been understood to be in a preferred position vis-à-vis merely useful governmental programs. Thus Justice Brennan, speaking for the Court in *Sherbert*, held that the infringement of a First Amendment right was justified only by a

> compelling state interest. . . . It is basic that no showing merely of a rational relationship to some colorable state interest would suffice. . . . For even if the possibility of spurious claims did threaten [important state interests]. . . it would plainly be incumbent upon the appellees to demonstrate that no alternative forms of regulation would combat such abuses without infringing First Amendment rights.[54]

While such an interpretation was severely challenged by the *Smith* free-exercise opinion in 1990 and has received little support in the establishment cases, if the Court should become convinced of the need for a coherent and consistent treatment of the religion clauses, it will have to accord them the same status as fundamental liberties it gives the other First Amendment rights.

The need for consistent treatment of religious liberty under both clauses as a preferred right is not a counsel of perfection. Either claim might be negated when to honor it would frustrate a paramount governmental or social interest. The concept does no more than assert that religious liberty, as well as the First Amendment's protection of speech and press, is the rule, and that infringement of the liberty must be a demonstrably justified exception. Strictly speaking, therefore, this first problem is less a matter of balance than of dominance; in resolving it, the task of the courts is to scrutinize and declare as winner either the individual's claim or society's countervailing value.

By contrast, the second problem is authentically one of balance, of equilibrium. This issue is resolved, not by acknowledging the superiority of one of two conflicting principles, but by according parity of treatment to conflicting claims under the single principle of fair and equitable treatment of all religious options. Balance in this sense might therefore suggest compromise rather than domination. Questions concerning this latter "internal" balance appear to be especially difficult, asking not "whether" but "how." How can establishment and free exercise claims be balanced? What weights, if any, should be assigned quantitative aspects? Does removal of religious practices from public schools, to protect the establishment liberty of the few, unduly restrict the free-exercise liberty of the many? These and similar questions are fundamental in a judicial quest for a balanced and effective protection of religious liberty among citizens committed to a wide variety of "religious" persuasions.

Thus a theory to maximize religious liberty must (1) recognize that societal interests will at times outweigh protections of the First Amendment, but (2) accord a prima facie preference to religious liberty under both clauses, since without such a preferred position legislation with minimal social utility will easily nullify the protection. Finally, (3) an adequate theory will have to cope with a long neglected problem: how to achieve effective "neutrality"—a carefully nuanced balance—among multiple religious claims.

Protecting Religious Liberty in the Positive State

The problems of balance are symptomatic and suggestive of an overarching issue related to the governmental "neutrality" that the Supreme Court has often sought in its religion decisions. An increasing threat to religious liberty during the past century has been the positive state: the welfare, warfare, regulatory state. The neutrality of the Lockean constable state, in which government is more an umpire than a participant, is relatively easy to achieve. A government that does little may not do much to protect liberty, but neither, it may be argued, does it do much to threaten it; the less it does, the more perfect its neutrality. It is when the state actively participates in the pursuit of human happiness that threats to religious liberty are prone to multiply, especially in a land of accelerating religious pluralism.

That the expansion of governmental activity has exacerbated the problem of protecting religious liberty via effective governmental neutrality in America is clear. None of the twentieth-century issues of religious liberty in education can be dissociated from the development of government as educator. The 1961 clash between "secular" blue laws and the claims of religious liberty could have occurred only in the context of the positive state, of government that accepts a major responsibility for the conditions of the good life, including leisure and recreation and the possibility of family togetherness. Affirmative government—government of parks and playgrounds, unemployment compensation and labor legislation, of military training and remedial education—has spawned most of the constitutional controversy in church/state relationships.

That the positive state increases threats to liberty may suggest to some that the appropriate solution is to do away with as much government as possible. However politically attractive this idea sounds, it does not represent a practical long-term goal; the positive state will surely continue for the foreseeable future.

Thus the reality of affirmative government requires an awareness of the real, if unintended, negative impact of governmental activity upon religious liberty. And an adequate theory must do more than recognize such infringements; it must, insofar as feasible, provide fair and balanced remedies.[55] For when government does so much for, to, and with its people, an adequate theory of the religion clauses must cope with this reality of our contemporary political systems. Unless relevant to conditions imposed by the positive state, a principle cannot hope to provide a balanced implementation of the religion clauses.

Testing the Principles under the Criteria

How well do the major theories meet our suggested criteria? As the following brief evaluation of the four principles indicates, significant problems exist.

Separation

Whether in its original strict version forbidding government officially to touch religion, to provide tax support for it, or to cooperate with it, or in its weakened version prohibiting only excessive entanglement, the separation mandate often contributes to religious liberty, at least in requiring the disestablishment of any official religion. Its focus, however, is on the governmental activity, not on the effective religious liberty. Thus it is not strange that the Court's separation/entanglement decisions, far from reconciling the two clauses, tend to exacerbate the conflict between them.

Does separation theory "define 'religion' broadly . . . to include alternatives to traditional theistic definitions of the term"? Here the answer, curiously, is yes *and* no. In practice, the Supreme Court has implicitly used two definitions of "religion" in its separation/entanglement decisions. For while it has quite properly allowed challenges brought by atheists and others whose ultimate commitments are "nonreligious" in the traditional sense, and by so doing has included them among the contending "religions" in the religious market-place, it has not, however, done so consistently. For its remedy separates government only from affirmative religion. Far from evenhandedly balancing the rights of all religious options, the separation rationale has in practice a built-in preference for nonreligion. Its two definitions of religion, one including and one excluding nonreligious options, together function to encourage secularism at the expense of affirmative religion. In failing to focus on religious liberty as such, separation theory has no occasion to weigh that liberty against its secularizing policy of separation. It sees no need to balance competing religious claims or to remedy problems associated with the development of the positive state.

Accommodation

As used here, "accommodation" refers to legislative encouragement or protection of religion, approved by the Supreme Court under the Establishment Clause when the governmental interaction with religion has the sanction of history and tradition, and if, under the *Lemon* test, it is deemed "nonexcessive."[56]

Does accommodation focus on "religious liberty as such"? The answer is a qualified yes. Since the relatively few establishment decisions approving such accommodation have in fact protected religious practices/exercises, they have appeared to reconcile the clauses. Because these accommodations are made by majority votes of legislative bodies, it is perhaps arguable that affirmative and mainline religions will be better protected than nonreligious and minority options, thus reversing the bias of the separation principle, as the New York *Zorach* decision undercut the Illinois *McCollum* holding in the released-time cases. On the other hand, legislative majorities have sometimes voted to protect minority religionists. Thus Congress has accommodated religion-based conscientious objections to war via draft exemptions (expanded by the Supreme Court's statutory interpretation to include nonreligious objectors); New York state similarly attempted to accommodate a community of Hasidic Jews by creating a tax-funded special school district to provide educational opportunities for its handicapped students (invalidated by the Court in the 1994 *Kiryas Joel* decision).[57]

When and if the Court approves legislative accommodation, its role is primarily judicial restraint. If in the draft-exemption cases the justices provided some balance among competing "religious" claims, they did so only when facing such claims; it would be impossible for legislators to anticipate the impact of all their laws on all religious options and practices. Legislators may well cope with some of the problems of religious liberty in the positive state, but they do not, and usually cannot, have the last word. The First Amendment rights of religious minorities are, in the long run, in need of protection by the courts.

Secular Intent

Governmental interaction with religion is acceptable, under the principle of secular intent, if it results from a law that does not classify in religious terms. Thus in the last decade, invoking secular intent to resolve free exercise as well as establishment cases, the Supreme Court has in one sense "met" several of our criteria: It has used the approach to reconcile the two clauses; and it has trumped the need to examine the impact of the positive state upon our many religions or to address what we have called problems of balance.

It has done so, however, at a high cost. Most crucial is the failure of the principle to (indeed its determination *not* to) "focus on the protection of religious liberty as such." Secular intent consistently protects government from religion, but only accidentally does it protect religion from government. The formal neutrality of secular intent will at times permit religious entities to share in broadly available secular benefits (for example, *Rosenberger* [1995], *Agostini* [1997], *Mitchell* [2000]), rather than to exclude them in the way that such strict separationist holdings as *Aguilar v. Felton* (1985) required. But in failing to address the actual impact of governmental activity on various religious options, it effectively rejects the concept that the religion clauses protect religious liberty.

Because it does not recognize nonreligion as a "religious option" in the religious marketplace but rather merges the meanings of "nonreligious" and "secular," the secular intent principle now favored by the Court closely resembles Kurland's "religion blindness" proposal. And, like the separation/entanglement principle, it has tended to reinforce the governmental secularism that Richard John Neuhaus has described as a "naked public square." While it does not separate government from religion, it does separate government from a real concern for religious liberty.[58]

Impact Analysis

That courts should, when governmentally feasible, exempt persons from laws that infringe on their religious practices is what we refer to as "impact analysis." Used by the Supreme Court in cases from the 1940s into the 1970s to protect free exercise of religion and favored by Congress in the ill-fated Religious Freedom Restoration Act of 1993, it has (1) focused on "the protection of religious liberty as such," (2) accepted the broad definition of "religion" that includes alternatives to traditional theistic definitions (in the conscientious objector cases), (3) accorded religious liberty "a prima facie preference over secular governmental policy," (4) provided "an equitable balance among competing religious claims" (though thus far only in the free-exercise context), and (5) often managed to supply sensitive remedies-by-exemption for problems posed by the positive state.

In terms of my suggested criteria, therefore, this principle has demonstrated considerable strength; as the appendix listings indicate (see pp. 169–71), impact analysis has protected non-mainstream religious persons in their differing practices in a variety of situations. It appears capable of providing the "effective neutrality"—equitable treatment, rather than equal treatment—that the religion clauses promise.

Impact analysis has not, however, been used by the Court to reconcile the two clauses; indeed, the justices have shown little interest in pursuing the rationale in establishment cases. Limiting their concern to the primary effect of laws challenged under the Establishment Clause, they appear unwilling to acknowledge, much less protect, the "establishment liberty" they created by incorporating the clause into the due process liberty of the Fourteenth Amendment. Whatever the conceptual strengths of impact analysis and its theoretical potential as a general theory of the religion clauses, its appeal to the Court has been waning during the 1990s, even as a rationale of the free-exercise clause.

Perhaps we should not be surprised about the reluctance of the justices to build on the rationale; a major problem is the analytical burden impact analysis imposes on the courts, a political burden far greater, to be sure, than that of the Court's current favorite, secular intent.[59]

An Unfinished Quest

Probably the only major conclusion observers can agree on concerning the Supreme Court's quest for religious liberty is that it is unfinished. Nor is this surprising; for nearly six decades the justices have been unable to resolve the meaning of the religion clauses or provide the means to apply them. Where then do we stand?

- That the quest for religious liberty is unfinished and that the Court's contradictory precedents in First Amendment religion cases are open to change are hopeful signs.
- The current Court's dependence on secular intent tends to support the secularization of American society, protecting freedom from religion better than freedom of religion.
- That the religious liberties protected by the two clauses are often treated as competing concepts is a major obstacle in the quest.
- Our courts and constitutional interpretations are not impervious to change. Informed citizens can sometimes—perhaps over a generation or two—make a difference.[60]
- However imperfectly the religion clauses have been and are being interpreted, the freedom of religion enjoyed by most Americans most of the time is impressive.[61] Thanks be to God!

6

We Must Spare No Diligence:
The State and Childhood Education

Marie Failinger

Not surprisingly, education continues to be one of the most persistent arenas of controversy about the relationship of church and state in the United States. As one of the few public functions that still involves significant local community input and strong parental involvement, education touches a large majority of American citizens as taxpayers, parents, students, teachers, and school officials. Controversies over K–12 education also expose most of the critical divisions remaining in American society on religion and values, reflecting diverse, incommensurable presuppositions about human nature and human well-being. The stakes in education are high, since education so strongly influences the individual's ability to be successfully involved in the social and economic world in a modern, literate culture and plays a critical role in any democratic nation's ability to govern itself and to prosper.[1]

Amid the paradoxes exposed by their faith and the pluralism of their culture, American Lutherans often find themselves pulled in two directions: toward active, prophetic criticism of public educational values discordant with their faith and toward support for education as an institution critical in the preservation of modern society. The American tradition of the separation of church and state so taxes Lutherans who attempt to live faithfully to the insight that the earthly and spiritual governances are radically different but wholly inseparable that it is difficult to construct *a* Lutheran position on decisions involving public and private education in the United States. This article will instead suggest how values and assumptions of Lutheran thought and American constitutional law might influence Lutheran citizens' thinking about public policy on education.

The separation of church and state, of religious teaching and disciplines concerned with "earthly" life, does have its positive side: Such separation might make it less likely for Christians to succumb to the temptation to believe they can "know God's will" or come to salvation or a state of perfection through the humanities, sciences, arts, and other subjects important for earthly governance. Moreover, the Establishment Clause prohibition against a state theology protects the freedom of religious conscience that occupies a high place in the Lutheran Reformation.[2] On the other hand, without intentional public work at religious education, the central task of education as Martin Luther saw it—to teach the Christian faith—might be lost, or families might come to believe that faith-learning is a private matter to be attended to at their discretion.

Because of these concerns, Lutherans are likely to approach educational policy somewhat differently than other Christians. Some Christians, termed *freewill separationists* by law professor Carl Esbeck,[3] believe that state involvement in religion will corrupt the Christian's understanding of God's will and God's way of life. They might ideally want to vest complete control over a child's religious, moral, and intellectual development with his or her parents and religious community. *Strict separationists* agree that the church and state-run institutions must be kept apart, but they think that religions bring quarrels into public schools and confuse children about their religious beliefs. In their view, religion is a private matter that must be kept out of public life.[4] Strict separationists, for instance, might insist that public school textbooks be stripped of any references to the religious views of the Pilgrims, or that schools celebrate only secular holidays, such as "winter solstice" rather than "Christmas."

Directly opposed to strict separationism, *restorationists* argue that the United States was founded as a Christian nation and that the state should favor and endorse the Christian faith in the classroom.[5] They would include school prayer and Bible reading during the school day, while permitting non-Christian students to stay silent or refuse to participate.[6] *Structural pluralists,* who champion religious diversity, claim that a secular ideology imposed by the state is just as coercive as any religious ideology, so the state must respect each religious belief, whether held by one individual or a longstanding religious community.[7] They therefore favor teaching *about* religion in public schools so long as every faith is given equal respect and attention in the curriculum and the rights of dissenting parents to choose their children's education are respected.

Lutheran Themes on Church and World

In discussing these thorny issues with others, Lutherans as Christians who distinguish God's creative activity from God's salvation given solely through Christ's work on the cross would recognize the partial truths embedded in each of these positions.

Restrained reason. Lutherans recognize the role of reason in seeking truth about the earthly realities of human existence, the requirements for human well-being, and the relationship between human beings and the material world. While reason is God's gift for discerning human callings on earth, it also must be viewed with some suspicion because of its prideful and disobedient insistence that we can substitute for God or know God's will. Thus, Lutherans affirm that the human power to reason—from observing the physical and human world to assessing, creating, and prescribing forms of government, social values, technologies, and economies—provides hope for creating a future with less injustice and fewer daily hardships. They agree that human reason can gain access to some of the truth about human existence and the physical world. At the same time, Lutherans acknowledge, with support from history, that human reason and human will often bury, distort, or neglect truth out of self-interest, self-delusion about human existence and well-being, and self-justification.

Critically situated responsibility. Unlike others who might try to protect Christians' moral and religious purity by separating themselves from the rest of the world, Lutherans have demanded education that recognizes that humans are situated in a complicated world and prepares them to take responsibility for the context in which they live. Luther, for example, advocated the study of science through direct observation of nature, because he viewed the world as God's activity accessible to every person through reason. He also was particularly fond of world history as "the story of divine providence and a practical guide for aiding the understanding of events of this world."[8] Yet a Lutheran view would couple an education that enthusiastically embraces and engages the world with one that teaches the perspectives and skills of valid critique, including the ability to expose and counter any ideology or "common sense" that purports to ultimacy or threatens the well-being of the created world.

Conscientious recognition of appropriate authority. Lutheran thought views authority with ambivalence. Lutherans accept the state as God's gift to restrain evil and order society, yet recognize that each human authority, or order, has its own competencies and limits, and that transgression of those limits brings great harm to human society. Thus for Lutherans, the state as an order of creation properly shares responsibility with the family and church to nurture and educate children and cultivate their moral development.[9] Yet Lutherans must speak up if the state usurps the responsibilities entrusted to other orders, such as the responsibility of family and church to teach children the gospel and what their Christian faith demands of them.[10] Lutheran thought also recognizes a tension between the right of conscience and the duty of loyal obedience to governmental authority. The freedom of

Christians to learn God's word and enter into personal relationship with God entails their duty to consider what they owe the world and therefore to refuse complicity even with state-authorized evil. As the Lutheran Church in America social statement on "Religious Liberty in the United States" explains:

> Religious liberty is rooted in our creation in the image of God and in God's continuing activity in the created world. . . . We are creatures to whom God speaks and from whom God expects a response. This is essential to our humanity. To deny religious liberty and other civil liberties, therefore, threatens to dehumanize us all.[11]

At the same time, Lutheran thought acknowledges that fallen persons need to recognize and obey authority that restrains them from the evil-doing they are so willing to justify. In education, Lutherans would be open to the conscientious decisions of dissenter parents or religions that challenge public educational authorities, yet they might need to ask whether these same decisions are tainted by ignorance, pride, power, or even indifference to their children's well-being.

Universal, humane education for vocation: recognizing and responding to the gift of creation. Because they believe that everything created is God's gift, Lutherans can affirm that each individual's life is entrusted to him, not earned, and from this gift entrusted to him flows the duty of delighted response to the world. In Lutheran terms, people are stewards of all creation and education is designed to give glory to God; stewardship implies a call to serve fellow human beings, the church, the state, and society.[12] Thus learning should help students understand how precious is the world given to their hand. Luther was unusual in his time in calling for this education to be universal. He considered it a necessity to enable each Christian to carry out his or her individual responsibility to learn about and worship God.[13] Such an education was not, in Luther's view, at the whim of parents who might have been preparing their children for the family business or who might have decided that their children did not need to be educated. Rather, he understood education not only as a right but as a compulsory duty for both parents and their children and even the state. Parents should make it possible for their children to attend school and to continue their learning as adults, and children should take their educational responsibilities seriously. But when parents defaulted through shortsightedness, greed, lack of teaching ability, or wherewithal to send them to private schools, Luther saw their responsibility falling on public leaders. In fact, he and his followers took on major responsibilities for creating a public education system, funded by taxes and contributions of both commoners and nobility.[14]

A God-centered education. As suggested previously, Luther believed that "the inculcation of faith in and fear of God" must come first.[15] The chief purpose for even the most elementary public education was, in Luther's view, to create and nurture Christians through the word of God. He initially advised that the public school curriculum must make the Bible central to all study, along with the liturgy, key religious books, grammar, writing, and music.[16] Indeed, Luther saw even the most abstract disciplines in his ideal liberal arts education—which included languages, logic, rhetoric, history, science, the arts, and mathematics—as first and foremost devoted to understanding and praising God. He focused on basic grammar, writing, and music to help people participate in the liturgy, and he thought the study of languages was most important for a better comprehension of the Bible and evangelism. In his view the liberal arts, even those brought to light by "heathens," were "serviceable and useful to people in this life, noble and precious gifts of Christ who used and uses them according to His good pleasure for the praise, honor and glory of His holy name."[17] Yet it cannot be said too often that Luther understood reason and learning as tools for faith and not the means to bring people to salvation or even an understanding of God's ultimate will.

These Lutheran themes can fruitfully be brought to bear in the discussion of three major disputed areas in American education: regulation of private religious education, religion and values in the public schools, and the state's duties to provide educational opportunity for both public and private school children.

State Regulation of Religious Education

Some Christians and other religious parents have sought to meet their duties to their children's religious education in parochial schools or home-school settings. Among them are freewill separationists, for whom parochial schools and home-schooling laws have offered a way to limit the influences of the "outside world" on their children without the need for constant parental involvement in monitoring those influences. Religious demands for separate schooling, either parochial or home schooling, have presented the fewest constitutional difficulties. Not only was religious schooling the norm early in our nation's history,[18] but the demand for separate parochial schools rests on the fundamental constitutional right to liberty, supported by the equally pro-tected constitutional right of parents to bring up their child as they see fit. This liberty right of parents was recognized in *Meyer v. Nebraska*, when the State of Nebraska unsuccessfully challenged Lutheran schools for teaching in the German language.[19] More recently, in *Wisconsin v. Yoder*, holding that Amish parents could withdraw their children from public school after eighth grade, the Court underscored that "the primary role of the parents in the upbringing of their children [including 'the inculcation of moral standards, religious beliefs, and elements of good citizenship'] is now established beyond debate as an enduring American tradition."[20]

Thus, the Supreme Court has held that under the Free Exercise Clause, the state may not interfere with the religious indoctrination of children by their parents, whether at home or in parochial school settings. Yet, as the Supreme Court said in *Cantwell v. Connecticut,* the Free Exercise Clause "embraces two concepts—freedom to believe and freedom to act. The first is absolute but, in the nature of things, the second cannot be."[21] Thus, the right of parents to control their children's education other than their religious upbringing has been limited by the state's responsibilities for its children.

In recent years stronger involvement by freewill separationist communities in education has triggered increased state monitoring of private education. In perhaps the largest area of controversy, home schooling, the courts have acknowledged that the state has the right and responsibility to set certain educational standards for private schools, so parents may not object to state regulation of private or home school curriculum,[22] reasonable teacher certification requirements,[23] regulation of the number of schooling days, or school inspections.[24] In some cases such as *People v. DeJonge,*[25] however, the courts have put the burden on the state to show that its requirements are necessary or even the "least restrictive means" of meeting the state's interests. Parochial school situations may raise the same issues, particularly about teacher credentials, although state-parochial education clashes have largely abated due to the increasing willingness of parochial schools to follow state standards in all but the religious aspects of their education. Yet a few objecting parochial schools have avoided extensive approval processes by the state, if not state regulation altogether.[26]

Lutheran tradition coincides in large part with the Court's view that parents have religious liberty, including the right to educate their children consonant with their religious beliefs, which is yet limited by the duty of the state toward each child. Luther thought that of all of the orders of creation, parents are the first stewards of their children, and their first and natural educators.[27] Although later in life he realized that the family was not going to be the ultimate solution to the educational needs he saw, Luther continued to focus on the family and the church as the places where the most critical nurturing of children's religious nature would be carried on.

The protection for parents' religious liberty is also consonant with Lutheran emphasis on the freedom of each person to engage in study and reflection on God's word, and to come to an understanding about the nature of the human person, God's will for the world, and God's relationship with him. From a Lutheran perspective, then, the claims of religious parents to be exempt from certain state laws in educating their children are entitled to serious respect, in order to further their freedom of conscience and their parental responsibilities. Yet, Lutheran doctrine also supports the right and responsibility of the state to be concerned about the child's vocation in the world. Lutherans would be wary of an argument by either the state or a parent demanding plenary power to control the child's educational destiny, for they recognize that either one can and will sometimes misuse its stewardship role, perhaps in order to vindicate self-interested ideologies or from a desire for power and control.

In a pluralistic democracy, Lutherans would take seriously the public criticism that some private school settings shield children from precisely the kinds of difference—socioeconomic, racial, and even religious—that are necessary for them to encounter the created world and to recognize the sanctity of every person. Lutherans would be among those who demand to know whether prejudice, elitism, or animus motivates people to choose and support private schools. While Lutheran theology does not dictate a clear constitutional baseline in such Free Exercise cases, Lutheran tradition would most likely support a balanced approach to the limits of parental rights in private and home schooling, which respects rights of conscience while probing the needs of a child and his or her responsibilities to society.

Religion in the Public Schools

Since the 1940s, when the Supreme Court held that Jehovah's Witness children could not be forced to salute the American flag against their conscience,[29] religious exercises such as prayer and Bible reading in public schools have been a political football. Yet, behind the sometimes inflammatory rhetoric on such subjects, the cases involving the separation of religion and the state in the public schools are a kind of public "watershed," signaling "the fact that the United States of America, like many other nations, is past the place where underlying Christian culture and beliefs are assumed in its life," and calling "for greater depth of conviction [displayed in the public life] in all Christian men and women."[30]

Arguments for and against religious teaching or practices in public school have rested on constitutional, religious, and practical grounds. Christians favoring such teaching and practice claim that

- religious piety pervades every aspect of life. To exclude religious references and rituals from the schools is to teach children that God is irrelevant to public life, and discourage them from living out their vocation as religious persons in all that they do.
- religion is the most effective way to inculcate moral behavior expected and needed in a democratic polity and therefore should be permitted in the schools
- religious exercises have been a traditional part of public schooling

since public schools were established; they have been molded to new circumstances and new religious groups of schoolchildren and have lost their objectionable character

- failure to permit a majority to exercise its right to practice religion through opening prayer, Bible readings, or worship, is a violation of the Free Exercise rights of that majority

Opponents of religious practice in public schools have argued that

- religious exercises can, even unwittingly, be offensive to religious minorities or those who have no religious convictions; they can be particularly coercive for children who are impressionable and might be confused by conflicting practices and beliefs at home and in the school. Children in the religious minority may feel branded as inferior and be excluded from full equal participation at school. They may even be persecuted by other children for being different.
- in order to be acceptable to a majority, religious exercises must be so watered down that they violate the beliefs of many people, even the majority of believers. Children may be led to believe there is no difference in theology and that one religion is as good as the next.
- religious exercises may cause fighting and divisiveness among parents, school officials, teachers, and even children over religion as they attempt to compose prayers and exercises for use in the schools.
- religious organizations may be tempted to mute some of their prophetic witness or conscientiously held beliefs in an attempt to have their religious views prevail with school officials.

As interpreted by the Supreme Court, the Establishment Clause of the First Amendment mandates that public schools not provide sectarian religious instruction. Specifically the federal courts have held that, under the Establishment Clause, schools

- may not require students to pray in school, make prayer an *official* part of school functions, or give legal permission to teachers to require prayer or any similar religious exercises such as devotionals, liturgies, or reading from sacred texts as a part of worship. Statutes that require a period of silence, whether for meditation or "meditation or prayer" at the opening of school have had mixed response from the courts, depending on whether the Court discerned a legislative purpose to reintroduce prayer itself into the schools, or whether the state could raise some plausible non-religious reasons for its period of silence, such as focusing student attention on the school day.[31]

- may not require students to attest to any creed, religious or secular.[32] Thus the state is disempowered from creating a set of beliefs, secular or religious, that a child must confess.

- may not teach or present *as truthful or correct* any religious or atheistic doctrine. Thus the Supreme Court has struck down laws mandating that the Bible be read to children in schools, or that the Ten Commandments be posted in school, or that laws requiring that creation of the world by God be taught, either alone or with other scientific doctrines such as evolution.[33] By contrast, school curricula that have merely *described* the doctrines of certain religious bodies (such as in a world religions course), *acknowledged* the religious beliefs of certain groups such as the Pilgrims or the 1960s civil rights movement, or *allowed* a variety of people to present their religious views have rarely been struck down.[34]

Thus, for example, a public school that celebrated Christmas as the birthday of Christ would be in violation of the Establishment Clause, while a school that taught children about the religious origins of a number of winter holidays, including Christmas, probably would not be. It is difficult to describe the precise borderline between acceptable and nonacceptable references to religion, because so much depends on the context—for example, what statements are made, the tone of the presentation, whether teachers and school administrators or outsiders such as pastors and parents are involved in the presentation, whether "equal time" is given to other religions, whether the materials are indeed offensive to minority religions or atheists or agnostics, and so forth. Despite the beliefs of many educators, however, it is surely *not* the case that schools are precluded from mentioning religion at all in texts, teaching, or activities.

The reasons for the limits on religious instruction in schools can be traced back to the purposes for the Establishment Clause. One goal of the clause is to prevent one religious belief from becoming the "official" state religion, primarily to avoid discrimination or persecution against minority faiths. The anti-discrimination provision is twofold: It protects both political equality and the freedom of conscience. Indeed Thomas Jefferson argued that it would be pernicious for the state to require religious conformity even if it could succeed, for such an outer conformity without inner conviction would "tend to beget habits of hypocrisy and meanness" in citizens.[35]

Supreme Court cases such as *Lee v. Weisman* and *Sante Fe Independent School Dist. v. Doe*,[36] holding that the Establishment Clause prohibits a public high school from sponsoring a nondenominational prayer in its graduation ceremonies and football games, have emphasized this twofold protection for equal citizenship and a free conscience. In the *Sante Fe* case, the Supreme Court particularly focused on the equality concern embodied in the Establishment Clause. In the view of Justice O'Connor and others, the government should not send a message of endorsement of any religion to citizens, lest they think that some religious peoples are political "insiders" and others are "outsiders."[37] In *Lee v. Weisman,* the Court focused more on the freedom of conscience concern. The state must not coerce people to believe or worship, not even through the psychological or "peer pressure" compulsion that a high school student might face in "going along with" school-sponsored prayers.

Apart from theological concerns, Lutherans may have a certain amount of historical sympathy with the Court's move to ensure that public school officials and teachers do not require religious indoctrination of and religious practice by their students. Originally Free-Exercise and Establishment-type provisions were vital to protect the dissenter Protestant religions of the Colonial period. For example, in the mid 1700s in Virginia, Lutherans were one of the groups, along with Presbyterians, Reformed, and Quakers, who had to apply for "dissenter" preaching licenses from the state and who were not permitted to perform marriages.[38] They also were forced to support Anglican churches with their taxes. By law, those persons who did not belong to officially recognized dissenting groups (Lutherans were "official" dissenters) also had to attend Anglican church services at least monthly.[39] While Lutherans in the twentieth century have not had to face the persistent persecution and restrictions visited upon other religious minorities, such as Jehovah's Witnesses, Seventh Day Adventists, Christian Scientists, Jews, Santeria, and even atheists and agnostics, Lutheran experience with religious oppression both in the United States and in Europe should counsel sympathetic caution with the claims of religious dissenters.

Even though Lutherans respect these religious freedom concerns, Luther's emphasis on the need for a Bible-centered education as critical to the Christian's ability to worship and learn of God's relationship with him pose difficult questions about education for Lutherans. Advocates for religious teaching ask, How will Lutherans ensure that children—not just their children, but all children—have a God-centered education, one in which God is at the heart and not the fringes of all learning, if religion is excluded in the public schools? They might worry that children will not be sure of the giftedness of their lives and their responsibility to care for the world if they receive conflicting messages from church, home, and school about God's presence in the world.

Weighing these contrasting concerns, Lutheran social statements have supported non-establishment of religion for some of the same reasons presented by pro-exclusion advocates in the constitutional debate. First, Lutheran social statements have made theological arguments against any coercion by any official of the state, including school authorities, upon children's' religious beliefs and practices:

> Christian faith asserts that God will not force anyone into communion with God. If, then, God refuses to impose divine will upon humanity, then

persons exceed their prerogatives if they try to use coercion of any kind on one another to obtain religious conformity. Religious liberty for all is thus not only a demand of civil justice but also an aid to our response to the Christian gospel.[40]

Second, Lutheran tradition recognizes that fallen human beings will always have difficulty according equal respect to persons who differ from them, the concern that lay at the heart of the *Lee* and *Sante Fe* opinions. As one Lutheran social statement acknowledges,

We make law and order ends in themselves or the means of preserving our privileged position. . . . We create invidious distinctions among persons, declaring some to be more human than others in defiance of the Creator who loves all equally. We allow our respect for institutions to degenerate into unquestioning obedience especially when such respect serves our own self-interest.[41]

These concerns—violation of the individual's conscience, discrimination against those who religiously differ, compelling outward religious conformity without inward confession, and the human desire to seek a privileged position by demanding a religious preference—are of particular concern in the school setting. Children, whose religious understandings are still in the process of being shaped, are particularly susceptible to the pressure of teachers and peers to conform with accepted practices, whether social or religious. Indeed, the social statements acknowledge that when the law, public authorities, and teachers combine to supervise religious exercises, there is an "indirect coercive force on young and impressionable children" to take part, even if they are excused.[42] Children are particularly likely to include or exclude, praise or harass other children based on whether they conform to the routine prescribed by school authorities.

The history of the Establishment Clause debate also has raised institutional concerns about the relationship between church and state that are especially keen in the public school setting.

Here the Lutheran theology of the orders of creation has something particularly helpful to contribute to the debate about religion in the public schools. Luther specifically distinguishes between the competence of the church with respect to God's use of law and gospel for salvation, and the state's use of the civil law. As one social statement describes it, the church's mission and competence is to proclaim the gospel, be a fellowship for Christian people, and minister to the world as critic, advocate for the needy, and in other roles. The state's "distinctive calling" is to "maintain peace, establish justice, protect and advance human rights, and promote the general welfare."[43]

In the public educational setting, Lutheran social statements have acknowledged that, given the state's distinctive calling and competence, religion taught by the state may not be faithful to the truth of God's word or may become a mere shadow, mocking the force of Christian confession and mutating into a civil religion dictated by the state:

> The Lord's Prayer is the supreme act of adoration and petition or it is
> debased. . . . The more we attempt as Christians or Americans to insist on
> common denominator religious exercise or instruction in public schools,
> the greater risk we run of diluting our faith and contributing to a vague
> religiosity which identifies religion with patriotism and becomes a
> national folk religion.[44]

The statement emphasizes that religious exercises separated from an atmosphere of adoration quickly become "a formal, mechanical exercise that neither reflects nor contributes to genuine religious piety and reverence." Further, they may "promote a vague or a syncretistic religion that conveys none of the substance, the depth, and cutting edge of the historic Christian witness."[45]

Consonant with the constitutional tradition as interpreted by Thomas Jefferson and James Madison, Lutherans also have recognized the potential for the corruption of religion if the state pretends to an office it does not hold. Like Lutherans, Jefferson notes the danger that may result if authorities are allowed to regulate the preaching or profession of belief: They will make their personal opinions the law "and approve or condemn the sentiments of others only as they shall square with or differ from [the ruler's] own."[46] Such a danger is present even with well-meaning teachers or school administrators who may believe that they have the child's best interests at heart, and dismiss their parents' objections as ill-informed or self-interested.

Third, the Lutheran churches have been realistic about the potential for political divisiveness in the prescription of government-sponsored prayer, noting that officially prescribed devotions "risk the intrusion of sectarian elements."[47] Community controversies over the language and delivery of public religious exercises may well become political battlefields if such exercises attempt to inject any meaningful specificity. Just as one danger comes from watered-down religion in the schools, another is that the state will select and impose values and beliefs in direct opposition to the church's doctrine. Most Lutherans, for example, would object to school prayers or curriculum that assumed that humans can perfect their own natures or societies, or claimed that one worldview was just as good as the next, even though some educators might believe that these values are vital for children participating in a democratic state.

Because American Lutherans have struggled with the dilemma of ensuring a God-centered education that also is sensitive to needs of democratic tradition, Lutheran church bodies have not agreed with strict separationists that all references to religion should be consigned to the private sphere and thus banned in public schools. Partly because of Lutheran dedication to an education that is truthful and partly to "do justice to the religious factor," Lutheran social statements have proposed that the study *of* religion be included where it is an appropriate part of the school curriculum, just as religious pluralists have done. One social statement, for instance, recognized the importance of "the objective study of religion and the Bible in the public schools" that "gives promise of a constructive approach to neutralizing secularist tendencies in public education."[48]

Similarly, Lutheran statements call for some recognition of religious customs of local communities, though the extent to which such recognition can be accorded by the schools is expressly left somewhat vague.[49] Yet the recognition of such actions might result in Establishment Clause problems if it were read to permit a local government to hold religious ceremonies simply because most residents shared the faith of government leaders. Where religious freedom is concerned, majority rule is not acceptable, according to the Court.

As suggested, however, there is an important constitutional difference between the government running religious celebrations and permitting them to occur. The accommodation of religious practices of parents and children in public school is not inconsistent with the Establishment Clause, so long as the government does not thereby endorse their religious beliefs in front of the entire community. It is important to remember that Establishment Clause jurisprudence governs *only* what school authorities (including teachers, principals, and students who appear to have school sponsorship) may do when they are acting in their official roles, such as leading classroom or lunchroom prayers. Both the courts and Congress have upheld the right of individual students, their parents, and others properly on school grounds to engage in religious speech so long as they do not disrupt the educational setting.[50] For instance, the federal Equal Access Act explicitly protects the right of school children to distribute religious literature and gives student religious groups the same rights to gather for religious education, worship, and prayer at public schools than are permitted any other school club or activity.[51]

The limits of students' rights to accommodation of their religious practices in the public school setting are still being tested in the courts, largely because they depend so much on context, including the message that particular activity sends about school endorsement. For example, school children's rights to have outside clergy come in for religious exercises or to distribute religious materials between classes, and teachers' rights to participate in extracurricular religious activity on school grounds continue to be litigated. Yet, many Christians have not taken full advantage of their *clearly established* rights to express religious beliefs and engage in religious exercises in the public school setting. More attention to exercising those rights might be the most fruitful path for addressing Christians' concerns about ensuring that God is a part of children's education.

Values Education in the Public Schools

Controversies about religion in the school are rarely so clear as whether or not a school can adopt the Muslim, Catholic, or Mormon faith as its official religion. Parents and school officials usually fight about whether schools should teach any values, religious or otherwise, and what values they should be. In recent years, public attention has been focused on the so-called secular humanism debate, which centers on whether public schools have adopted an implicit "secular" (godless) theological position directly contrary to Christian (and other) traditions. In the view of some Christian parents, traditional religious education in the public schools has been replaced by a new quasi-religious system of values improperly stressing individualism, noncritical tolerance of all people's beliefs (even false ones), humans' ability to achieve perfection and happiness through their own will, and other beliefs that oppose their faith.

Again, Lutherans might well have difficulty fully supporting either side of the secular humanism debate without knowing how a particular school is handling such issues. Luther himself was sympathetic to many of the humanists' criticisms of education, and expressed his own frustration with medieval education for its focus on uncritical recitation, suggesting that teachers should go beyond memorization to discuss the meaning of what students read.[52] Lutheran social statements follow this theme, recognizing the need for education to teach children to reason logically and critically and "to understand the customs, ideas and beliefs which unite the community and undergird the responsibilities of citizenship."[53] Education also should help children appreciate "the possibilities in human life and relationships so that they will wish to continue growing and sharing in life's opportunities and responsibilities." Recognizing that theology cannot be explicitly taught in public schools, the social statements call for the schools to "teach respect for the spiritual and moral values that reflect the community consensus," many of which have Christian and Jewish origins.[54] This need for moral education in public schools is certainly consistent with Luther's attacks on Latin schools in Germany for their refusal to educate people for the "real world" or work on forming Christian character.[55]

Yet such education in the public schools raises a conundrum for Lutherans precisely because teaching moral behavior must contain at least implicit value premises, some of which may be starkly at odds with Lutheran beliefs. It is not necessary for Christians to agree that the public schools "establish a religion" of "secular humanism" for them to be concerned that public school authorities may find the teaching of values contrary to the Christian witness—such as ethical relativism and the human autonomy (values going well beyond teaching respect for ethical diversity)—the only palatable solution to teaching a diverse student body.

Most of the "values education" lawsuits that have raised Establishment Clause objections to teaching "secular humanism" have been unsuccessful.[56] For instance, parents in San Mateo County, California, failed to block what they deemed objectionable family-life and sex education in the schools.[57] The court in that case found that curriculum guides adequately stressed the diversity of family lifestyles and religious viewpoints on the nature of the family, urging teachers to send students to their parents or religious advisers if they raised questions.[58] Particular books such as *Slaughterhouse-Five*[59] and *The Learning Tree*[60] have also been attacked as unsuitable. The courts, however, generally refuse to find that values being taught in the public schools, such as respect for others, gender equality, independent moral decision-making, and tolerance are so distinctively identifiable with secular humanism or any other religious tradition that they would set up an establishment of religion. Even such topics as magic or witchcraft that would seem to implicate religion, at least if they are used in light-hearted ways to spark the imagination, have not been successfully attacked. By contrast courts have been somewhat more willing to find Establishment Clause violations when a religiously based system of behavior and beliefs, such as transcendental meditation, is involved.[61]

Courts have had more difficulty with parental requests that under the Free Exercise Clause their children should be permitted to have an alternative to objectionable work, since they touch directly on parents' right to control their children's education. In one well-publicized case, *Mozert v. Hawkins County Board of Education*,[62] parents raised a series of complaints about the "secular humanist" values in their children's English readers, which included stories on pacifism, telepathy, use of children's imagination, "futuristic supernaturalism," the achievements of women outside the home, the desirability of a "one world" community, and the absence of life after death.[63] The appeals court in *Mozert* ultimately decided that required reading of objectionable materials or viewing student class exercises on the materials did not constitute a violation of the Free Exercise Clause,[64] so students could not constitutionally demand to opt out of this work. In this court's view, if parents wanted to prevent their children from exposure to these materials, they should transfer to private schools. Other cases have held that exposing students to "humanist" or other religious values throughout the curriculum is not a violation of their religious freedom rights so long as the teacher does not try to indoctrinate the student, that is, to force or encourage him to believe that such ideas are true. Thus it would be permissible for a teacher to say, "Wiccans believe that . . . " but not to say, "You should believe what witches believe." Textbook challenges requesting a personal opt-out for individual students have been successful in some cases, though not always.[65]

A Lutheran response to the public school curriculum will probably be more nuanced than that of parents who demand the right to expunge all offensive material from the curriculum or, on the other side, those who would label any attempts to criticize school officials' choices as censorship. As critically situated Christians, Lutherans will view religious and moral diversity not only as a possible threat to their children's Christian identity but as a divine gift that is, sadly, touched by finitude and the willfulness of sin.

Thus Lutherans will recognize the complexity of the questions public education raises, manifesting both respect and critical engagement with all sides of the debate. They will recognize the appropriate authority and expertise of school officials to design curriculum and select teachers and materials, while conscientiously challenging them about the value assumptions informing school life. When educational critics, even those with whom they are at odds on other issues, appropriately criticize values embedded in books or teaching, they will be willing to support the message while still confronting the messenger on other areas of disagreement.

The State's Responsibility for Providing Education

Lutherans also must be concerned about a third question: the ability of children to receive an appropriate vocation-directed education, in both the public schools or in parochial/private schools. Three sorts of disputes that arise in public discussions of schools are linked by this concern:

- The right of children to equal respect in the provision of public education. This issue has arisen most momentously in school desegregation but also has come into focus in other contexts, such as single-sex education, provision of services for gay and lesbian students, and disability accommodations.
- The ability of all children to receive a well-rounded education that adequately prepares them to be active and able citizens in a democratic culture shaped by a free-market economy. Lutherans have supported public education because of its essential role in inculcating values necessary for service to the community and the nation.[66]
- The realistic opportunity for all parents and their children to choose an adequate religious education for their children if they desire one.

In modern America, the right of children to a basic education is virtually without question, even as controversies about the appropriate type of education abound. Mandates for the states to provide public education, usually a free K–12 education, can be found in every state's constitution or statutory laws. The language of these laws differs from state to state, perhaps mandating " a 'thorough and efficient system of public education,' a 'general and uniform system of Common Schools,' or a 'system of free common schools.'"[67]

The public's responsibility to provide education is echoed in the views of early Lutheran reformers. Some of the impetus in early Lutheran calls for a public system of education were pragmatic: Luther believed that society needed educated men and women "for the maintenance of civil order and the proper regulation of the household."[68] But he also claimed that the devil would "secretly sap the strength of the cities" and "starve out a . . . land and destroy it without a battle" if children were not educated.[69] Luther even took his pleas for a public educational system to the princes themselves, arguing to Elector Johann of Saxony that he had both the right and duty to step in where families and localities failed to educate their children and to compel them to do so.[70] Otherwise, warned Luther, if children were left to their parents' desires, they would "poison and pollute the other children until at last a whole city is ruined."[71]

Lutherans have traditionally stressed the importance of high educational quality as well. As suggested previously, from the earliest days, the reformers sought to transform German education from its focus on rote learning and earning a good living to a system concentrating on critical primary texts and active inquiry.[72] Modern-day church statements have reiterated the necessity of quality education for children in public schools, which contributes "to renewing the vitality of communities," as well as the promotion of high standards "in all aspects of school life—behavioral, social, academic and spiritual" in Lutheran parochial schools.[73] Echoing Luther's understanding of vocation, Lutheran schools have found their calling as holistic institutions, dedicated to Christian nurture, mission outreach, and quality education that will "strive for excellence in the development and use of all God-given gifts."[74]

While modern-day America has accepted that universal public education is necessary to ensure that children gain the virtues and skills needed for active citizenship, the quality, extent, financing, and variety of such education vary significantly from state to state. Because of a tradition of local control over public schools, regulation and taxing schemes for schools reflect local commitments to education and values. Some school districts stress diversity through a range of schools from magnet and charter schools to neighborhood schools; others offer a fairly uniform, no-frills system of public education.

Despite this significant recognition of public responsibility for the education of children, the courts have not gone so far as to hold that each child has a right to an adequate and appropriate education that respects his or her vocation and potential for contribution as a citizen. Perhaps the most progress, albeit far from full progress, has been made in recognizing the principle that children are entitled to equal respect in the provision of public education. *Brown v. Board of Education*,[75] which banned racially unequal or separate education, is most notable in this respect, although its emphasis on the need for a quality education that awakens all children to the values of their culture has been largely overlooked.[76] Similarly, Lutheran social statements on education have spoken forcefully about the need to provide for the poor in education and to resist racial and other discrimination in education. Lutherans have called for assurances that "all children [receive] educational opportunity, justice and achievement in an environment of racial, religious, social and economic pluralism."[77]

The Lutheran commitment to equal respect does not resolve the problem of what educational financing and systems will best respect these values. For instance, new public policy alternatives to provide more opportunity and choice in education, such as tax credit and voucher systems, have come under attack by both Christians and non-Christians because of concern that self-interested, prejudiced parents will use them as an excuse to abandon the other children in the public schools.[78] Others believe that more school choice, especially with adequate financial assistance for low-income families, will permit *more* integration because poor minority parents will have a more realistic opportunity to send their children to parochial schools with a tradition of welcoming students of all races and socioeconomic backgrounds.

These debates require both the distinctive voice of Lutheran values and the commitment of Lutheran people to work with others using their gifts of reason and experience to make the best possible choices for all of the community's children. In a complex world, involving human beings whose motivations and actions may be both well-intentioned and sinful at the same time, the Lutheran commitment to equal respect and fitting all students for their intended vocations through a humane educational system may conflict with Lutheran emphasis for a God-centered education, as the debates about tax breaks for parochial school children show. The call for Christian engagement in the world would be hollow if parochial systems are used to distance Lutherans from the needs of their neighbors, including children who might be left behind, or encourage people to act on biases against the poor, minorities, or others.

Yet Lutheran tradition would seem to require energetic efforts by Christians to ensure that Christian education is pervasively available and easily accessible to all children, no matter what public policy is in place. Luther affirmed that the most important objective in education was study of the Holy Scriptures, and emphasized the importance of education as a means to help young people to lead a prayerful life in communion with God, training for God's service and the development of character.[79] In a religiously pluralistic culture, the responsibility for ensuring that children can grow in faith, develop awareness of God's gift of dignity and worth, and become mature decision-makers whose moral actions are rooted in Christian conviction must rest largely on parochial educational programs, including but not limited to Christian day schools.[80]

Considering the extent to which the public tax or education systems should be utilized to make it realistically possible for parents to choose a religious education for their children has been a tortured task for the Supreme Court. Ever since the Court first held in *Everson v. Board of Education*[81] that the state could not assist parochial schools directly, case law interpreting the government's responsibility under the Establishment Clause to be neutral toward religion has not followed a bright-line course, and its decisions have often seemed hair-splitting. The Court's test for reviewing public financial aid that reaches parochial schools once focused on whether the state is motivated by a secular purpose and whether the primary effect of its plan is to advance or inhibit religion. The "effects" test for auxiliary aid currently asks whether (1) the program results in governmental indoctrination or (2) it defines recipients by reference to religion or (3) the state is "excessively entangled" with the church, that is, intrusively supervises parochial schools.[82] Political divisiveness caused by the state's action, such as fights between Protestants and Catholics on state tuition credits, may constitute "entanglement."

While it is sometimes difficult to understand the legal lines drawn by courts, in general, the more "public" the service, the more likely such aid has been held constitutional, although recent Supreme Court decisions have shown a decided turn in favor of permitting more types of assistance. Currently, services provided by a public employee, which are "objective" enough to prevent any religious influence (such as state-written tests, remedial education, or diagnoses of speech and hearing problems) and are ancillary to the main curriculum will probably be permissible. By contrast, direct subsidies to schools which have not been diverted there by parental choice are probably unconstitutional.[83] In the past, criteria employed by the courts and commentators to determine constitutionality included whether the money went to the school or parents (because the former suggests symbolic approval of religious activities),[84] whether the aid put the school in a better financial position or simply bought services that students would have been provided in the public school,[85] and whether state aid preferred some parents or simply equalized the position of parochial and public school parents.[86] State constitutional amendments have restricted assistance to religious institutions even more than Supreme Court decisions, sometimes even forbidding state money to be used for public transportation of parochial students and textbook loan programs.[87]

Past Supreme Court cases suggested that the permissible constitutional limits to public financing in aid of parochial education also depended on the form and amount of aid that is provided. However, at least some forms of tuition assistance to parents, such as government vouchers for low-income parents who want to send their children to private schools, have recently been approved in *Zelman v. Selman-Harris. Zelman* expanded on the court's ruling in *Mueller v. Allen,* where the Supreme Court upheld a tax deduction program for private school tuition and expenses, finding that Minnesota had secular purposes and effects—it would relieve the public system of the cost of educating such children and provide a private benchmark for public school performance, much as public school educational choice has done. Where the *Mueller* Court stressed that that parents received the benefit through a deduction, rather than a direct payment to the school and noted the deduction was given to all parents, including public school parents with educational expenses.[88] *Zelman* requires only that vouchers to schools are truly parental choices, not "deliberately skewed incentives toward religious schools and that they provide aid to "a broad class of citizens without reference to religion.[89]

The American context, with its separation of church and state, imposes a burden on all Christians to make sure that an education centered on the gospel is available to all children, particularly where parochial schools are not accessible to everyone because of distance, finances, or other barriers. Because education centrally focused on God's word is so critical to Chris-tian freedom, Lutheran tradition would call on every Christian to insist upon and sacrifice to provide that education. Especially in cultures that embrace church and state separation, Lutheran theology will counsel that education in God's word must go beyond a privatized, unimportant moment in the week and become a daily part of children's lives not only in the home, but also through organized and subsidized programs available to all children. Because children are God's gift and every Christian's responsibility, all forms of Christian education, including parochial school and Sunday school, are the responsibility of the whole church, not just those who teach or administer the programs or have children in them. If Luther saw early that parents' responsibilities and skills limited their ability to rear their children as Christians, citizens, workers, and parents, modern demands on parents in dual-employment and single-parent households, civic responsibilities, and a difficult and sometimes unsafe climate for children make it critical for Christians to assume these duties toward their neighbors, most especially those who are strangers to them and those who are overlooked because they live in rural or urban areas overwhelmed by human need.

In summary, although there is much room for debate among Christians about how the public can best be involved in educating children, Lutherans must keep in mind three elements of their tradition:

- Luther understood education as a critical but insufficient, tool in enabling children to take their place as Christians and citizens. These citizenship responsibilities have not lessened since Luther's time; indeed, they have grown greater as both church organizations and the state have moved to more participatory democratic models for governance, so that the need for a well-rounded education is vital.

- Children are God's gift to the world, not simply burdens or even the property of their parents or the state. In educational reform discussions, therefore, Lutherans must keep in mind their responsibility for all of God's children, not just their own. They must search for solutions that will respect God's gift in all of its diversity, setting aside biases based on race, class, gender, and other stereotypes that do not respect the unique talents and potential of its children.

- Children must be equipped for the vocation God has for them, rather than for what use they are to parents or others surrounding them. Lutherans will therefore demand that the state respect the variety of vocations to which people are called in order to create an orderly, peaceful, and just society. They will expect the state and the church to educate people to participate in a world where those vocations are honored and the ability of children to fulfill them is taken seriously.

Finally, and perhaps most importantly, Luther insisted that the gospel be at the center of children's learning and growth. Above all else, young people, he claimed, must learn to know God and understand God's Word. While he was not naive about the presence of sin from the moment of birth, Luther once claimed that if the Christian Church were ever to rise again, "[W]e must make a new beginning with children."[90]

[A note on the title of this chapter: In the discussion of the Fourth Commandment in the Large Catechism, Luther says, "For if we wish to have excellent and apt persons both for civil and ecclesiastical government, we must spare no diligence, time or cost in teaching and educating our children, that they may serve God and the world, and we must not think only how we may amass money and possessions for them.]

7

Love Thy Neighbor:
Churches and Land Use Regulation

Robert W. Tuttle

Consider the following three cases:

1. *Cornerstone Bible Church v. City of Hastings*[1]
In 1983, Cornerstone Bible Church formed and began to hold worship services in the home of its pastor. As the congregation grew, it moved first to the local high school and then leased space for worship in an office building located in the city's central business district. When the city's planning director learned of the church's move, he ordered the church to stop using the office building for worship services: the city's zoning ordinance excludes religious uses from commercial districts. The church then started to look for other worship space. It attempted to purchase a former theater, also located in the business district, but the city denied the church permission to use the theater for religious services. The congregation met with the same response in several other attempts to convert commercial space into a church. The city argued that religious uses would interfere with economic development of the central business district, and that churches were free to locate in residential zones, which made up nearly half the city. The church claimed that it could find no suitable sites in the residential areas, which were already well developed, and sued for permission to locate in the commercial zone.

2. *Western Presbyterian Church v. Board of Zoning Adjustment*[2]
Western Presbyterian Church, located just blocks from the White House, sponsored a feeding ministry that served breakfast to homeless men and women. In 1989, the International Monetary Fund and the church exchanged parcels of property: the IMF wanted to expand onto the church's site, so the

IMF agreed to build a new structure for the congregation at a site it owned several blocks away. The new site was in the middle of an expensive residential area, across the street from the Watergate condominium complex. Claiming fear of increased crime and harassment from homeless people visiting the church, the church's new neighbors asked the city to stop the church from reopening its feeding ministry. The city agreed with the neighbors: although the zoning ordinance permitted religious use of the site, serving meals to the homeless did not constitute an approved "accessory" use of the property. After the zoning board upheld the city's decision, the church brought suit in federal court for the right to continue the feeding ministry.

3. *City of Boerne v. Flores*[3]
St. Peter Catholic Church had outgrown its small sanctuary. Sunday morning masses were packed with overflow crowds, so the church made plans to expand, plans that involved demolishing part of the old sanctuary. Before the church applied for a building permit, however, the City of Boerne established an historic district in order to preserve significant properties, and St. Peter's— a fine example of mission style architecture—was included within the historic district. Based on the historic landmark designation, the city denied the church's application for a building permit. The church brought suit in federal court, claiming that the landmark status infringed on the church's right to religious liberty.

Introduction

How should we understand these cases? The churches involved experience the land use regulations as barriers to core aspects of their mission, indifferent— and perhaps even hostile—to their free exercise of religion. To the regulators, on the other hand, the churches' claims sound like "special pleading," a claim that laws applying to others should not bind churches. Regulators ask why Western Presbyterian should be able to open a feeding program when a non-religious charitable institution (or a for-profit restaurant) would be prohibited at that location. Why should St. Peter's be exempt from historic preservation laws when a similarly historic theater would not be exempt? These questions and competing perceptions lead us to one of the most difficult topics in the relationship between church and state: the extent to which religious believers or institutions must (or may) be excused from compliance with laws that burden their religious practice, even though the laws do not discriminate against religion.[4]

Land use regulation proves especially fruitful for exploring this topic of "free exercise exemptions." Conflict between churches and land use regulators seems on the rise in recent years, attracting the attention of courts and legislatures across the country, and providing the factual setting for development of the exemption doctrine. At the federal level, the U.S. Supreme Court used the *City of Boerne* case to strike down Congress's first statutory enactment of free exercise exemptions, the Religious Freedom Restoration Act. After several years of legislative hearings, which included detailed studies of religious institutions' zoning cases, Congress passed a new exemption statute focused on land use, the Religious Land Use and Institutionalized Persons Act.[5] After a survey of the basic types of land use regulation, I will discuss judicial and legislative protections for religious land use and conclude with some thoughts on how we might construct a more faithful approach to religious liberty in the land use context.

Regulation of Religious Land Uses

Prior to this century, conflict between churches and their neighbors would have fallen under the law of nuisance, which constrains uses of property that "unreasonably interfere" with others' use and enjoyment of their property. Claims of excessively loud or frequent bell-ringing provided the most common ground for nuisance suits against churches, though particularly exuberant tent meetings could attract lawsuits as well.[6] Early land use legislation attempted to regulate "noxious uses," activities likely to cause nuisances if located in inappropriate areas—such as a factory or livery stable in a residential community. By 1920, however, the new city planning movement had a broader goal for land use regulation. Through categorical zoning, land use planners intended to rationalize the urban and suburban landscape, separating residences from the noise and congestion of commerce and the dangers and pollution of industry.[7] In a famous 1922 decision, *Euclid v. Ambler Realty,* the U.S. Supreme Court upheld the power of localities to create categorical zoning schemes. The Court held that government's "police power" extends beyond the control of nuisances; government may regulate land uses to serve the general welfare even if the regulated uses do not cause direct harm to their neighbors.[8]

Early zoning ordinances, often modeled on one drafted by Edward M. Bassett for New York, did not exclude churches from residential areas. In 1936, Bassett wrote:

> When, in 1916, the framers of the Greater New York building zone resolution were discussing what buildings and uses should be excluded from residential districts, it did not occur to them that there was the remotest possibility that churches, schools and hospitals could properly be excluded from any districts. They concluded that these concomitants of civilized life had a place in the best and most open localities.[9]

Bassett's words represent more than just his reflections on the early ordinances; they also indicate his awareness that the early attitude toward churches was no longer unquestioned. While most jurisdictions continued to permit churches in any residential zones, some localities started to place limits on religious institutions. The end of World War II brought about dramatic shifts in the patterns of American life, including worship life. Church construction boomed along with the suburbs. Where Bassett envisioned parishioners walking to their neighborhood churches, suburban planners realized that most worshipers in the new churches would arrive by car, bringing traffic congestion and parking problems along with them.[10]

In a 1949 case, *Church of Jesus Christ of Latter-Day Saints v. City of Porterville,* California courts became the first to uphold the exclusion of churches from a residential zone. The court of appeals found that the city had sufficient reason to keep public buildings, including churches, out of neighborhoods designated exclusively for single-family homes. Public buildings invite crowds, the court said, and crowds mean noise and congestion in residential enclaves. The California decision, implicitly approved by the U.S. Supreme Court, was soon followed by cases in several other states that reached the same result: churches need not be permitted in all residential neighborhoods.[11]

The *Cornerstone Bible Church* case discussed in the introduction reveals a different problem of exclusion, one that may be more important for churches today. While most cases and legal commentary deal with churches' exclusion from residential neighborhoods, that focus often proves misplaced. As Douglas Laycock, a leading scholar of constitutional law, writes:

> A right to locate a church in built-up residential neighborhoods is illusory for all but the tiniest congregations. Unless your congregation can meet in a single house, the only way to build a church in a residential area is to buy several adjacent lots and tear down the houses. But several adjacent lots never come on the market at the same time, and if they did, any church pursuing this strategy would likely provoke an angry reaction from the neighborhood. It is only in commercial zones that significant tracts of land are bought and sold with any frequency. . . . To exclude new churches from commercial zones goes far to exclude them from the city, while allowing them to locate as of right in residential neighborhoods goes far to fool uninformed judges into believing that a complaining church has ample opportunity to locate.[12]

Commercial zones usually offer the infrastructure necessary to address concerns about traffic congestion and parking produced by religious uses, and noise should present fewer problems outside residential neighborhoods. But zoning regulators, even in jurisdictions that traditionally favor religious uses, often argue that churches should not be allowed to displace revenue-generating uses in commercial districts.[13]

Regulation of religious land uses typically takes forms that are more subtle and complicated than categorical exclusion of churches. Zoning ordinances commonly treat churches as "conditional uses," permitted in a given zone only with the approval of land use administrators. Conditional use (sometimes called "special use") permit schemes developed out of zoning authorities' desire for greater discretion in regulating land uses: rigid categories do not always work well with the distinct features of specific uses or sites. Some uses, such as a gas station, may be appropriate for only some sites in a zone. Even where appropriate the regulators may impose additional conditions to harmonize the use with surrounding properties.[14]

For land use authorities, churches seemed a natural subject of conditional use permits. Most planners did not want to exclude churches from residential districts but recognized that some sites for religious uses would be better than others. A church at the end of a cul-de-sac in the middle of a subdivision creates more congestion, noise, and parking problems than a church located on a busy street at the edge of the subdivision. By the 1950s, conditional use permits were commonly applied to churches. With very few exceptions, courts approved the permit requirements for religious uses, often applauding the permits as a means for ensuring a fair balance of competing values.[15] Although this case-by-case balancing seems desirable, permit processes raise special problems when applied to religious institutions, especially the risk that regulators will discriminate against unpopular religious groups. Protection of religious uses is especially important under conditional-use permit schemes, but as we will see, the schemes differ widely in the standards used to guide administrators' discretion.

Along with migration to the suburbs, which was accompanied by categorical and conditional-use regulation of churches, another shift in religious life also attracted the attention of land use authorities. Churches became centers of daily activity, providing day care for children and seniors, gathering places for teenagers and young adults, shelters and soup kitchens for the homeless, and dormitories for those on spiritual retreat.[16] Long common in Roman Catholic parishes, private religious schools grew up in other faith communities as well. This increased range and intensity of religious land uses provoked conflicts with neighbors and regulators. *Western Presbyterian* reflects this sort of conflict: the church had already established a permitted religious use of the property, but the legal question was whether the challenged activity—in *Western Presbyterian*, a meal ministry for homeless persons—represented a legitimate "accessory use" to the primary religious use, typically defined as religious worship and assembly.

Zoning ordinances, by implication or express language, permit accessory uses of religious property. To determine whether a proposed use qualifies as "accessory," zoning administrators require the church to show that the use is "related, subordinate, and customarily incidental to the principal use."[17] With an ordinary residential use, the accessory use test should be noncontroversial. A zoning board or court is perfectly competent to decide whether domestic workers' quarters or tennis courts are "customarily incidental" to the primary residential use. Churches pose a more difficult challenge. May a government official decide whether sheltering the homeless or living in community is "related" and "customarily incidental" to religious assembly and worship? Western Presbyterian Church emphasized the gospel command to feed the hungry in arguing that this social ministry was integrally related to the church's worship. The regulators countered by focusing on the "customarily related" element, suggesting that because no other Presbyterian church in Washington, D.C., had a similar feeding ministry, the one run by Western Presbyterian could not be deemed customary. As we will see, the question of who gets to decide whether an activity constitutes a permitted "accessory use" of a religious institution raises significant constitutional and practical difficulties.

In addition to restrictions on the location and accessory uses of their property, some churches may find themselves regulated by historic preservation laws, as St. Peter's did in the *City of Boerne* case. Historic preservation ordinances usually establish a commission whose first task is to designate neighborhoods or particular structures as historically significant. Property owners typically have the legal right to challenge this designation, but most ordinances give the commission the authority to "landmark" the property or include it in a historic district even if the owner objects. Once a property is designated by the commission, the property's owner may not modify or destroy the exterior (and in some cases the interior) of the structure without the commission's approval. The owner must also preserve the structure in its historic condition. Although historic landmark ordinances stand at some distance from the origins of land use regulation in the law of nuisance, the Supreme Court has recognized historic preservation as a legitimate exercise of government power.[18]

Think of the most historically important structures in any town, and the list will invariably include churches. As Angela Carmella writes, "it is not at all surprising that many houses of worship have been designated landmarks. . . . They are often magnificent examples of architectural styles, sites of significant historic events and anchors of cultural stability within neighborhoods."[19] Many churches welcome their designation as historic landmarks. Designation reflects the community's appreciation for the congregation's home, and it may make the church eligible for assistance in preserving the structure—a considerable help given the high cost of maintaining or restoring an older building.[20] But landmark status can also impose heavy burdens on a congregation, especially when the structure is no longer adequate for the church's needs. In the *City of Boerne* case, the historic district commission denied the church's request for permission to expand the sanctuary. Although the church and the commission eventually reached a compromise, St. Peter's was faced with the prospect of dividing its congregation or selling the historic sanctuary and moving to larger space outside the city. And the latter option, selling the sanctuary, would have been made more difficult because of the landmark designation: any buyer would have been bound by the same requirement to maintain the historic church, thus substantially reducing the market value of the property.

Protection of Religious Land Uses

Our reflections on the interaction between churches and land use regulators are guided by basic theological commitments that are well summarized in the 1979 statement of the Lutheran Council in the U.S.A., "The Nature of the Church and Its Relationship with Government."

> As one of God's agents, government has the authority and power in the secular dimensions of life to ensure that individuals and groups, including religious communities and their agencies, adhere to the civil law. The churches and their agencies in the United States are often subject to the same legislative, judicial, and administrative provisions which affect other groups in society. When necessary to assure free exercise of religion, however, Lutheran churches claim treatment or consideration by government different from that granted to voluntary, benevolent, eleemosynary, and educational nonprofit organizations in society.[21]

The statement's first clause affirms the legitimacy of civil government as a divine agent, a "mask of God" in Luther's phrase, called "to maintain peace, to establish justice, to protect and advance human rights, and to promote the general welfare of all persons."[22] To the extent that land use regulation orders human community toward the common good—by coordinating the location of uses that would otherwise conflict, by reducing congestion and promoting safety in residential neighborhoods, and by supporting preservation of the community's history—it merits respect as a proper exercise of the state's authority.

The state's divine calling serves not only to legitimate but also to limit: the state is not God but an agent of God, a subordinate and not ultimate authority. In a liberal, pluralistic political community, the state recognizes this limitation by respecting its citizens' religious liberty. The temporal welfare achieved through land use regulation may be outweighed by the needs of religious communities. Respect for religious liberty, however, cannot entail the political sovereignty of religious believers and institutions. With his acute understanding of human sinfulness, Luther recognized that an absolute right to violate laws that conflict with religious conscience invited chaos and anarchy.[23] The question, then, is how to safeguard the work of religious institutions while maintaining the benefits of properly regulated land uses.

Courts and legislatures have been wrestling with that question for the last fifty years, using a wide range of approaches to reach an equally wide range of answers. I will first describe judicial responses to religious land uses in the four contexts outlined above: categorical exclusion, conditional-use permits, limitation of accessory uses, and historic preservation. I then turn briefly to legislative protections for religious land uses.

Religious Land Use in the Courts

Religious land use cases arise in both federal and state courts. The state decisions rest on several different grounds, including federal and state constitutional law, state administrative procedures, and judicial interpretation of the land use ordinance at issue; federal courts generally have jurisdiction only when a church alleges a violation of its rights under the U.S. Constitution. Yet even state cases that focus on narrow technicalities in a land use ordinance reflect some concern with the religious liberty of churches regulated by the ordinance.

From the early 1960s to 1990, a church's religious freedom claim would have been decided under the standard developed in *Sherbert v. Verner*, a case involving the denial of unemployment benefits to a woman whose religious beliefs forbade her to work on Saturdays. The Supreme Court held that if the claimant could show that the state regulation imposed a "substantial burden" on her "sincerely held" religious beliefs, the claimant would be exempted from the regulation unless the state proved that the regulation was the "least restrictive means" of advancing a "compelling governmental interest."[24] The *Sherbert* compelling interest test was embraced by the ELCA's predecessor bodies as the appropriate mechanism for reconciling legitimate government interests with religious liberty.[25] Courts—particularly the Supreme Court—were somewhat less enthusiastic about the test, applying it unevenly. In 1990, the Supreme Court severely limited the reach of the *Sherbert* test in *Oregon v. Smith*, holding that religious conduct is entitled only to neutral treatment, not special exemptions. Congress has twice attempted to restore the *Sherbert* standard, most recently in a statute that applies the compelling interest test to land use and institutionalized persons, but the test's future in the courts remains uncertain at best.[26]

Categorical Exclusion[27]

Categorical exclusion of churches from residential areas provided the context for most early court decisions and legal commentary on religious land uses. Both courts and commentators tended to describe the alternatives in stark terms: either churches were preferred land uses and could not be excluded from residential districts, or churches were entitled to no special protection and thus could be excluded. New York courts led the "no exclusion" group, an approach shared by a majority of states, holding that categorical exclusion of churches from residential zones represents an arbitrary and irrational exercise of the zoning power because religious uses are "clearly in furtherance of the public morals and general welfare."[28] Categorical exclusion of such beneficial uses cannot serve the general welfare. A minority of states, following California's *City of Porterville* case, permitted categorical exclusion of religious uses based on the noise and congestion often created by religious uses. The desire to create a quiet residential enclave free from heavy traffic constituted a rational basis for the exclusion.[29]

Closer inspection of these cases reveals not two diametrically opposed camps, with one elevating religion above all else and the other subordinating religion for the convenience of neighbors, but a surprising degree of commonality. Through legislation, a few states—Massachusetts is the best example—exempted religious institutions from the reach of zoning ordinances. Most of the remainder, however, sought a balance. New York and other "no exclusion" states do not bar religious uses from residential areas, but they often subject churches to conditional-use permit requirements. "No exclusion" really means "exclusion only after a specific determination that the religious use would be inappropriate for a given site."[30] Conversely, courts in California and other "pro-exclusion" states may uphold categorical restrictions but typically require land use authorities to have good cause for excluding churches and also to show that churches remain free to locate in a significant portion of the jurisdiction. In *Porterville*, for example, the court emphasized the fact that no other place of assembly—such as a school, library, or theater—was permitted in the residential district, and that the restricted area comprised a very small part of the city.[31]

Although state courts decided a substantial number of religious land use cases after 1950, federal courts ruled on very few such cases until the early 1980s. From the *City of Porterville* case through the 1980s, however, the U.S. Supreme Court consistently rejected the appeals of churches that lost land use cases in state courts.[32] While one should be cautious about reading too much into denials of review (the Supreme Court accepts only a tiny portion of cases seeking its review), the Court has never indicated that it regards exclusion of religious land uses from particular zones to be a serious infringement on religious liberty. Consider Chief Justice Vinson's remarks about the *Porterville* case, made in a later opinion:

> When the effect of a statute or ordinance upon the exercise of First Amendment freedoms is relatively small and the public interest to be affected is substantial, it is obvious that a rigid test requiring a showing of imminent danger to the security of the nation is an absurdity. We recently

dismissed for want of substantiality an appeal in which a church group contended that its First Amendment rights were violated by a municipal zoning ordinance preventing the building of churches in a residential area.[33]

A survey of federal decisions since 1980 reveals a similar attitude toward religious land use cases: federal courts tend to regard application of the *Sherbert* test in this context as "an absurdity" and rarely exempt the religious use from land use regulation.

Federal courts have employed two strategies for avoiding the *Sherbert* compelling interest test. *Lakewood, Ohio, Congregation of Jehovah's Witnesses v. City of Lakewood* demonstrates the first of these strategies.[34] In a case involving exclusion of religious uses from a residential district, the U.S. Court of Appeals for the Sixth Circuit held that the zoning restriction placed no significant burden on the religious beliefs of the congregation: "building and owning a church is a desirable accessory of worship, not a fundamental tenet of the Congregation's religious beliefs."[35] As an inquiry into the religious significance of "building and owning" a Kingdom Hall for these Jehovah's Witnesses, the court's analysis surely must be found wanting. Like most congregations, the particular design and (absence of) ornamentation of the worship space is loaded with religious meaning. But for Jehovah's Witnesses, even the act of constructing the worship space is theologically charged: most Kingdom Halls are built by church members, and construction is interspersed with prayer and fellowship.[36]

In *Messiah Baptist Church v. County of Jefferson,* the church was denied a conditional-use permit to locate its house of worship on land zoned for agricultural use.[37] The court followed *Lakewood* and held that the zoning restriction imposed no "substantial burden" on the congregation's religious exercise. Then the *Messiah Baptist* court continued on to a second strategy. The court concluded that even if Messiah Baptist had been able to show a substantial burden on its religious exercise, the county zoning ordinance constituted a sufficiently compelling interest to outweigh the burden on the church. "[W]ithout question, the zoning district plan, one of true differentiation and upheld as sound under the due process analysis, cannot be implemented effectively without the resulting financial burden on the church."[38] *Porterville* involved "true differentiation," but *Messiah Baptist* surely did not: the agricultural zone at issue in *Messiah Baptist* did not categorically exclude religious uses; it allowed them subject to a conditional-permit process. How could the county have a compelling interest in "true differentiation"—drawing clear lines that exclude religious uses—when the ordinance itself created exceptions?

The *Lakewood* court's narrow reading of "religious burden" and the *Messiah Baptist* court's willingness to accept questionable rationales as compelling interests can be found in most federal court decisions involving religious land uses.[39] What explains courts' reluctance to apply a robust version of the compelling interest test to religious land use disputes? Part of the explanation can be traced to the test itself, which originates in contexts quite different from typical burdens on religious exercise.[40] When the government classifies people based on their race or imposes restrictions on the content of peoples' speech, we strongly presume that the regulation will be unconstitutional. The compelling interest test captures this presumption and demands that the government justify its "extraordinary" need to impose such restrictions. Laws that place incidental burdens on religious exercise do not attract our suspicions in the same way: we do not believe that such laws are valid only in extraordinary cases, but recognize that a wide variety of otherwise quite useful laws may conflict with someone's religious beliefs. For example, laws requiring vaccination of children confer significant individual and public benefit, but some religious traditions object to such treatment. Should courts regard vaccination laws as skeptically as they would view a law that established racially segregated schools? The compelling interest test does not match our intuitions about the validity of laws affecting religious exercise, so it should come as no surprise that courts—and most notably the U.S. Supreme Court—granted religious exemptions under the test only on rare occasions.[41]

Specific features of the land use context highlight this defect in the compelling interest test. All free exercise exemptions, of course, impose some additional burdens on others. Tax exemptions place a greater tax burden on the rest of the community; *Sherbert* raises the cost of the unemployment insurance system, an expense passed along to employers and consumers; exemptions from drug laws increase the dangers posed to society by having people under the influence of such substances; and military draft exemptions impose a higher risk of selection on non-objectors. But each of these costs is relatively diffuse. No one person in society bears a substantially higher burden of the exemption than anyone else.

Land use is different. When a church is allowed to locate in a residential neighborhood, the church's neighbors must put up with the noise, parking problems, and increased traffic that accompany the church. The exemption's costs are entirely local. The problem is magnified by a perception of the religious institution as "other," a perception more common in our days of greater religious pluralism and "megachurches" that draw people from well beyond the affected neighborhood. Unlike hospitals or schools—or even retail stores—which have an obvious connection to the local community, churches may appear to impose costs on the neighborhood without significant counterbalancing benefits.[42] We should not be surprised, then, when courts fail to subject land use restrictions on churches to the searching review demanded by the compelling interest test.

We may not be surprised by *Lakewood*, *Messiah Baptist*, or the other federal cases that avoid applying the compelling interest test, but the courts veer from one extreme to the other. After finding that the *Sherbert* test does not apply, these courts invariably moved to the least searching standard of judicial review, one requiring only that the government show a "rational basis" for imposing the burden—a requirement that the government invariably meets.[43] As we shall see, the *Cornerstone Bible Church* case recognizes an important middle ground in constitutional review, an alternative to the "all-or-nothing" approach of *Lakewood* and its followers. The *Cornerstone* court draws this middle ground from two constitutional sources that are not religion specific: the Equal Protection Clause of the Fourteenth Amendment and the Free Speech Clause of the First Amendment.

Equal Protection Analysis

Two different strands of equal protection doctrine can be implicated in religious land use cases. The first, more common strand is known as "suspect classification" analysis: when a regulation imposes burdens on someone because of that person's race, national origin, or religious beliefs, the Equal Protection Clause requires courts to provide close scrutiny of the regulation. Categories such as race and religion are deemed constitutionally impermissible bases for imposing burdens. In a 1993 decision, *Church of the Lukumi Babalu Aye v. Hialeah*, the Supreme Court illustrates suspect-classification analysis. Residents of Hialeah opposed the Santerian church's practice of ritual slaughter of animals, and so the city council passed a law prohibiting the ritual killing of animals. The Court held that the ordinance singled out the Santerians' religious practices for mistreatment—other ways of killing animals were exempted from the ordinance—and by singling out an activity for regulation *because of its religious character*, the ordinance violated the church's constitutional rights.[44]

Unlike the *Lukumi Babalu Aye* case, the *Cornerstone* case did not involve a religious activity targeted for mistreatment because of its religious character; churches were among a number of other land uses excluded from the business district. The *Cornerstone* court turns to a second strand of equal protection doctrine, the "fundamental rights" analysis. This strand asks courts to scrutinize regulations that burden basic liberties, such as the right to travel, marry, or procreate. Judicial review in fundamental rights analysis focuses primarily on underinclusion, that is, where burdens are imposed on the exercise of fundamental rights that are not imposed on relevantly similar conduct. *Lukumi Babalu Aye* again provides a helpful illustration. The ordinance banned the Santerians' ritual sacrifice of animals yet permitted hunting, experimentation on animals, and even kosher slaughter—all conduct that is relevantly similar to the Santerians' sacrifices.[45]

In *Cornerstone*, the court found that while the city excluded churches from the business district, claiming that religious uses hinder commercial development, the zoning ordinance permitted a substantial number of noncommercial uses in that district. In order to exclude churches from that zone, the court held, the city needed to justify "this apparent unequal treatment of similarly situated entities."[46] Although the court did not impose the compelling interest test's "strict scrutiny" on the city's land use regulation, it did apply a review more intensive than the highly deferential rational basis test. Commentators sometimes describe this intermediate scrutiny as a "hard look" test, a description perfectly appropriate to the court's approach in *Cornerstone:* the court demanded that the city provide more than "conclusory statements" in justifying its distinction between churches and other noncommercial uses. The city must show a factual basis for the distinction, a showing that the city failed to make at the trial. After this appellate court decision, the city settled the case and allowed religious uses in the commercial zone.[47]

Free Speech Analysis

The *Cornerstone* court also looks to the Free Speech Clause of the First Amendment as a source for protection of religious land uses. In turning to the Free Speech Clause, the *Cornerstone* court follows a long tradition in constitutional law. Much of our modern free speech jurisprudence was developed during the 1930s and 1940s in cases involving public preaching and proselytizing by Jehovah's Witnesses.[48] In recent years, the Supreme Court has turned to the Free Speech Clause (and not to the Free Exercise Clause) in a series of cases that have guaranteed religious groups' equal access to public schools and other public meeting facilities.[49] Although the overlap between speech and religious exercise is not perfect—worship and religious instruction fit easily, but day-care programs or homeless shelters may not fit as well—*Cornerstone* demonstrates the important place of free speech analysis for religious land use disputes.

The Free Speech Clause, at its core, prohibits government censorship. Whenever the state discriminates among speakers based on the content of their speech, it has the heavy burden of showing that the restriction is the "least restrictive means" of achieving a "compelling government interest." Very few content-based restrictions survive this strict constitutional scrutiny. Thus, in *Widmar v. Vincent,* the Supreme Court held unconstitutional a state university's rule that barred student religious groups from using student meeting space for prayer and worship. The rule impermissibly singled out religious speech for a burden (exclusion) not imposed on other kinds of speech.

At first glance, the zoning ordinance at issue in *Cornerstone* would seem to be content-based and thus deserving of strict scrutiny. Like the student groups in *Widmar v. Vincent,* the state excluded religious groups from an area open to other "speakers." Citing a body of case law involving the regulation of adult theaters, the *Cornerstone* court found that the zoning ordinance did not target the religious speech of religious land uses, but rather the "secondary effects" of religious uses on the surrounding area. Just as adult theaters can be controlled because they bring in crime and blight, religious uses can be regulated because they bring traffic and noise to residential zones—or, in *Cornerstone*, because churches fail to stimulate commerce in a business district.

The "secondary effects" explanation may avoid strict constitutional scrutiny of most zoning restrictions on religious uses, but it does not insulate such restrictions from all constitutional review. Again following the adult theater cases, *Cornerstone* turns to the intermediate constitutional scrutiny traditionally applied to "indirect burdens" on speech. This intermediate scrutiny has two prongs: an ends-means test and a requirement that the restriction still leave open "reasonable alternatives" for the regulated speech. First, the ends-means test: unlike the strict scrutiny applied in *Widmar v. Vincent* (and in the *Sherbert* free-exercise test), intermediate scrutiny demands only an important, not a compelling, governmental objective; and the means for reaching that objective need only be "narrowly tailored," not the "least restrictive means" of achieving the state's end. Nevertheless, the state still must define clearly the harms the regulation addresses and show that the regulation does not "burden substantially more speech than is necessary to further the government's legitimate interests."[50] In *Cornerstone*, the court found that the city had failed to present sufficient evidence that churches would cause actual harm to the economic vitality of the central business district, and so reversed a lower court's judgment for the city.[51]

The second aspect of intermediate scrutiny, which requires the state to demonstrate that the regulation "allows for reasonable alternative avenues of communication,"[52] is designed to keep indirect limitations from becoming complete bans on the regulated speech. Several cases involving zoning of religious uses have explored the reasonable alternatives analysis. The *Lakewood* case, noted above, gives a constricted reading to this requirement:

> The effect of the Lakewood ordinance is not to prohibit the Congregation or any other faith from worshiping in the City. Although the Congregation may construct a new church in only ten percent of the City, the record does not indicate that the Congregation may not purchase an existing church or worship in any building in the remaining ninety percent of the City. Furthermore, unlimited numbers of churches may be constructed in the appropriately zoned areas, confined only by the number of lots. The lots available to the Congregation may not meet its budget or satisfy its tastes, but the First Amendment does not require the City to make all land or even the cheapest or most beautiful land available to churches.[53]

With respect to the 90 percent of the city closed to new religious uses, the *Lakewood* court seriously understates the obstacles facing the congregation. The court suggests that the congregation could worship in a private home, but conflicts over parking and noise almost invariably arise when attendance grows beyond a handful of members (and sometimes even well before that point).[54] And conversion of a nonreligious use (for example, a theater) into a church typically involves the same zoning issues as constructing a new church in the zone.[55] The reasonable alternatives analysis turns on the remaining 10 percent of the city. The court rejected the congregation's claim that land in the commercial district was too expensive and "not conducive to worship," finding such considerations constitutionally irrelevant.[56]

To counter *Lakewood*'s narrow reading of the reasonable alternatives analysis, churches can look to an unlikely source—constitutional review of land use restrictions on adult theaters. Though the leading Supreme Court case interpreting the reasonable alternatives requirement, *Renton v. Playtime Theaters*, takes a similarly narrow reading, lower federal courts have provided significantly more robust scrutiny of zoning exclusions. In *Topanga Press v. City of Los Angeles*, the Ninth Circuit Court of Appeals held that Los Angeles's zoning restrictions on adult theaters failed to provide reasonable alternative sites. While acknowledging that real estate prices were not a constitutionally relevant factor, the *Topanga Press* court held that "reasonable alternatives" means that the area zoned for adult uses must be reasonably accessible, have proper infrastructure (such as roads and sidewalks), and suited for ordinary commercial development. In short, *Topanga Press* requires courts to take a close look at the particular sites offered by the government as reasonable alternative places for the protected speech. Churches can demand the same sort of scrutiny. If a congregation can show that land zoned for religious uses is not practically available—the sites are unlikely to become available (for example, an airport, heavy industry, or a sports stadium) or lack basic infrastructure— the Free Speech Clause's reasonable alternatives requirement should offer some protection.

Although the Free Exercise Clause does not immunize churches from land use regulation (and has frequently offered little protection, even under the most robust tests for free-exercise exemptions), we have seen that other constitutional provisions offer significant resources for religious institutions that are categorically excluded from particular zones. Equal protection analysis ensures that religious uses are not restricted more than other similarly intensive land uses, while the free speech tests require the government to prove that the zoning exclusion responds to actual harms caused by the religious uses—not just anti-religious animus—and that reasonable alternative sites are available within the jurisdiction.

Conditional-Use Permits

As I described earlier, many jurisdictions—including those that treat churches as preferred land uses—regulate the location of churches through conditional (or special) use permits, a process that allows the locality to designate certain areas as potentially appropriate for religious uses, depending on a closer examination of the site and the specific proposed use. At one level, judicial review of conditional-use regulation of churches proceeds in the same manner as categorical zoning. Courts have almost unanimously upheld conditional-use permit requirements against free-exercise challenges, and several courts have suggested that conditional-use permits offer a valuable framework for reconciling the religious liberty of churches with the land use interests of the broader community.[57]

The equal protection and free-speech analyses outlined in the previous section apply to conditional-use permits as well as categorical zoning. Using the Equal Protection Clause, churches can challenge a zoning ordinance that requires religious uses to obtain conditional-use permits when relevantly similar or more intensive land uses (such as social clubs or theaters) are allowed without permits.[58] The Free Speech Clause's intermediate scrutiny also requires the state to show that a conditional-permit scheme is a narrowly tailored means of achieving important interests, while leaving open reasonable alternative avenues for expression. In *Church of Jesus Christ of Latter-Day Saints v. Jefferson County,* the court struck down a zoning ordinance that failed to provide reasonable alternative locations for religious uses: any church desiring to locate on any site in the jurisdiction was first required to obtain approval of the neighbors. By subjecting new religious uses to "neighborhood whim," the ordinance effectively excluded unpopular religious groups from the community.

The *Latter-Day Saints v. Jefferson County* case suggests an important difference between conditional and categorical zoning of religious uses, a difference that requires a deeper level of constitutional review. Zoning administrators and courts recite the benefits of conditional-use regulations—closer scrutiny of proposed uses to determine their appropriateness for a particular lot, the ability to adjust uses through conditions on zoning approval—but these benefits can become constitutional liabilities in cases like *Latter-Day Saints v. Jefferson County.* Particularized inquiries, and the administrative discretion that usually accompanies them, invite arbitrary or discriminatory judgments. Again, equal-protection and free-speech analyses prove important sources of constitutional scrutiny. Equal-protection concerns are the most obvious: zoning administrators may employ conditional-use permits to exclude disfavored religious uses while approving more traditional groups. In *Islamic Center v. City of Starkville,* a Muslim community complained about discriminatory application of a conditional-permit process: no permits—aside from the Islamic Center's—had ever been denied, and the zoning administrators tolerated more disruptive religious uses without enforcing the permit requirement. The case was particularly egregious: a much larger Christian center was located next to the Islamic Center, operated a better-attended and more intensive schedule of activities than the Islamic Center, yet received zoning approval while the Islamic Center's request was denied.[59]

The Free Speech Clause offers a different type of constitutional scrutiny to conditional-permit schemes. In a long line of cases, from *Lovell v. Griffin* and

Cantwell v. Connecticut to *Shuttlesworth v. City of Birmingham* and *City of Lakewood v. Plain Dealer Publishing Co.*,[60] the Supreme Court considered the constitutional implications of "prior restraints" on speech—laws that require speakers to ask government permission before engaging in speech or other expressive action (for example, parades, public performances, demonstrations). A government official is then vested with authority to decide whether the speech or parade will take place, and on what terms. Conditional-use zoning restrictions on religious uses display features similar to these prior restraints on speech: the ordinance requires religious land users to obtain prior government permission before locating a place of worship on a particular site.

The Court's prior restraint analysis addresses two harms with permit schemes. First, any such restraint must establish reasonable time limits for administrative decision, without which an administrator could hold the permit application indefinitely, effectively barring the activity. Although uncertainty about zoning can impose significant costs on churches looking for new property—a clause making sale or lease contingent on zoning approval often will be part of the church's property agreement, and such clauses make contracts more expensive for churches and less attractive to potential sellers or lessors—zoning ordinances generally impose time limits on administrators' permit decisions. The second aspect of prior-restraint analysis proves more significant for churches subject to conditional-use permits: any regulation that imposes a prior restraint on free speech must have "narrow, objective, and definite standards" for administrative decision. Determinate standards ensure that applicants will know the conditions they must fulfill for approval, and reviewing courts can decide whether the administrator has acted for constitutionally sufficient reasons (and not arbitrarily or discriminatorily). Again, churches can look to constitutional principles developed in adult theater zoning cases. Courts repeatedly strike down adult-use permit schemes for lack of definite standards. Conditions such as "essential or desirable to the public convenience or welfare" or "detrimental to the public health, safety, or welfare" have been found constitutionally defective when used as requirements for adult use permits.

Measured by the requirement of "narrow, objective, and determinate standards," many conditional-use permit schemes applied to churches will be found deficient. With this standard, *LDS v. Jefferson County* was an easy case: the obligation to seek neighborhood approval before locating a religious use provided no standards for decision at all and invited the worst sort of discrimination against minority religious communities. *Christian Gospel Church v. City and County of San Francisco* should have been an easy case, but the church lost. After the church's conditional-use permit application sparked neighborhood opposition, zoning authorities denied the application on grounds that the use would increase congestion and "adversely affect the character of the neighborhood." The latter grounds reflect the broad discretion the ordinance accorded to zoning authorities—precisely the same requirement that the use not be "detrimental to the public health, safety, or welfare" found unconstitutionally broad in adult-theater cases—but the court never considered the implications of the Free Speech Clause for the matter. The court looked only to the *Sherbert* test for free exercise exemptions, found that the zoning ordinance imposed no substantial burden on religious exercise, and ruled in favor of the city.

In contrast to the court's truncated analysis in *Christian Gospel*, a more robust constitutional analysis of conditional-use regulation of a religious use would require (1) that the religious use is not subjected to more burdensome regulation than similar non-religious uses, (2) that this particular religious applicant is being treated equally with similar religious applicants, and (3) that the criteria for approval of the permit application are objective, determinate, and focused on the religious use's actual impact on the community— such as parking and noise—rather than vague (and easily manipulated) invocations of "public convenience or welfare."

Accessory Uses

Should a homeless shelter or feeding program be considered a "religious use" of property? The question, at the heart of *Western Presbyterian Church v. Board of Zoning Adjustment*, has been asked in cases across the country.[61] Strictly speaking, the question usually asked is whether homeless shelters should be considered "accessory uses" to the primary religious use of the property (defined, in turn, as a place for worship or assembly of a religious group). Zoning ordinances typically define accessory uses as those that are "related, subordinate, and customarily incidental to the principal use."[62] Is feeding and sheltering the homeless "related" and "customarily incidental" to religious worship?

Courts have taken two approaches to untangling the thicket of religious, political, and legal implications of this question. The first, "objective" approach emphasizes the "customarily incidental" nature of accessory uses and determines whether the proposed use is actually common among religious land uses. Under the objective standard, parking lots, day-care centers, and parsonages fit, but nontraditional uses—such as homeless shelters or drug treatment facilities—do not. The objective test has the advantage of avoiding close (and constitutionally dubious) investigation of a religious group's beliefs to assess the significance of the use within the group's ministry. But equating "customarily incidental" with "widely practiced" normalizes traditional religious groups, often at the expense of nontraditional faiths or newer practices of established communities.

The second, "subjective" approach answers the limits in the objective approach by focusing on the relationship between the proposed accessory use and the group's religious mission. Because of constitutional (and practical limits) on judicial inquiry into a group's theology, the subjective approach turns on the group's sincerity: is the accessory use necessary to the flourish-ing of the members' ministry *as the members understand that ministry?* This approach has the advantage of according full respect to nontraditional reli-gious groups and practices. But this respect comes with a serious cost: because the religious community alone is competent to judge the importance of the proposed accessory use, the property is open to any use the religious commu-nity desires.[63]

Homeless-shelter cases, like *Western Presbyterian,* offer a useful test of these two approaches. Under the objective test, shelters and feeding programs tend to fare poorly. Homeless shelters have not traditionally been part of churches and other houses of worship and so may not qualify as "customarily inciden-tal" to the primary religious use.[64] The subjective test leads in the opposite direction: acts of hospitality and care for the poor belong to the heart of reli-gious commitment—some consider it an affront even to have these uses clas-sified as "accessory" rather than "primary" religious uses.[65]

Though churches celebrate the victories in *Western Presbyterian* and similar cases, the subjective approach rests on uncertain footing. The uncertainty is both practical and jurisprudential. On the practical side, the absence of meaningful boundaries that can be known and assessed in advance gives zon-ing authorities even greater incentive to limit the location of religious land uses. If "religious use" potentially encompasses the full range of possible land uses, from schools to radio broadcast towers to printing presses for religious literature, zoning authorities will be justified in restricting churches to areas that can tolerate the most intensive uses (that is, large lot sizes distant from residential neighborhoods). The jurisprudential uncertainty of *Western Presby-terian* stems from its reliance on the *Sherbert* strict scrutiny test for free exercise exemptions, a test that has met with very little success in the land use context (at least in part because of concerns about limiting the reach of religious immunity from zoning regulations).

The search for firmer footing in the accessory use context leads us in a familiar direction, to equal protection principles and the intermediate scrutiny of free speech analysis. But our first step takes us beyond the objective and subjective approaches outlined above, which share a common flaw. Both examine the religious nature of the proposed accessory use and differ only in their understanding of religion. A sounder approach assumes that the reli-gious community has (or can give) a religious justification for its desired accessory use, and turns to a more focused inquiry: does the proposed use materially change the intensity of the existing land use, making the new use incompatible with its surroundings? Consistent with the equal protection analysis outlined earlier, this inquiry compares the proposed accessory use with other existing or approved uses within the zone. As long as the accessory use is no more intensive than other uses, it carries a significant presumption of legitimacy. Although *Western Presbyterian* adopts the subjective approach,

Judge Sporkin's decision draws its logical power from equal protection analysis. The judge asked the city's attorney whether the church would be allowed to host regular breakfast meetings of its members, and the attorney indicated that such meals would fit within the normal definition of "religious use." The city's objection, then, was to the identity of those attending the meal. Members would be welcomed in this upscale neighborhood, but not homeless people. The distinction revealed the weakness of the city's asserted interest in closing the feeding ministry, and the city later conceded that it lacked a "compelling interest" in the matter.[66]

Judge Sporkin's demand that the city define the actual harm threatened by Western Presbyterian's ministry also recalls the test for indirect burdens on free speech. Because accessory use determinations typically focus on particular uses and sites, the prior restraint test's requirement of definite and objective standards for administrative judgments should also apply in this context as well. When considering a proposed accessory use, zoning authorities must articulate in advance determinate criteria for approval, criteria that reflect the state's legitimate interest in maintaining the religious use's compatibility with its surroundings, but avoid the unnecessary and controversial judgments about which are the truly "religious" accessory uses.

Historic Preservation

In an important sense, historic preservation ordinances impose the same kind of burden on churches as do limitations on accessory uses: rather than restricting the location of the church, these regulations limit the congregation's ability to develop fully its ministry at its existing site. As in *City of Boerne v. Flores*, the ordinance may prevent the church from expanding its structure to accommodate a growing congregation, even though the church's lot is large enough to support the expansion. The obligation to repair and maintain an aging structure may burden the congregation with heavy costs, diverting needed resources and requiring the congregation to forgo more economically advantageous development of the property (which would, in turn, support the church's mission).[67] At their most intrusive, historic preservation ordinances may even force the church to retain a configuration of worship space—such as the placement of an altar—that no longer conforms to the church's liturgy.[68]

The Supreme Court has made it clear that the U.S. Constitution's Free Exercise Clause offers churches little protection from historic-preservation ordinances. After the Washington Supreme Court held, in *First Covenant Church v. City of Seattle*, that historic landmark designation of a church's exterior violates the Free Exercise Clause, the U.S. Supreme Court—which had just rejected the *Sherbert* strict scrutiny test in *Oregon v. Smith*—told the Washington court to reconsider *First Covenant* in light of the *Smith* rereading of free exercise law.[69] On the same day, the Supreme Court declined to review

St. Bartholomew's Church v. City of New York, a case that denied a church's free-exercise claim to exemption from the historic-landmark designation of its "community house," a designation that prevented the church from tearing down the structure and building a much larger office tower on the site.[70] In *City of Boerne v. Flores,* the Court used the historic preservation case to strike down the Religious Freedom Restoration Act, reaffirming its holding in *Oregon v. Smith* that the Free Exercise Clause only protects churches from intentional religious discrimination, not the indirect burden of "neutral and generally applicable" laws. In historic-preservation cases, churches' sole victory in federal courts came in *Archbishop Keeler v. Cumberland,* a district court case that dealt with a city's refusal to allow a church to demolish a historic monastery. The court held that the landmark ordinance was not a "neutral and generally applicable" law, but instead focused narrowly on the church, and thus deserved stricter scrutiny than *Oregon v. Smith* provided. Using the stricter scrutiny, the court found that denial of the demolition permit placed a substantial burden on the church's free exercise of religion by requiring the church to support a structure that was expensive to maintain and inappropriate for the church's mission, and that this substantial burden was not justified by any compelling interest of the city.[71]

State courts have provided religious land uses somewhat greater protection from historic-preservation ordinances. The *First Covenant* case offers the starkest contrast between federal and state approaches to this question. After the U.S. Supreme Court returned *First Covenant* to the Washington Supreme Court for reconsideration in light of the *Smith* decision, the Washington Supreme Court ruled that the Washington State Constitution's Religion Clause provided strict scrutiny for burdens on religious liberty—they adopted the *Sherbert* test as a matter of state constitutional law, placing religious liberty decisions outside the U.S. Supreme Court's reach. Using this new state constitutional standard, the Washington Supreme Court then reaffirmed its earlier decision that the historic-landmark designation of a church's exterior violates the church's right to free exercise of religion.[72] In *Society of Jesus v. Boston Landmarks Commission,* the Supreme Judicial Court of Massachusetts also found that its state constitution's religion clause, unlike the federal Free Exercise Clause, provided strict scrutiny for burdens on religion. The Massachusetts court then held unconstitutional the historic-landmark designation of the Jesuits' worship space, finding that the state had no compelling interest in controlling the interior of the church.[73]

Neither the Washington State decisions nor the federal cases (apart from *Keeler*) represent constitutionally adequate responses to historic-preservation cases involving churches. In their blanket exemption of all religious uses from historic-landmark designation, the Washington court (like the California legislature, considered below) provides religious institutions with a benefit difficult to justify under either the Establishment Clause or basic principles of equal treatment. Without regard to the religious institution's reason for objecting to landmark designation—the statute itself exempted architectural changes made for liturgical reasons—the Washington court relieved churches of a burden to which all other landowners are subjected. Under the Washington court's reasoning, a church that wanted to demolish its sanctuary in order to sell the vacant lot for development would be free to do so, while a nonreligious institution that purchased the church for nonreligious uses would be denied a demolition permit and required to maintain the structure. It is hard to see such a broad exemption as anything other than a direct benefit conferred on religious institutions alone.

The Supreme Court's indifference to religious liberty claims of landmarked churches is equally flawed, reflecting the Court's blindness to free exercise considerations other than intentional religious discrimination. Attention to free speech and equal protection parallels would prove fruitful in this context as well. The *Society of Jesus* case offers a useful starting point. The Boston Landmarks Commission designated the church's interior as a historic site, requiring the church to obtain the commission's approval to change the worship space (including placement of the altar). The commission's landmark designation raises a host of First Amendment concerns. First, the liturgical configuration of worship space undoubtedly expresses theological commitments of the church—an altar against the wall means the priest celebrates the Eucharist with his back to the congregation, whereas an altar pulled away from the wall means that the priest may now face the congregation, symbolically assuming a quite different role in worship. The requirement to leave the altar against the wall is a form of "compelled speech," expression mandated by the government, which is a fundamental violation of free-speech rights.[74] Second, and intertwined with the "compelled speech" concern, the commission's power to regulate the church's interior invites the kind of government-church entanglement prohibited under the Establishment Clause. B Courts typically forbid government officials to become immersed in the self-governance of religious institutions.[75] Third, the commission's authority also represents a kind of prior restraint on the church's free speech, entitling the church to close review of the standards imposed and their relation to "important governmental interests." Although the Massachusetts court relied on its state religion clause, the same result would have been reached through the approach I have outlined: given the dangers of government "commandeering" the religious community by regulating its worship space, and the fact that the interior was not publicly visible, the state's interest in maintaining the historic interior seems quite weak.

Unlike *Society of Jesus,* the *City of Boerne* case involved only the exterior of the structure, and the church's reasons for desiring a change were not directly expressive (that is, they raised no theological objection to the design and were willing to preserve the facade) but clearly theological: the church needed to expand or it would be forced to split the congregation. Under traditional free speech analysis, this burden on the congregation would need to be justified as a narrowly tailored means of reaching an important government interest. Should historic preservation count as an important government interest? It may be less significant than basic public health or safety, or public welfare considerations like noise and congestion that are typically involved in church-zoning cases, but securing a community's historic legacy is increasingly recognized as a valuable public purpose, even when the buildings are privately owned. Although a church should have concerns about becoming solely a cultural artifact—like the cathedrals of many European towns, empty of worshipers but full of tourists—being seen as a community treasure can equally enhance the religious mission of a congregation. The reasonable alternatives prong of free-speech analysis could help to clarify the distinction between sterile artifact and vibrant treasure: where historic preservation would render the structure practically unusable for the ordinary purposes of a congregation, such as a structure with worship space too small or too oddly configured to sustain a viable community, landmark-preservation concerns may need to give way or at least compromise with the religious community's right to worship.[76]

St. Bartholomew's offers a quite different type of conflict, though it proves equally helpful in outlining a more nuanced approach to free exercise in the landmark context. The church's desire to demolish a historic building and replace it with a much larger skyscraper is hardly unique to religious communities; indeed, it echoes the Supreme Court case that established the constitutionality of historic-preservation ordinances, *Penn Central v. City of New York*.[77] So what other claims might the church make? The church lacked a distinctive theological reason for demolishing the structure; it wanted more space and money, but churches are regularly thwarted in those desires. Equal protection analysis, ineffectively addressed by the *St. Bartholomew's* court, represents the most promising alternative. To prevail on an equal protection claim, the church would need to show that the burden of historic preservation was not spread equally among similar properties. For example, if an architecturally comparable structure had been exempted from landmark designation, the church would be entitled to close judicial review of the reasons that the church's structure was not also exempted. Churches may not often prevail on such discrimination claims, but that merely reflects the relative weakness of the church's claim to relief from a burden equally shared by similarly situated landowners.

Legislative Protection for Religious Land Uses

Following the *City of Boerne* case and the accompanying demise of the Religious Freedom Restoration Act, Congress attempted to place legislative protection for religious liberty on more solid constitutional footing. Because the Supreme Court had held that RFRA lacked sufficient evidence of discrimination against religion to justify its assertion of federal power over the states,

Congress looked for such evidence, and seemed to find it in several studies of religious land uses. In the summer of 2000, this search for new protections for religious liberty resulted in the Religious Land Use and Institutionalized Persons Act (RLUIPA). Like RFRA, RLUIPA emphasizes "restoration" of the *Sherbert* strict scrutiny test for free-exercise exemptions: whenever a regulation substantially burdens a free exercise of religion, the burdened believer or institution is exempted from the regulation unless the government can show that the regulation is the "least restrictive means of furthering a compelling government interest." But RLUIPA also borrows from the equal-protection and free-speech analyses I outlined earlier: it prohibits discrimination against particular religious groups or religious uses in general, and forbids the exclusion of religious uses from a jurisdiction.[78]

RLUIPA faces an uncertain future in the courts. Though the new statute responds to some of the defects in RFRA that the Supreme Court identified in *City of Boerne,* the Court's deep skepticism about the *Sherbert* test and its expanding protection of states against Congress's jurisdiction do not bode well for RLUIPA's future. Even if RLUIPA survives constitutional scrutiny, however, the *Sherbert* test's limited success in land use cases is already evident in several of the early cases to apply the new law. In both *C.L.U.B. (Civil Liberties for Urban Believers) v. Chicago* and *City of Chicago Heights v. Living Word Outreach Full Gospel Church,* the courts found that zoning limitations on churches did not constitute "substantial burdens on religion" necessary to invoke the protections of RLUIPA.[79] The legacy of *Lakewood* and *Messiah Baptist* persists.

At the state level, protections for religious land use come in several forms. A number of states have enacted their own version of RFRA (though, like the federal version, these have not guaranteed significant protections for religious land uses).[80] In addition, states frequently exempt religious institutions from certain types of land use regulation, such as restrictions on development of schools or day-care centers.[81] Most cases interpreting these statutory exemptions for religious land uses deal with narrow questions of the scope of the exemption. But in the past year, courts have decided two major cases on the constitutionality of religious land use accommodations. *Boyajian v. Gatzunis* and *East Bay Local Development Corporation v. California* both addressed Establishment Clause challenges to statutes that exempted religious institutions from land use regulation. Though both cases upheld the disputed regulations, and cite the basic principle that government may accommodate religious exercise without violating the Establishment Clause, the differences between the challenged statutes and the courts' rationales in upholding the statutes are significant.

At issue in *Boyajian* was the Dover Amendment, which exempts religious or educational uses from zoning restrictions in Massachusetts, though it does permit "reasonable regulation" of such uses for height, building density, and parking.[82] Plaintiffs challenged the amendment as an impermissible benefit to religious institutions in violation of the Establishment Clause. The court acknowledged that statutory exemptions could constitute a kind of regulatory support for religion, exemplified by the U.S. Supreme Court decision in *Texas Monthly v. Bullock*, which held unconstitutional a Texas law that exempted only religious periodicals from a state tax.[83] But the court distinguished the Dover Amendment from *Texas Monthly* by pointing to the significant number of other land uses also protected under the same amendment. Religious uses are treated the same as educational institutions, group homes for the handicapped, child care facilities, and agricultural uses. Like the U.S. Supreme Court's decision in *Walz v. Tax Commission*, which upheld New York's tax exemption for religious uses of property—as part of an ordinance that also exempted other educational and charitable uses—*Boyajian* looks at churches as one among many types of beneficial institutions in the community. Rather than singling out religious uses for special treatment, the Dover Amendment treats churches equally with other similarly situated land uses.

In *East Bay*, however, the California Supreme Court upheld against an Establishment Clause challenge the state's exemption of religious institutions from historic preservation laws. The statute in question provided that religious institutions could avoid the reach of historic landmarks for all noncommercial buildings they owned by making a unilateral (and unreviewable) declaration of "substantial hardship."[84] Unlike *Boyajian* (and *Walz*), this exemption was not part of a broader scheme involving nonreligious charitable and educational uses. Religious institutions alone were relieved of the burdens of historic landmark designation. The *East Bay* court recognized that the statutory exemption extends well beyond the claim religious institutions could make for free exercise protection from landmark designation but ruled that the scope of legislative accommodations for free exercise could be broader than the scope of judicially created exemptions without infringing the Establishment Clause. While that statement (invoked in *Boyajian* as well) is correct, the Constitution requires a material relationship between the free exercise burden alleviated and the statutory protection for religion. Protections that are too broad can become unconstitutional support for religious entities.

At first glance, the statutory accommodation in *East Bay* is hard to distinguish from the tax exemption scheme found unconstitutional in *Texas Monthly*: the law relieves a burden on religious institutions that is primarily financial,[85] and this relief is not extended to secular analogues (that is, other nonprofit charitable or educational institutions). Though the point is not adequately developed in the *East Bay* decision, the California historic preservation exemption differs from *Texas Monthly* (and, indeed, *Boyajian* and *Walz*) in one important respect: where historic preservation is concerned, religious uses and secular nonprofit institutions may not be "similarly situated." Property used for religious purposes—including "pervasively sectarian schools"—may be ineligible for certain forms of government assistance with maintenance and repair of historic structures.[86] To the extent that the Establishment Clause concerns bar religious institutions' participation in public support for historic preservation, the Establishment Clause surely should not prohibit government exemption of churches from the burdens of historic preservation. Seen from this perspective, however, the California exemption still seems overbroad, encompassing properties clearly eligible for government assistance (such as religious hospitals, nursing homes, and other facilities open to the general public) as well as those that are arguably ineligible (that is, houses of worship).

Land Use and Free Exercise

How should we regard these developments in the land use regulation of churches? The legal doctrines I have described stand in some tension with understandings of religious liberty advanced in the statements of the ELCA's predecessor church bodies. The tension is manifested most clearly in two aspects of religious liberty articulated in the 1979 ALC statement "The Nature of the Church and Its Relationship with Government." The first aspect can be seen in a description of the church's institutional free exercise right:

> Government exceeds its authority when it defines, determines or otherwise influences the churches' decisions concerning their nature, mission, and ministries, doctrines, worship and other responses to God, except when such decisions by the churches would violate the laws of morality and property or infringe on human rights.[87]

The structure of this claim follows the *Sherbert* compelling interest test for free exercise exemptions (a test specifically endorsed in the 1968 LCA social statement "Religious Liberty in the United States"). The claim starts by defining "substantial burden" on churches' free exercise right as government action or regulation that "defines, determines or otherwise influences the churches' decisions" about religious matters. It then recognizes the limit on this right, the state's "compelling interest" that may outweigh free exercise claims.

Our survey of free exercise in the land use context should raise two concerns with this claim of institutional religious autonomy. One concern is prudential. At least in land use cases, the *Sherbert* compelling interest standard (both at the federal and state levels, and in both statutory and judicial form) has rarely provided the kind of protection for religious land uses that one might expect from the stringent review the test purports to offer. Indeed, as I indicated above, the test might even be counterproductive: courts familiar with the compelling interest test from circumstances where offending laws truly deserve a presumption of illegitimacy—racial discrimination or content-based regulation of speech—find it difficult to apply the standard to regulations that seem, on the whole, generally beneficial. As we saw, courts refuse to concede that churches' free exercise rights have been substantially burdened, or else accept as "compelling interests" an expansive range of government purposes (including "exceptionless administration of the laws"). Paradoxically, religious land uses seem to receive more searching constitutional scrutiny when courts employ a less rigorous standard of review—one that acknowledges the general validity of the rule in question but asks whether that rule has the indirect effect of burdening religious expression or has been applied in a discriminatory fashion.

The other concern has prudential implications as well but addresses the deeper justification for the LCUSA statement's claim of institutional religious autonomy. The "substantial burden" part of the claim encompasses a broad—one might even say unlimited—range of decisions for which the church claims a presumptive regulatory autonomy, that is, any decision that concerns the churches' "nature, mission, and ministries, doctrines, worship and other responses to God." The range recalls zoning administrators' difficulties with the accessory uses of religious institutions. If the church reserves to itself the power to determine what is religious, can it truly expect to receive the presumptive regulatory autonomy that it claims? Lawyers for the church (including myself) are tempted to answer "yes": a broad religious privilege makes the church's dealings with the government much easier, as the state needs to justify any regulatory intrusion on the church's self-described mission as a governmental interest of the highest order.

But our Lutheran theological understandings of the state's responsibility and our own obligations as citizens and neighbors counsel against the litigator's quick response. Not all of our "ministries . . . and other responses to God" merit the same degree of legal protection. In addition, the current unsettled state of free-exercise law gives us the opportunity to attempt a more nuanced—and, I believe, more faithful—articulation of the churches' institutional autonomy and the state's coordinate obligation of deference. I offer here only the roughest sketch of a hierarchy of free-exercise claims, all focused on the religious land use context. The items in each category are meant to be illustrative, not exhaustive.

To the highest order of free-exercise claims belong

- a right to a reasonable opportunity to plant new churches (subject, of course, to the existing market for real estate), rather than a right not to be excluded—"zoned out"—from particular jurisdictions
- a right to be free from intentional government discrimination on the basis of religion—thus, for example, conditional-permit regulations especially should receive close scrutiny to ensure that minority religious communities are not being disfavored in the regulatory process

- a right to definite and objective conditions for approval of a use permit
- a right to determine the time and nature of the church's worship and assembly—the "primary" religious use
- a right to be free from regulatory control over the appearance of worship space, except that necessary to meet reasonable fire and building safety ordinances, and a right to determine the external appearance of houses of worship in conformity with the church's theological understanding

Regulation of these core free-exercise claims must be justified by governmental interests traditionally defined as compelling—public health, safety, and order, and the civil rights of others—and the government must show that the compelling interest cannot be achieved by any less restrictive means.

To an intermediate level of free-exercise claims belong

- a right to meaningful judicial review when churches are excluded from a particular zone, which should include attention to churches' relevant similarities to other uses permitted in that zone
- a right to have the conditions of any use permit scheme narrowly tailored to the harms posed by the religious use at issue
- a right to zoning regulations—such as lot-size restrictions, building-size limits, and parking requirements—that are narrowly tailored to the burdens imposed by religious uses
- a right to determine the nature of any accessory use of religious property
- a right to determine the architectural configuration of church property used for worship and religious assembly

Regulation of this intermediate level of free-exercise claims must be justified by "important" governmental interests, determined by evidence of the actual harms that the religious exercise will cause. The regulation must not be significantly more intrusive on free-exercise rights than necessary to achieve the government's objectives. Thus, for example, regulation of an accessory use of a church could only proceed through government proof of the harms such use would cause, and some showing that compromise with the church would frustrate the government's purposes.

Finally, to those aspects of the church's work that merit the least searching free-exercise review

- regulations or use permit conditions that focus specifically on public health and safety, such as fire-code regulations on building occupancy

- conditional-use permit regulations for religious uses (so long as the permit processes meet the requirements noted above)
- historic-landmark designation of the exterior of buildings owned by religious institutions but not used for religious worship or instruction

Government regulations of this sort enjoy a strong presumption of legitimacy, a presumption that the church can overcome only if it can show that the regulation at issue is being administered in a discriminatory matter (for example, property owned by religious institutions is being disproportionately singled out for historic landmark designation).

This tentative hierarchy of free-exercise claims leads us back to the second aspect of the ALC's social statement's understanding of religious liberty, a claim of the legal distinctiveness of religious institutions: "When necessary to assure free exercise of religion, however, Lutheran churches claim treatment or consideration by government different from that granted to voluntary, benevolent, eleemosynary, and educational nonprofit organizations in society." If one starts with the expansive definition of free exercise given in the earlier claim made by the ALC statement, this assertion of religious distinctiveness is implausible. The broad claim would privilege religious institutions over their secular analogues in areas where the two are virtually indistinguishable, such as education or the provision of social services. But if the legal distinctiveness of religious institutions is refocused on the core aspects of free exercise—religious worship and assembly—the privilege returns to solid ground. To ensure the rights of citizens to gather for worship, government may be required to leave space for religious institutions even when it excludes other institutions. Because of the threat of religious discrimination, zoning authorities may be required to give more precise reasons for denials of land use permits to religious institutions than to others, and face more searching judicial review of such denials as well.

As the ALC statement recognizes, the state is called primarily to the fair, equal, and just execution of the laws, promoting "the general welfare of all persons." In our pluralistic society, the state's religious witness is quite limited but nonetheless significant. Our government is most faithful to its traditions when it acknowledges its own penultimacy, its temporally bounded horizon, and respects the fact that its citizens' horizons may not be so bounded. In land use law, the state enacts this respect by making space—both physically and within the law—for citizens to gather and witness to that which lies beyond the state's grasp.

Appendix: Major Religion Decisions, 1940–2000

Case by Dominant Rationale	Subject	Holding of the United States Supreme Court
Separation: Government must not engage in religion, provide tax support for it, or cooperate with it.		
McCollum v. Board of Education (1948)	Education	Invalidated released time religious education taught in the Illinois public schools.
Engel v. Vitale (1962)	Education	Invalidated NY Regents' "nondenominational" public school prayer.
Abington v. Schempp (1963)	Education	Invalidated reading of the Bible and praying the Lord's Prayer in public schools.
Epperson v. Arkansas (1968)	Education	Invalidated state law prohibiting teaching of evolution in the public schools.
Lee v. Weisman (1992)	Education	Invalidated clergy prayer at public school graduation ceremony.
Santa Fe Indep. School Dist. v. Doe (2000)	Education	High school may not authorize a pre-football game prayer by elected student volunteer.
Accommodation: Legislative governmental encouragement of religion, if based on history and tradition, is acceptable.		
Zorach v. Clauson (1952)	Education	Upheld "off campus" public school released time religious education.
Walz v. Tax Commission (1970)	Property Taxes	Upheld exemption of churches from payment of local property taxes.
Marsh v. Chambers (1983)	Legislative Prayer	Upheld right of Nebraska legislature to employ chaplain offering Judeo-Christian prayer.
Secular Intent: Governmental interaction with religion is acceptable if resulting from a law that does not classify in religious terms.		
Prince v. Massachusetts (1944)	Child Labor	Refused to exempt child who was selling religious literature from child labor laws.
Everson v. Board of Education (1947)	Education	Upheld state reimbursement to bus children to public and nonpublic schools.
Torcaso v. Watkins (1961)	Test Oaths for Officials	Forbade state requirement that office holders acknowledge existence of a Supreme Being.
McGowan v. Maryland (1961)	Sunday Closing Laws	State's failure to exempt sabbatarian did not violate the Establishment Clause.
Braunfeld v. Brown (1961)	Sunday Closing Laws	State's failure to exempt sabbatarian did not violate the free exercise of religion.
Board of Education v. Allen (1968)	Education	Upheld state provision of "secular" textbooks used in parochial schools.
Trans World Airlines v. Hardison (1977)	Labor Relations	Statutory holding subordinating sabbatarian's religious obligation to union seniority.
Jones v. Wolf (1979)	Church Property	"Neutral principles," not church practices, should resolve church property conflict.
Larkin v. Grendel's Den (1982)	Alcohol Licensing	Invalidated law allowing churches, synagogues & schools to veto nearby liquor sales.
Employment Division v. Smith (1990)	Labor Relations	Rejection of claimed exemption from drug laws of sacramental use of peyote.
Church of Lukumi Babalu Aye v. Hialeah (1993)	Animal Sacrifices	Municipal law regulating religious slaughter of chickens violated sect's free exercise.
Zobrest v. Catalina Foothills School District (1993)	Education	Tax funded sign interpreter for deaf student in Catholic H.S. doesn't violate Estab. Clause.
Board of Education of Kiryas Joel v. Grumet (1994)	Education	Tax funded special school district for handicapped Hasidic students does violate Estab. Clause.
Rosenberger v. University of Virginia (1995)	U. Students/Free Speech	Student activities funding to publish religious group's paper doesn't violate Estab. Clause.

Secular Intent (continued)

Agostini v. Felton (1997)	Education	Overturned Aguilar v. Felton (1985); okayed public school classes taught in church schools.
Boerne v. Flores (1997)	Church Property Use	Invalidated Congress's Religious Freedom Restoration Act that favored impact analysis.
Mitchell v. Helms (2000)	Education	Upheld state provision of computers and other instructional equipment to parochial schools.

Impact Analysis: Courts should, when governmentally feasible, exempt persons from laws that infringe on their religious practices.

Cantwell v. Connecticut (1940)	Proselytizing	Included free exercise in 14th Am. due process liberty; forbade state proselytizing permit.
Murdock v. Pennsylvania (1943)	Soliciting Sales	Exempted Jehovah's Witnesses selling religious literature from solicitor's license requirement.
Follett v. McCormick (1944)	Bookselling	Exempted Jehovah's Witnesses clergy who sold religious books from a bookseller's tax.
United States v. Ballard (1944)	Criminal Fraud	Upheld special exemption for religious sincerity in a United States mail fraud trial.
Niemotko v. Maryland (1951)	Use of a Public Park	Upheld right of Jehovah's Witnesses to use city park without prior approval.
Kedroff v. St. Nicholas Cathedral (1952)	Church Property	Rejected "Cold War" state interference with Russian Orthodox Church polity.
Fowler v. Rhode Island (1953)	Public Parks	Like Niemotko, but specified protection under both establishment and free exercise clauses.
Sherbert v. Verner (1963)	Unemployment Comp.	State must compensate sabbatarian who for religious reasons refused Saturday work.
Welsh v. United States (1970)	Military Draft and COs	On statutory grounds accorded conscientious objector status to nontheist pacifists.
Gillette v. United States (1971)	Military Draft and COs	Refused to exempt selective ("unjust war") COs because of "compelling" U.S. interest.
Wisconsin v. Yoder (1972)	Education	Exempted Amish children from compulsory school attendance after the eighth grade.
Goldman v. Weinberger (1986)	Military Service	Held that Orthodox Jewish Air Force officer had no right to wear his yarmulke indoors.

The Lemon Test: "First, the statute must have a secular purpose; second, its principal or primary effect must be one that neither advances nor inhibits religion; finally, the statute must not foster 'an excessive government entanglement with religion.'"

Lemon, as thus formulated, combines weakened remnants of all four theories in its formulation of the Establishment Clause requirements:

1. **Separation** is required, but only when church-state entanglement is "excessive."
2. **Accommodation** is permitted when the entanglement is less than excessive.
3. **Secular Purpose** is required of legislation; it is a necessary but not a sufficient measure of nonestablishment.
4. **Impact Analysis** is required, but remedies for effects on religions are available only if the problems are caused by the primary or principal effect of the law; threats to religious liberty from secondary effects of the statute are ignored.

Case	Subject	Holding of the United States Supreme Court
Lemon v. Kurtzman (1971)	Education	Invalidated some subsidies to parochial schools as excessive entanglement.
Tilton v. Richardson (1971)	Education	Upheld U.S. grants, loans, for academic purposes at church-related colleges.
Levitt v. Committee (1973)	Education	Invalidated state subsidy to parochial schools to test students as excessive entanglement.
Committee v. Nyquist (1973)	Education	Invalidated tuition reimbursement to parents of nonpublic school children.
Sloan v. Lemon (1973)	Education	Invalidated tuition reimbursement as excessive entanglement.
Hunt v. McNair (1973)	Education	Upheld state revenue bonds to finance buildings at private and church-related colleges.
Meek v. Pittenger (1975)	Education	States may provide textbooks, but no auxiliary services, to parochial schools.
Roemer v. Board (1976)	Education	States may provide nonsectarian grants to private (including church-related) colleges.
Wolman v. Walter (1977)	Education	Upheld some auxiliary services by state to parochial schools; invalidated other services.

McDaniel v. Paty (1978)	Elections	Invalidated law forbidding election of clergy to state constitutional convention.
NLRB v. Catholic Bishop (1979)	Education/Labor	Statutory holding; NLRAct does not clearly apply to church school teachers.
Committee v. Regan (1980)	Education	States may reimburse nonpublic schools for mandated functions.
Stone v. Graham (1980)	Education	Display of Ten Commandments in public school classroom violates establishment.
Widmar v. Vincent (1981)	Education	State U's prohibition of use of its buildings and grounds for rel. worship, teaching invalidated.
Lynch v. Donnelly (1984)	Christmas Display	City of Pawtucket could have a secular—mixed Santa and crèche—Christmas display.
Wallace v. Jaffree (1985)	Education	Invalidated state authorization of minute of silence "for meditation or voluntary prayer."
Grand Rapids School District v. Ball (1985)	Education	Invalidated "shared time" teaching of public teachers in nonpublic church-related schools.
Aguilar v. Felton (1985)	Education	Ended funding of teachers of deprived low income children in church schools in NYC.
Edwards v. Aguillard (1987)	Education	Invalidated state requirements to pair teaching of evolution with "creation science."
Corporation of Presiding Bishop v. Amos (1987)	Church Employees	Exempted church from Civil Rights Act that protects employees from religious test.
Texas Monthly v. Bullock (1989)	Tax Exemption	Sales tax exemption for religious journals violates Estab. Clause; not required for free exercise.
County of Allegheny v. ACLU (1989)	Holiday Displays	Crèche in courthouse is too religious; menorah next to large evergreen is sufficiently secular.
Board of Education v. Mergens (1990)	Education	Facilities available for chess or scuba clubs are equally available for Christian groups.

Notes

1. The Confessional Basis of Lutheran Thinking
on Church-State Issues

Note: All references to *The Book of Concord* (*BC*) in this chapter are to the Tappert (1959) edition.

1. I am using the term "confessional perspective" to encompass more than the text of the confessions. Wilhelm Maurer, in his commentary on the Augsburg Confession (*CA*), makes clear how important it is to look at the ideas developed in Wittenberg in the 1520s to understand the *CA*. See Wilhelm Maurer, *Historical Commentary on the Augsburg Confession*, trans. H. George Anderson (Philadelphia: Fortress Press, 1986).

2. See the explanation of the Third Article of the Apostles' Creed in Luther's Small Catechism (*SC*), *Book of Concord* (*BC*), 345.

3. Apology of the Augsburg Confession (Ap), Articles VII and VIII, *BC* 169.5: "The church is not merely an association of outward ties and rites like other civic governments, however, but it is mainly an association of faith and of the Holy Spirit in men's hearts. To make it recognizable, this association has outward marks, the pure teaching of the Gospel and the administration of the sacraments in harmony with the Gospel of Christ."

4. *CA* VII, *BC* 32.1.

5. "On the Councils and the Church," *Luther's Works* (*LW*) 41:150: "Now, wherever you hear or see this word preached, believed, professed, and lived, do not doubt that the true *ecclesia sancta catholica*, 'a Christian holy people,' must be there, even though their number is very small. For God's word 'shall not return empty,' Isaiah 55[:11]. . . . And even if there were no other sign than this alone, it would still suffice to prove that a Christian, holy people must exist there, for God's word cannot be without God's people, and conversely, God's people cannot be without God's word."

6. "Gospel" can be used in two senses. When "gospel" is used to designate the entire Christian message, the term includes both the proclamation of repentance (law) and the forgiveness of sins. When "gospel" is opposed to law, the term is limited to the proclamation of the forgiveness of sins and reconciliation with God. See the Formula of Concord (FC) Epitome (Ep), article 5, "Law and Gospel." *BC* 477–79.

7. "We believe, teach, and confess that, strictly speaking, the law is a divine doctrine which teaches what is right and God-pleasing and which condemns everything that is sinful and contrary to God's will." FC-Ep V, *BC* 478.3.

8. See the explanation of the Ten Commandments in the *SC*, *BC* 342–44.

9. Explanation of the Second Article of the Apostles' Creed, *SC*, *BC* 345.3, 4.

10. FC-Ep V, *BC* 478.1.

11. *CA* XVI, *BC* 37–38.

12. Explanation of the Fourth Commandment in Luther's Large Catechism (LC), *BC* 385.150.

13. Protest may arise that Art. XXVIII is not a doctrinal article. Maurer notes that "*CA* XXVIII offers the most fundamental statements about the doctrine of the two ways of governing (two kingdoms). They must be compared with Luther's statements; only in that way can their binding theological force be recognized." While he identifies *CA* XXVIII as a "strategy for negotiation" at the Augsburg Diet, Maurer notes that the doctrine of the two ways of governing provides the theological basis for this strategy (Maurer, *Historical Commentary*, 64). After reviewing the key themes defining the doctrine of the two authorities in *CA* XXVIII, Maurer notes the limitations of *CA* XXVIII and states that to understand the divinely willed connection between the two authorities "one must go beyond *CA* XXVIII and evaluate the whole tenor of the *CA*. There the relationship of the two kingdoms forms a basic theme that defines the Confession's total structure" (ibid., 70).

14. *CA* XXVIII, *BC* 82.11.

15. *CA* XXVIII, *BC* 83.18.

16. LC, *BC* 385–86.150: "The same may be said of obedience to the civil government, which, as we have said, is to be classed with the estate of fatherhood, the most comprehensive of all relations. In this case a man is father not of a single family, but of as many people as he has inhabitants, citizens, or subjects. Through civil rulers, as through our own parents, God gives us food, house and home, protection and security. Therefore, since they bear this name and title with all honor as their chief glory, it is our duty to honor and magnify them as the most precious treasure and jewel on earth."

This explanation of the Fourth Commandment goes into detail on the duty of parents and, by extension, other authorities. It should not be interpreted as requiring obedience to such authorities in all things. Earlier, Luther writes: "If God's Word and will are placed first and observed, nothing ought to be considered more important than the will and word of our parents, provided that these, too, are subordinated to obedience toward God and are not set into opposition to the preceding commandments" (LC, *BC* 381.116).

17. Luther complains in his explication of the Fourth Commandment in the LC, *BC* 388.170, 171: "Everybody acts as if God . . . gave us subjects to treat them as we please, as if it were no concern of ours what they learn or how they live. No one is willing to see that this is the command of the divine Majesty, who will solemnly call us to account and punish us for its neglect. . . ."

18. See, for example, "Secular Authority: To What Extent It Should Be Obeyed" (1523), *LW* 45:75–129.

19. For a discussion of the law that the state is to uphold, see page 4.

20. The confessions mention three such orders: government, family, and the church. As Robert Benne points out, later Lutheran ethics recognized four orders or "places of responsibilities": marriage and family life, work, public life (citizenship and voluntary associations) and church. See Robert Benne, "Lutheran Ethics: Perennial Themes and Contemporary Challenges," in *The Promise of Lutheran Ethics*, ed. Karen L. Bloomquist and John R. Stumme (Minneapolis: Fortress Press, 1998), 13–17.

21. *CA* XVI, *BC* 38.5: "The Gospel does not overthrow civil authority, the state, and marriage but requires that all these be kept as true orders of God and that everyone, each according to his own calling, manifest Christian love and genuine good works in his station of life."

22. "It is taught among us that all government in the world and all established rule and laws were instituted and ordained by God for the sake of good order, and that Christians may without sin occupy civil offices or serve as princes and judges, render decisions and pass sentence according to imperial and other existing laws, punish evildoers with the sword, engage in just wars, serve as soldiers, buy and sell, take required oaths, possess property, be married, etc.

. . . Also condemned are those who teach that Christian perfection requires . . . the renunciation of such activities as are mentioned above . . ." (*CA* XVI, *BC* 37–38.1, 2, 4).

23. Ap XVI, *BC* 222.1.

24. Sometimes the terms *realm, sphere,* or *domain* are used rather than *kingdom, rule,* or *reign.* I will not explore the nuances and differences that some writers have found in these terms.

25. This discussion should not be interpreted to contradict earlier Lutheran statements such as the LCA social statement "Church and State: A Lutheran Perspective" (1966), which affirmed "both institutional separation and functional interaction as the proper relationship between church and state."

26. Ap XVI, *BC* 222–23.3,6: "The Gospel does not introduce any new laws about the civil estate, but commands us to obey the existing laws, whether they were formulated by heathen or by others, and in this obedience to practice love. . . . The Gospel does not legislate for the civil estate but is the forgiveness of sins and the beginning of eternal life in the hearts of believers. It not only approves governments but subjects us to them. . . ."

27. *CA* XXVIII, *BC* 83.12, 13.

28. John Calvin, *Institutes of the Christian Religion,* ed. John T. McNeill, trans. Ford Lewis Battles (Philadelphia: Westminster Press, 1960), Bk. IV, chap. 20 (9), 1495.

29. Calvin, *Institutes,* Book IV, chap. 20 (2), 1487.

30. FC-Ep, *BC* 499.12, 13, 14 condemns several errors of the Anabaptists in this regard including: "1. That government is not a God-pleasing estate in the New Testament. 2. That no Christian can serve or function in any civic office with a good and clear conscience. 3. That as occasion arises no Christian, without violating his conscience, may use an office of the government against wicked people, and that subjects may not call upon the government to use the power that it possesses and that it has received from God for their protection and defense."

31. *CA* XVI, *BC* 38.6, 7.

32. See Reinhard Hütter, "The Twofold Center of Lutheran Ethics: Christian Freedom and God's Commandments," in *The Promise of Lutheran Ethics,* ed. Karen L. Bloomquist and John R. Stumme (Minneapolis: Fortress Press, 1998), 48–52.

33. Ap IV, *BC* 108.7.

34. *BC* 419.67.

35. Ap XVI, *BC* 222.1–223.3: "The Gospel does not introduce any new laws about the civil estate, but commands us to obey the existing laws, whether they were formulated by heathen or by others, and in this obedience to practice love."

36. The distinction between civil and spiritual righteousness is discussed in Ap, Articles IV and XVIII.

37. Ap IV, *BC* 110.22.

38. Ap IV and XVIII, *BC* 110 and 225.

39. Ap IV, *BC* 110.24.

40. *CA* XXIII, *BC* 53.14: ". . . in these last times of which the Scriptures prophesy, the world is growing worse and men are becoming weaker and more infirm."

41. "The Babylonian Captivity of the Church," LW 36:100. "Nor would I agree to that

impediment which they call 'disparity of religion,' which forbids one to marry an upbap-
tized person, either simply, or on condition that she be converted to the faith. Who
made this prohibition? God or man? Who gave to men the power to prohibit such a marriage?" FC-Ep XII, *BC* 499.19 condemns the Anabaptist idea that a difference of faith is
sufficient ground for divorce.

42. The literature on this is extensive. See, e.g., Mark U. Edwards Jr., *Luther's Last Battles: Politics and Polemics: 1531–1546* (Ithaca, N.Y.: Cornell University Press, 1983). Chapter 6 is particularly applicable.

43. Luther commented in the preface to *SC, BC* 339.13: "Although we cannot and
should not compel anyone to believe, we should nevertheless insist that the people learn
to know how to distinguish between right and wrong according to the standards of those
among whom they live and make their living. For anyone who desires to reside in a city
is bound to know and observe the laws under whose protection he lives, no matter
whether he is a believer or, at heart, a scoundrel or knave."

2. Toward a Lutheran "Delight in the Law of the Lord": Church and State in the Context of Civil Society

1. ELCA Constitution, chap. 4.03.n. Toward the end of my inquiry I will raise the
question of the adequacy of the precise words "institutional separation" and "functional
interaction." This formulation of "institutional separation and functional interaction"
animates other sections of chap. 4 of the ELCA constitution; 4.02.c says: "To participate
in God's mission, this church shall: Serve in response to God's love to meet human
needs, caring for the sick and the aged, advocating dignity and justice for all people,
working for peace and reconciliation among the nations, and standing with the poor
and powerless and committing itself to their needs." Section 4.02.e says: "To participate
in God's mission, this church shall: Nurture its members in the Word of God so as to
grow in faith and hope and love, to see daily life as the primary setting for the exercise
of their Christian calling, and to use the gifts of the Spirit for their life together and for
their calling in the world." Section 4.03.g says: "this church shall: Lift its voice in concord
and work in concert with forces for good, to serve humanity, cooperating with church
and other groups participating in activities that promote justice, relieve misery, and reconcile the estranged." Section 4.03.l and 03.m say respectively: "this church shall: Study
social issues and trends, work to discover the causes of oppression and injustice, and
develop programs of ministry and advocacy to further human dignity, freedom, justice,
and peace in the world . . . [and] Establish, support, and recognize institutions and
agencies that minister to people in spiritual and temporal needs."

2. When addressing the constellation of questions regarding "church and state," we
should remember that the modern notions of "state" diverge from notions before the
modern era. For one influential rendition of the modern notion of state, see Quentin
Skinner, *The Foundations of Modern Political Thought* (Cambridge, N.Y.: Cambridge University Press, 1978), 2:349–58. George Forell has emphasized maintaining a clear distinction between the notions of "political authority" and "state" in "The State as Order
of Creation," in *God and Caesar: A Christian Approach to Social Ethics*, ed. Warren Quan-
beck (Minneapolis: Augsburg, 1959), 43–45.

3. I use the term *predilection* in the sense of a diligent, reflectively purposeful preference and delight—even love—that derives from one's core identity.

4. The Augsburg Confession and Luther's Small and Large Catechisms are confessional documents of the Evangelical Lutheran Church in America and, along with other

confessional writings, are contained in *The Book of Concord: The Confessions of the Evangelical Lutheran Church,* ed. Robert Kolb and Timothy J. Wengert (Minneapolis: Fortress Press, 2000); hereafter cited as *BC.* All references in this chapter are to this edition of the *BC.*

5. Luther himself noted that the form of Anabaptism under discussion and perfectionist monasticism were "joined at the tail, even though they have different heads." See *Luther's Works,* American ed. 55 vols. (Philadelphia: Fortress Press; St. Louis: Concordia, 1955–86), 27:149 (hereafter *LW*).

6. There are of course many excellent discussions of justification by faith alone. Among the more incisive American Lutheran explications are: Robert W. Bertram, "'Faith Alone Justifies': Luther on *Iustitia Fidei,*" in *Justification by Faith: Lutherans and Catholics in Dialogue VII,* ed. H. George Anderson, T. Austin Murphy, Joseph A. Burgess (Minneapolis: Augsburg, 1985), 172–84; Robert W. Jenson, "On Recognizing the Augsburg Confession," in *The Role of the Augsburg Confession: Catholic and Lutheran Views,* ed. Joseph A. Burgess (Philadelphia: Fortress Press, 1980), 151–66.

7. John Stumme also employs the term "critical participation" to describe an American Lutheran tradition on church and state (see this volume, p. 56); also see Stumme, "A Tradition of Christian Ethics," in *The Promise of Lutheran Ethics,* ed. Karen L. Bloomquist and John R. Stumme (Minneapolis: Fortress Press, 1998), 4. Interpreters of great traditions are particularly vulnerable because they are considering big ideas over grand expanses of time and social space and often asking not only questions of origin but also of patterns, survivals, influences, adaptations, mutations, transformations, and so forth. When this is the case, as it is here, we should heed medieval historian Brian Tierney's careful determination to go forward even when faced with the genuine hazards of a "whig interpretation of history"—Herbert Butterfield's phrase—whereby someone merely reads present-day ideas back into the past. *Religion, Law, and the Growth of Constitutional Thought, 1150–1650* (Cambridge N.Y.: Cambridge University Press, 1982), vii–x. When considering Lutheran heritage, I find helpful Alasdair MacIntyre's notion that a living tradition exists as a "historically extended, socially embodied argument." See his *After Virtue: A Study in Moral Theory,* 2nd ed. (Notre Dame, Ind.: University of Notre Dame Press, 1984), 221–23.

8. My typology has similarities to Stumme's fourfold typology; see his "Lutheran Tradition," 55, 73.

9. Here we can see the confessors constructing their theological claims according to their fundamental hermeneutical distinction of law and gospel. They articulate this hermeneutic most fully in Art. IV of the Ap. See Mary Jane Haemig's "Confessional Basis," 4–6. Also see n. 6 above.

10. For one widely read survey of the notion of God's continuing creational agency from a contemporary Lutheran perspective, see Philip J. Hefner, "The Creation," in *Christian Dogmatics,* 2 vols., ed. Carl E. Braaten and Robert W. Jenson (Philadelphia: Fortress Press, 1984), 1:341–51.

11. Perhaps we can conceptualize the "orders of creation" as enduring relational configurations and systems that are essential, beneficial, historical, and critical for God's creating, preserving, and governing of a thriving temporal life. See Haemig, "Confessional Basis," 7–8. For two other brief sketches see, Robert Benne, "Lutheran Ethics: Perennial Themes and Contemporary Challenges," in Bloomquist and Stumme, *Promise of Lutheran Ethics,* 13–16; and William Lazareth, "Orders," in *A New Dictionary of Christian Ethics,* ed. James Childress and John Macquarrie (Philadelphia: Westminster Press,

1986), 440–41. For a more extensive analysis and construction in the face of Karl Barth's critique of the notion, see Carl E. Braaten, "God in Public Life: Rehabilitating the 'Orders of Creation,'" *First Things* (December 1990): 32–38. While the immediate context of Edward Schroeder's examination is Lutheran Church–Missouri Synod theology, he offers an important analysis and reconstruction of the category in "The Orders of Creation—Some Reflections on the History and Place of the Term in Systematic Theology," *Concordia Theological Monthly* 43 (March 1972): 165–78. Max Stackhouse, from a Reformed theological perspective, creatively connects the Reformation's "orders of creation" with "civil society" in a manner resembling the proposal in part four below, though I have differences with him on other issues; see his "Christian Social Ethics in a Global Era: Reforming Protestant Views," in *Christian Social Ethics in a Global Era*, ed. Max Stackhouse, et al. (Nashville: Abingdon Press, 1995), 26ff.

12. For Luther's understanding of the integrity of various orders see *LW* 46:181–83. Stumme also uses the term "integrity"; see his "Lutheran Tradition," 56ff. See also Karl Hertz's compendium of nineteenth-century Lutheran, frequently German, reflection, which is inclined toward more absolutist interpretations of Lutheran theology, in *Two Kingdoms and One World: A Sourcebook in Christian Social Ethics* (Minneapolis: Augsburg, 1976), 68–91.

13. See Haemig, "Confessional Basis," 4–6, 8. See also W. D. J. Cargill Thompson's helpful discussion of the various terms and relationships that Luther employs in his two-or-both-kingdoms teaching, *Studies in the Reformation* (London: Athlone Press, 1980), esp. 42–59. For Thompson's fuller interpretation of Luther on many of the issues covered in our inquiry, see *The Political Thought of Martin Luther* (Sussex, U.K.: Harvester, 1984).

14. Of course, for the Lutheran confessors, the very reason for properly distinguishing "alien righteousness" and "proper righteousness" is so that they might be evangelically linked together rather than being confused or severed one from the other or one or the other being collapsed into the other. The confessors usually perceived the ultimate source of such false relationships to be Satan. The confessors discuss this crucial aspect of their confession in *CA* VI under the rubric of "faith and works" and in Ap IV.22–24, a discussion lying beyond the scope of this inquiry. See Haemig's "Confessional Basis," 15–16.

15. While the formulation "institutional separation" remains grounded in the kind of constitutional integrity for which *CA* XVI argues, this does not mean that "institutional separation" might not have other problems. The notion of "separation," filtered through Thomas Jefferson's famous metaphor of a "wall of separation," has a long and problematic history in the constitutional jurisprudence of the United States. Better than "institutional separation" in the ELCA constitution would be the phrase "constitutional integrity." See Lutheran theologian Ronald Thiemann's helpful discussion of the problematic issues surrounding "separation" and the metaphor "wall of separation" in *Religion in Public Life: A Dilemma for Democracy* (Washington, D.C.: Georgetown University Press, 1996), 42–66.

16. See *BC* 126.40–127.47 regarding the gospel as unconditional promise. For a poignant discussion of the gospel as the unconditional promise that creates faith, see Eric W. Gritsch and Robert W. Jenson, *Lutheranism: The Theological Movement and Its Confessional Writings* (Philadelphia: Fortress Press, 1976), 7–10, 36–44. On December 6, 1536, Luther and other Wittenberg theologians issued a *Gutachten*—an official, expert opinion—in which they argued that the gospel "confirms" and "values highly" temporal

authority (cited by Thompson, *Studies in the Reformation,* 31). I concur with Wilhelm Maurer that while Melanchthon builds Luther's two-kingdoms teaching also into *CA* Art. XXVIII, there unfortunately the teaching suffers from a theological "lack of depth." See Maurer's *Historical Commentary on the Augsburg Confession,* trans. H. George Anderson (Philadelphia: Fortress Press, 1986), 85.

17. See Haemig's discussion of both the scripture's and the Lutheran confessors' use of "gospel" in both a "broad" and "strict" sense ("Confessional Basis," 172 n. 6) and the significance that this twofold use of the term "gospel" has for the proclamation of law and gospel.

18. Charles Taylor, *Sources of the Self: The Making of the Modern Identity* (Cambridge, Mass.: Harvard University Press, 1989), 211–18. That the confessors in *CA* XVI do not specifically thematize the notion of vocational callings in relation to the corporate Christian life of congregations does not, of course, forbid such reflection. I will explore this corporate dimension in the fourth part below.

19. See Marc Kolden, "Creation and Redemption; Ministry and Vocation," *Currents in Theology and Mission* 14 (February 1987): 31–37; Gustav Wingren, *Luther on Vocation* (Philadelphia: Muhlenberg Press, 1957). For the two different ways that Luther defines "good works," see Paul Althaus, *The Ethics of Martin Luther,* trans. Robert C. Schultz (Philadelphia: Fortress Press, 1972), 7ff. That I emphasize in this context the publicness of vocational love does not in any way detract from the public nature of the gospel. For a poignant portrayal of the latter, see Patrick Keifert's *Welcoming the Stranger: A Public Theology of Worship and Evangelism* (Minneapolis: Fortress Press, 1992).

20. In the catechisms Luther does not employ his often-used phrase, "masks of God" *(larvae dei),* but the notion here is the same. For instances of Luther's notion of "masks of God," see *LW* 14:112–15ff. and *LW* 26:94–96. See Gustav Wingren, *Luther on Vocation* (Philadelphia: Muhlenberg Press, 1957), 117, 123–43; also Philip Watson, *Let God Be God! An Interpretation of the Theology of Martin Luther* (Philadelphia: Muhlenberg Press, 1948), 76–80. Many if not most people in our own era acquire and exercise primarily a psychological imagination of parenthood. That is, we tend to understand parenthood as a life-cycle stage of our lives. By contrast Luther, through his immersion in the Bible, acquires and exercises a *theological* imagination regarding parenthood. That is, he retains a heightened mindfulness for what the triune God is up to through parenthood. For Luther's notion of divine immanence, see George Forell, *Martin Luther, Theologian of the Church: Collected Essays,* ed. William Russell (St. Paul, Minn.: *Word & World* Supplement Series 2, 1992), 72–74, 193–95, 260–62. In classic post–Reformation theology these issues were taken up quite thoughtfully under the topic of God's concurrence with human action: see Heinrich Schmid, *The Doctrinal Theology of the Evangelical Lutheran Church,* 3rd ed. (Minneapolis: Augsburg, 1961 [1875, 1899]), 170–94. For a contemporary discussion of divine concurrence with particular reference to theology and natural science, but not to the social world, see Wolfhart Pannenberg, *Systematic Theology,* 3 vols. (Grand Rapids, Mich.: Eerdmans, 1991, 1994, 1998), 2:46–52.

21. Luther notes in the *LC:* "Although their [parents and other authorities] responsibility is not explicitly presented in the Ten Commandments, it is certainly treated in detail in many other passages of Scripture. God even intends it to be included precisely in this commandment in which he speaks of father and mother" (*BC* 409.167). I return below to this duty of political authority under the rubric of the criterion of justice. In his *Commentary on Psalm 82* from 1530, which Luther composed as an essay on the office of

the virtuous prince, he quite specifically invokes the Fourth Commandment's "honor demand." See *LW* 13:44–45. He highlights two aspects: it signifies the immanence of the triune God's agency mediated through political authority, and equally, the high degree of accountability to which God holds political authorities. More than once does Luther, when admonishing princes, prominently recall King Jehoshaphat's charge to his official representatives in 2 Chron. 19:6–7: "Consider what you are doing, for you judge not on behalf of human beings but on the Lord's behalf; he is with you in giving judgment. Now, let the fear of the Lord be upon you; take care what you do, for there is no perversion of justice with the Lord our God, or partiality, or taking of bribes." See *LW* 13:44 and *LW* 45:121. I inquire more fully below into this crucial issue of accountability.

22. Thompson, *Political Thought*, 1–13. For examples of a reductionistic interpretation of Luther's notion of law as serving "only negative functions: it convicts us of our sins, and it helps keep order among sinful people who without some law would just murder each other," see William Placher's widely read, *A History of Christian Theology: An Introduction* (Philadelphia: Westminster Press, 1983), 221; also see Stewart Herman, "Luther, Law and Social Covenants," *Journal of Religious Ethics* 25.2 (Fall 1997), 257–75.

23. "The sword" was that synecdochal figure of speech used most often in Luther's day and before to refer to political authority in reference to coercive power. At times Luther recommends "the breadloaf" as a more appropriate comprehensive synecdoche for political authority; see, e.g., the *LC*, Fourth Petition of the Lord's Prayer (*BC* 449–52). By using "the breadloaf," Luther acknowledges other fundamental, socially generative powers of political authority besides the more restraining power of "the sword," without, of course, ever excluding coercion from the parameters of political authority. Carter Lindberg especially has highlighted the socially constructive aspect of Luther's view of political authority against the reductionistic interpretations of Luther by Ernst Troeltsch, Reinhold Niebuhr, and others, which have dominated and skewed the hermeneutical imaginations of many interpreters of Luther particularly in North America. See Carter Lindberg, *Beyond Charity: Reformation Initiatives for the Poor* (Minneapolis: Fortress Press, 1993), 95–127, 161–69. It seems to me that Luther addresses these more socially generative aspects of the political use of the law when the context is more "civicly" situated. Perhaps we might call this side of our heritage "civic Lutheranism," whose complexion would also diverge from that of "civic Calvinism." See Heinz Schilling, *Civic Calvinism* (Kirksville, Mo.: Sixteenth-Century Journal, 1991).

24. Thompson, *Political Thought*, 5.

25. See Gerhard Ebeling, *Word and Faith* (Philadelphia: Fortress Press, 1963), 73–74.

26. Of course Luther invariably knows that because the old Adam always clings to this life, he is describing Christians qua Christian, that is, "to the extent that he is a Christian" (*LW* 26:134). See also, for example, Luther's reflections on baptism and holy communion in the LC, *BC* 465, 469.

27. See Gustav Wingren's admonition against those who would reduce Luther's notion of the civil use of the law to "too narrow an association with politics," which Luther himself sometimes did: *Creation and Law* (Philadelphia: Muhlenberg Press, 1961), 153. In *Temporal Authority* Luther also takes up the second theological or spiritual use of the law, which is pivotal for Luther though not our primary concern in this inquiry.

28. See Luther's exposition of the Second Table of the Decalogue in his catechisms as an imaginative way to construe the lively dialectic of boundaries and bridges that the triune God provides for the ongoing flourishing of temporal life.

29. Indeed, this distinction is ubiquitous in Luther's theological and ethical reflection. For instance, in *Temporal Authority* see *LW* 45:95, 96, 101, 103, et al.

30. "For the hand that wields this sword and kills with it is not man's hand, but God's; and it is not man but God who hangs, tortures, beheads, kills, and fights. All these are God's work and judgment" (trans. from the *Weimar Edition of Luther's Works* [WA 41:639] in Althaus, *Ethics of Martin Luther*, 113 n. 12).

31. See Stumme, "Lutheran Tradition," 64–68.

32. At certain historical junctures Luther appears to situate the competencies of political authority, including the sword, not only with reference to the Second Table of the Decalogue but also with reference to the Second and Third Commandments. Because the Second Commandment pertains to behaviors of the tongue, Luther at times thinks that political authority has God-given competencies and thus responsibilities in this arena. He worked out the rationale for this position in 1524 and again in the later 1530s under the very different circumstances of the question of armed military resistance to the emperor. See Thompson, *Political Thought*, 155–62 and *Studies in the Reformation*, 31–32. This rationale also accompanies his 1543 advice that the political authorities have the duty to discipline and even forcefully expel the Jewish population from Christian territories since these Jews verbally and willfully deny the divinity of Christ. See *LW* 47:262–65; see Martin Bertram's helpful introduction to this treatise, 123–36; also see Heiko Oberman's comprehensive *The Roots of Anti-Semitism: In the Age of Renaissance and Reformation*, trans. James Porter (Philadelphia: Fortress Press, 1984). The error and evil of Luther's appraisal in these matters remains beyond dispute! See, for instance, *Luther, Lutheranism, and the Jews*, ed. J. Halperin and A. Sovik (Geneva: Department of Studies, The Lutheran World Federation, 1984) esp. 5–32; and "Declaration of the Evangelical Lutheran Church in America to the Jewish Community," ELCA, Department for Ecumenical Affairs, website: www.elca.org/ea/interfaith/jewish/declaration.html.

33. See his *Treatise on Good Works* (1520), *LW* 44:100.

34. See Althaus, *Ethics of Martin Luther*, 128.

35. Luther violates his thinking here regarding heresy and the limits of political authority when in 1543 he advised the political authorities to use coercion against the Jews because they denied the divinity of Christ and other doctrines. See n. 32 above.

36. Luther features some of his most provocative, critical thinking on these issues in *How Christians Should Regard Moses* (*LW* 35:161–74). His notion of situated, prudential justice, equity, and human reason can be seen in *Whether Soldiers, Too, Can Be Saved* (*LW* 46: 100–103). See in this volume Marie Failinger's apt description of a Lutheran notion of "restrained reason," 121. A well-known discussion of Luther and reason appears in Brian Gerrish, *Grace and Reason: A Study in the Theology of Luther* (Chicago: University of Chicago Press [1962] 1979). For more extensive interpretations of Luther's notion of justice see Althaus, *Ethics of Martin Luther*, 132–37; also see Reinhart Hütter's discussion of natural law in Bloomquist and Stumme, *Promise of Lutheran Ethics*, 48–52.

37. "Very wide admonitory power" is Cargill Thompson's phrase in *Political Thought*, 7. Also see Althaus, *Ethics of Martin Luther*, 120, 147–54. In *A Sermon on Keeping Children in School* (1530), Luther again extols the role that the office of preaching plays vis-à-vis

political authority, *LW* 46:226–27. He investigates at length the obligation that the admonitory obligation of the office of preaching be exercised in a fully public and open forum. See *Dr. Martin Luther's Warning to His Dear German People* (1531), *LW* 47:21–29.

38. See Wingren, *Luther on Vocation*, 156–61; and Althaus, *Ethics of Martin Luther*, 155–60.

39. Shortly after the failure of the 1530 Diet of Augsburg to bring peace within the empire, Luther readies the German people for just such a "raising up" by God. Increasingly he invokes the figure of Judas Maccabeus as he does in his 1531 *Dr. Martin Luther's Warning to His Dear German People. LW* 47:17.

40. While the significance of common people's "regard" for the basic form of political authority did lie beyond Luther's political imagination, his ecclesial imagination about the importance of common people's judgment for the form of authority in the church was quite fertile. In this he was an heir to traditions of conciliar ecclesiology. See, for example, *That a Christian Assembly or Congregation Has the Right and Power to Judge All Teaching and to Call, Appoint, and Dismiss Teachers, Establish and Proven by Scripture* (1523), *LW* 39:305–14; also see the seventh mark of the church in *Concerning the Ministry* (1523), *LW* 40:31–44. For the medieval conciliarist traditions, see Skinner, *Modern Political Thought*, 113–22 and Brian Tierney, *Foundations of the Conciliar Theory* (New York: Brill, 1998 [1955]). After the *Augsburg Confession* of 1530, Luther incorporates the notion of common Christian discernment or "testing" into his developing understanding of public confessing. See Robert Bertram, "*Confessio:* Self-Defense Becomes Subversive," *Dialog* 26.3 (1987): 201–8. For Luther, therefore, "confessing" becomes a newly retrieved mode of ecclesial existence. Many interpreters of Luther overlook, under appreciate, or ignore altogether this innovative retrieval of confessing ecclesial existence.

41. For an account of the Reformers' medieval forerunners regarding the question of resistance, see Cynthia Shoenberger, *The Confession of Magdeburg and the Lutheran Doctrine of Resistance* (Ann Arbor, Mich.: University Microfilms, 1975), 6–27.

42. See Thompson, *Studies in the Reformation*, 4.

43. Ibid., 26.

44. Ibid., 31; this is Thompson's translation.

45. Ibid., 211–12, n. 124; I also concur with Thompson's opinion that "it must be considered doubtful whether he [Luther] ever fully accepted it in his own mind." *Vim vi repellere licet* literally means "it is lawful (or permitted) to repel (or resist) force with force." This natural law of armed self-defense was usually restricted to a private sphere of self-defense.

46. Ernst Troeltsch, *The Social Teaching of the Christian Churches* (Louisville: Westminster John Knox, 1992 [1931, 1912], 2:529, 530, 537, 543; Troeltsch, for instance, cites J. N. Figgis, who claims, "we must bear in mind that Luther never allowed the right of overt resistance." See Figgis, *Political Thought from Gerson to Grotius*, 2nd ed. (New York: Harper and Bros., 1960 [1900]), 74. Troeltsch was, of course, right that many Lutherans, particularly in Germany during the nineteenth and early twentieth centuries—tragically from our point of view—interpreted Luther in just these ways.

47. Reinhold Niebuhr, *The Children of Light and the Children of Darkness: A Vindication of Democracy and a Critique of Its Traditional Defense* (New York: Scribners, 1946), 43–44.

48. William Shirer, *The Rise and Fall of the Third Reich* (New York: Simon and Schuster, 1960), 236.

49. See Stumme, "Lutheran Tradition," 51–56. Quentin Skinner boldly scolds noted political theorists for their reductionistic interpretations of Luther on the question of resistance: "Despite the availability of these judgments [that Luther's political thinking developed], however, most textbooks on the Reformation continue to insist" on the interpretive trajectory represented by Figgis, Troeltsch, and Niebuhr (Skinner, *Modern Political Thought*, 74). In addition to Figgis, Skinner has in mind the influential works by John W. Allen, *A History of Political Thought in the Sixteenth Century* (London: Methuen, 1957) and especially Michael Walzer, *The Revolution of the Saints* (Cambridge, Mass.: Harvard University Press, 1965).

50. Quotation taken from Skinner, *Modern Political Thought*, 208.

51. A host of research now exists that traces this historical development and that brings out the significance of the insights offered by the Magdeburg confessors. The best and most accessible digest of research is Skinner's. Also see Robert Kingdon, "The First Expression of Theodore Beza's Political Ideas," *Archiv für Reformationsgeschichte* 46 (1955): 88–100; Oliver Olson, "Theology of Revolution: Magdeburg, 1550–1551," *Sixteenth Century Journal* 3 (1972): 56–79; Esther Hildebrandt, "The Magdeburg Bekenntnis as a Possible Link between German and English Resistance Theories in the Sixteenth Century," *Archiv für Reformationsgeschichte* 71 (1980): 240–52; and Luther Peterson, "Melanchthon on Resisting the Emperor: The *Von der Notwehr Unterrichte [Instruction Concerning Self-Defense]* of 1547" in *Regnum, Religio et Ratio,* ed. Jerome Friedman (Kirksville, Mo.: Sixteenth Century Journal, 1987), 133–44.

52. This is Shoenberger's translation, *Confession of Magdeburg,* 143.

53. See Skinner, *Modern Political Thought,* 206–24.

54. Luther addresses the question of the relation between ruler and ruled as a matter of the attitude and virtue—and, indeed, of the Christian identity—of the prince. That is, he does not imagine this relationship to be a matter of the very form, structure, and procedure of political authority itself, as eventually would become the case in the West. Luther does, however, realize that while "it is not impossible for a prince to be a Christian . . . it is a rare thing and beset with difficulties" (*LW* 45:121).

> Christ himself describes the nature of worldly princes in Luke 22[:25], where he says, "the princes of this world exercise lordship, and those that are in authority proceed with force. For if they are lords by birth or by election they think it only right that they should be served and should rule by force. He who would be a Christian prince must certainly lay aside any intent to exercise lordship or to proceed with force. For cursed and condemned is every sort of life lived and sought for the benefit and good of self; cursed are all works not done in love. They are done in love, however, when they are directed wholeheartedly toward the benefit, honor, and salvation of others, and not toward the pleasure, benefit, honor, comfort, and salvation of self." (*LW* 45:118)
>
> And, "First, he [the Christian prince] must give consideration and attention to his subjects, and really devote himself to it. This he does when he directs his every thought to making himself useful and beneficial to them; when instead of thinking, 'The land and people belong to me, I will do what best pleases me,' he thinks rather, 'I belong to the land and the people, I shall do what is useful and good for them. My concern will be not how to lord it over them and dominate them, but how to protect and maintain them in peace and plenty.' He should picture Christ to himself, and say, 'Behold, Christ, the supreme

ruler, came to serve me; he did not seek to gain power, estate, and honor from me, but considered only my need and directed all things to the end that I should gain power, estate, and honor from him and through him. I will do likewise, seeking from my subjects not my own advantage but theirs. I will use my office to serve and protect them, listen to their problems and defend them, and govern them to the sole end that they, not I, may benefit and profit from my rule.'" In such manner should a prince in his heart empty himself of his power and authority, and take unto himself the needs of his subjects, dealing with them as though they were his own needs. For this is what Christ did to us [Phil. 2:7]; and these are the proper works of Christian love. (*LW* 45:120)

Subsequent Western political reflection rightly did not remain satisfied with the rare and thereby undependable appearance of princes with such cruciform lives and practices that Luther described. Rather, it set about to develop a more dependable and sustainable form of political government with more rigorous procedures for the discernment of and accountability to the norms of divine law.

55. Skinner, *Modern Political Thought,* 326–59.

56. See n. 11 above for analyses of the notion of "order of creation."

57. Jürgen Habermas, *The Structural Transformation of the Public Sphere* (Cambridge, Mass.: MIT Press, 1989 [1962]), 5–12. For a fuller account of the historical emergence of civil society, see my *Critical Social Theory: Civil Society, Prophetic Reasoning, and Christian Imagination* (Minneapolis: Fortress Press, 2001). In the early nineteenth century Hegel used the term "civil society" to refer to the private economic sector. Hegel's "civil society" is terminologically different from our non-economic use of "civil society" in this inquiry and in the present-day explorations of "civil society."

58. Habermas, *Public Sphere,* 20. Also see Alvin Gouldner, *The Dialectic of Ideology and Technology* (New York: Oxford University Press, 1976), 91–117.

59. Habermas, *Public Sphere,* 23; also see Habermas, *Between Facts and Norms: Contributions to a Discourse Theory of Law and Democracy* (Cambridge, Mass.: MIT Press, 1996 [1992]), 329–87.

60. Several articles in *Habermas and the Public Sphere,* ed. Craig Calhoun (Cambridge, Mass.: MIT Press, 1992), are instructive regarding various types, historical development, and overlapping interaction of other public spheres in the West. See Nancy Fraser, "Rethinking the Public Sphere: A Contribution to the Critique of Actually Existing Democracy"; Michael Schudson, "Was There Ever a Public Sphere? If So, When? Reflections on the American Case"; Mary Ryan, "Gender and Public Access: Women's Politics in Nineteenth-Century America"; Harry Boyte, "The Pragmatic Ends of Popular Politics"; and given our concern for the Christian church and its significance, see esp. David Zaret, "Religion, Science, and Printing in the Public Spheres in Seventeenth-Century England."

61. In 1992 Habermas noted, "One searches the literature in vain for clear definitions of civil society that would go beyond such [analytically unrefined] descriptive characterizations" (*Between Facts and Norms,* 367). Not until 1992 does Habermas himself enter into an extended analysis of civil society and its crucial tasks for the health and ongoing development of constitutional states of deliberative democracy (*Between Facts and Norms,* 329–87).

62. See my "Civil Society and Congregations as Public Moral Companions," *Word & World* 15 (Fall 1995): 420–27.

63. See the opening pages of my "Civil Society and Congregations" and chapter 5 of my *Critical Social Theory* for a look at factors contributing to an impoverishment of civil society.

64. The burgeoning literature regarding civil society is due precisely to the heroic part

played by civil society in the 1989 fall of the iron curtain and the emergence of democracies in Eastern Europe. Besides Habermas, see John Keene, ed., *Civil Society and the State: New European Perspectives* (London: Verso, 1988); Michael Walzer, "The Idea of Civil Society: A Path to Social Reconstruction," *Dissent* 38 (Spring 1991): 293–304; Jean Cohen and Andrew Arato, *Civil Society and Political Theory* (Cambridge, Mass.: MIT Press, 1992); Adam Seligman, *The Idea of Civil Society* (New York: Free Press, 1992); Robert Wuthnow, *Christianity and Civil Society: The Contemporary Debate* (Valley Forge, Pa.: Trinity Press International, 1996); Elisabeth Ozdalga and Sune Persson, *Civil Society, Democracy and the Muslim World* (Istanbul: Swedish Research Institute, 1997); Alan Mittleman et al., ed., *Jewish Polity and American Civil Society: Communal Agencies and Religious Movements in the American Public Sphere* (Landham, Md.: Rowan and Littlefield, 2002).

65. See Stumme, "Lutheran Tradition," 51, 69, though Stumme also recognizes in a preliminary way the significance of civil society, 57, 71. The major drawback of an otherwise excellent book by Robert Bellah and his colleagues is the abiding shadow of the one-on-one intersection of church and state. See Robert Bellah, et al., *The Good Society* (New York: Knopf, 1991), esp. 179–92.

66. This poster is also the photo on the front of the brochure of the Division for Church in Society of the ELCA entitled "Christian Faith and U.S. Political Life Today" (1995).

67. A clear focus on "civil society," with its overlapping spaces with the constitutional state, would also free us to think about "church" in ways that do not unduly restrict, or tend to restrict, our ecclesial imaginations to denominational or church-wide notions, as presently is the case. Without this ecclesial restriction the sociological reality and theological integrity of "congregations" could begin again to achieve a vibrancy in regard to political realities together with confessional notions and denominational configurations. A tendency toward a denomination or ecumenical bureaucracy restriction is one of the four weaknesses that I find in Robert Benne's, in many ways, stimulating *The Paradoxical Vision: A Public Theology for the Twenty-first Century* (Minneapolis: Fortress Press, 1995). A second weakness of Benne's proposal concerns the absence of "civil society" as a meaningful, institutional, and structural component of his political imagination. The closest he comes is to locate institutional religion within the "cultural sphere" (4–7), which is not the same as "civil society." A third weakness is the need for an analysis of public reason more extensive than his brief look at "intelligibility" (212–15). A fourth weakness lies in his—sometimes—overly shrill, not quite right-wing, ideological discourse that too easily divides political positions binarily.

68. I suggest that the notion of public reason and a communicative civil society represent significant and necessary, though not sufficient, components of a general, yet contextually attentive, "natural law" approach to "delight in the law of the Lord." There is, I propose, a more specifically Christian "delight in the law of the Lord," a "*dilectio legis* of Christian freedom," one might say. This is the theme of a forthcoming essay, "Critique, Christology, and the *Dilectio Legis* of Christian Freedom." For a preview of some of the issues involved, see my "Daunting, Indeed! A Critical Conversation with *The Promise of Lutheran Ethics*," *Word & World* 29 (Spring 1999): 187–200.

69. Habermas, *Public Sphere*, 24–27.

70. See Thiemann, *Religion in Public Life*, 80–173, for a vigorous and suggestive proposal for the combination of religion (construed very generally), public reason, and democratic politics. See also Michael Perry's very readable and suggestive *Religion in Politics: Constitutional and Moral Perspectives* (New York: Oxford University Press, 1997), esp. 43–104.

71. Seyla Benhabib, "Models of Public Space," in Calhoun, *Public Sphere,* 73–98. I give a fuller account of different models of civil society in "Civil Society and Congregations as Public Moral Companions," 424–25.

72. Benhabib, "Models of Public Space," 87.

73. See my "Human Nature and Communicative Ethics," *Dialog* 33 (Fall 1994): 280–87, for an introductory essay on communicative ethics and communicative reason, and for a more complete bibliography of this emerging trajectory of moral reflection. Also see my *Critical Social Theory,* chap. 4.

74. See Nancy Fraser, "Talking about Needs: Interpretive Contests as Political Conflicts in Welfare-State Societies," *Ethics* 99 (January 1989):291–313.

75. In twentieth-century North American Christian ethics, Reinhold Niebuhr, like Luther before him and communicative ethics after him, exercised a sharply double focus on both human moral resources and self-interested limitations. See especially Niebuhr's *Moral Man and Immoral Society* (New York: Scribners, 1932), xxiv. Niebuhr's subtitle, *A Study in Ethics and Politics,* manifests the weakness of his account, which overlooks the public space of civil society as well as the communicative access to that space.

76. This is the core imagination of the widely read sectarian "church as colony" proposal offered by Stanley Hauerwas and William H. Willimon in *Resident Aliens: Life in the Christian Colony* (Nashville: Abingdon, 1989). Walter Pilgrim has recently published a comprehensive exegetical investigation of "church and state in the New Testament" entitled *Uneasy Neighbors* (Minneapolis: Fortress Press, 1999). He utilizes a contextually contoured paradigm for church-state relations that "coheres" with his New Testament survey of an "ethic of subordination," an "ethic of critical distancing," and an "ethic of resistance." Depending on what a government is up to, the church should position itself with a "critical-constructive stance" or a "critical-transformative stance" or a "critical-resistive stance" (181–210). Besides the total lack of attention to the emergence of civil society and its contextual significance for the dynamics of "state" and "church," my uneasiness with his proposal lies largely in his metaphor "uneasy neighbors." The qualifier, "uneasy," tends to connote neighborliness as something that the neighbors would rather not be involved with but will, "uneasily," if they must (see 211–12).

77. See Martin E. Marty, "Public and Private: Congregation as Meeting Place" in *American Congregations,* vol. 2: *New Perspectives in the Study of Congregations,* ed. James P. Wind and James W. Lewis (Chicago: University of Chicago Press, 1994), 133–66.

78. Others who have recently been using the metaphor of companion in reference to the church's publicness are Roman Catholic feminist theologian Elizabeth A. Johnson in *Friends of God and Prophets: A Feminist Theological Reading of the Communion of Saints* (New York: Continuum, 1999), esp. 114–22, 163–218; and the Division for Global Mission (ELCA), "Companion Synod Program" (www.elca.org/dgm/csp/index.html) and "Global Mission in the Twenty-first Century: A Vision of Evangelical Faithfulness in God's Mission" with its extensive theology of accompaniment and companionship (www.elca.org/dgm/policy/index.html). The latter document notes "The model of *accompaniment* and its resulting terminology can remind us to avoid language that implies mission as conquest, pioneering take-over of frontier territory, making people objects of mission, engaging in a 'numbers game' evangelism strategy, and taking inappropriate initiatives as outsiders. *Accompaniment* language continually pulls us back to the image of walking alongside one another." See "Global Mission," 39.

79. See Carl Braaten, "Protestants and Natural Law," *First Things* (January 1992): 20–26.

80. See my "No Trinity, No Mission: The Apostolic Difference of Revisioning the Trinity," *Word & World* 18 (Summer 1998): 264–71.

81. Kolden, "Ministry and Vocation," 36.

82. This is, of course, a complex issue that is worth much greater examination than we can do here. See n. 40 above. Also see the ELCA's (1991) foundational social statement, "The Church in Society: A Lutheran Perspective," with its important notion of the church as "a community of moral deliberation."

3. A Lutheran Tradition on Church and State

1. Constitution of the Evangelical Lutheran Church in America (ELCA), 4.03.n.

2. "Church and State: A Lutheran Perspective"—hereafter "Church and State" (Philadelphia: Board of Social Ministry, Lutheran Church in America, 1963). Although this was a Lutheran Church in America (LCA) study, two members of the American Lutheran Church (ALC) served on the commission that produced it, and the first ALC statement on church and state (see n. 3) recommended it as "a particularly valuable, carefully prepared, currently relevant booklet" (8). The landmark importance of this study can be noted in heavy reliance on it in the theoretical section of the 1979 statement from the Lutheran Council in the USA (LCUSA—see n. 3). Although it is not an official statement, I refer to it often because it elaborates on what the briefer social statements say.

3. "Institutional separation and functional interaction" first appeared in the LCA statement, "Church and State: A Lutheran Perspective," 1966 (hereafter CSLP). The ALC statement "Church-State Relations in the USA," 1966 (CSR), did not use the phrase but conveyed much of the meaning by speaking of the "separation" and the "interrelation" of church and state. LCUSA's 1979 statement "The Nature of the Church and Its Relationship with Government" (NCRG) gives the most extensive description of the phrase. For the most part, I treat the statements as a unity. While there are differences in nuance among them, they contain a very similar attitude toward church and state relations. When in the text I speak of Lutherans, I am referring to the Lutheran churches whose statements these are. These statements continue to provide guidance to the ELCA.

4. See E. Clifford Nelson, *Lutheranism in North America 1914–1970* (Minneapolis: Augsburg, 1972); Lloyd Svendsbye, "The History of a Developing Social Responsibility Among Lutherans in America from 1930 to 1960, with Reference to the American Lutheran Church, the Augustana Lutheran Church, the Evangelical Lutheran Church, and the United Lutheran Church" (Th.D. diss., Union Theological Seminary, New York, 1966); and Christa Klein with Christian D. Von Dehsen, *Politics and Policy: The Genesis and Theology of Social Statements in the Lutheran Church in America* (Philadelphia: Fortress Press, 1989).

5. Svendsbye, "Social Responsibility Among Lutherans,"19. Cf. Anson Phelps Stokes, *Church and State in the United States* (New York: Harper & Brothers, 1950), 499ff.

6. Frederick W. Stellhorn, "Church and State," *The Lutheran Cyclopedia,* ed. Henry Eyster Jacobs and John A. W. Haas (New York: Scribners, 1905), 107–9.

7. Stellhorn adds, "Its strict and perfect execution would, of course, do away with offi-

cial prayer in Congress and Legislatures, with the reading of the Bible, or any religious book, in the public schools, and the like, and also render impossible any interference on the part of the State with the education of children demanded by the conscience of parents, as long as those children learn what the State has a right to demand its citizens should know."

8. *Reynolds v. United States,* 98 U.S. 145, in Robert S. Alley, *The Supreme Court on Church and State* (New York: Oxford University Press, 1988), 353.

9. E. Theodore Bachmann, "The Church and the Rise of Modern Society, 1830–1914," in *Christian Social Responsibility,* vol. 2 of *The Lutheran Heritage,* ed. Harold C. Letts (Philadelphia: Muhlenberg Press, 1957), 133.

10. Martin E. Marty, *The Irony of It All, 1893–1919,* vol. 1 of *Modern American Religion* (Chicago: University of Chicago Press, 1986), 169.

11. "A Free Church in a Free Nation," *Augustana Quarterly* (January 1946): esp. 69–71.

12. *Lutheran Quarterly* 5.3 (August 1953): esp. 282–85.

13. The authors insist that the separation of church and state in the United States does not have the "absolute" connotation that is sometimes attributed to it; instead, "it has usually meant just the separation of the external ecclesiastical organization from the government." This notion is found later in "institutional separation."

14. Ibid., 287–90.

15. LCA, "Church and State," viii.

16. CSLP, 3.

17. CSR, 1.

18. See Karl Hertz, ed., *Two Kingdoms and One World: A Sourcebook in Christian Social Ethics* (Minneapolis: Augsburg, 1976); and James M. Childs Jr., "Ethics and the Promise of God," in *The Promise of Lutheran Ethics,* ed. Karen L. Bloomquist and John R. Stumme (Minneapolis: Fortress Press, 1998), 98–104.

19. Franklin Sherman, "Church Social Pronouncements—Open Questions" in *To Speak or Not to Speak?* ed. Eckehart Lorenz (Geneva: Lutheran World Federation, 1984), 92.

20. LCA, "Church and State," viii.

21. CSLP, 1.

22. LCA, "Church and State," viii; cf. CSR, 2.

23. LCA, "Church and State," viii.

24. CSR, 2.

25. CSLP, 2.

26. LCA, "Church and State," viii.

27. See, for example, Ronald F. Thiemann's criticism of "separation" in *Religion in Public Life: A Dilemma for Democracy* (Washington, D.C.: Georgetown University Press, 1996), esp. 55ff. and 166ff.

28. LCA, "Church and State," viii.

29. NCRG, 2 (emphasis added).

30. CSLP, 2 (emphasis added).

31. CSR, 3.

32. CSLP, 1.

33. Ibid.

34. CSR, 3.

35. CSLP, 1.

36. NCRG, 1. Lutherans do not equate God's rule through the law with government. Government is one agency through which God governs and blesses creation in "the old age of Adam." See the social statement "The Church in Society: A Lutheran Perspective" (Chicago: Evangelical Lutheran Church in America, 1991), 3.

37. LCA, "Church and State," 35–36.

38. Ibid., 33–34. CSLR speaks of "the sacredness of secular life," 3.

39. CSLP, 2; cf. CSR, 3.

40. See NCRG, "Statement of Affirmation," 1–4. Cf. LCA, "Church and State," 36–47.

41. Cf. with the statement's earlier affirmation: "The government is to make no decisions regarding the validity or orthodoxy of any doctrine, recognizing that it is the province of religious groups to state their doctrines, determine their policies, train their leaders, conduct worship, and carry on their mission and ministries without undue interference from or entanglement with government." The longest part of the statement, "Public Policy Recommendations," raises a number of specific issues involving government intervention of religious bodies, 5–11.

42. Seen in light of this 1979 statement, an earlier characterization of relations of church and state in the United States as "a flexible, friendly cooperation" appears too benign. Cf. CSR, 4. Note that the Lutheran critical edge is presented in the spirit of democratic negotiation.

43. "Prayer and Bible Reading in the Public Schools," LCA, 1964; "Public Schools and Religious Practices," ALC, 1984. The latter brings together three documents from 1971, 1980, and 1984. CSR also discusses this topic, 6–7.

44. "Prayer and Bible Reading," 3; "Public Schools," 2. The statements also use other arguments such as religious divisiveness and unfairness to those who do not share the religious beliefs or practices.

45. "Prayer and Bible Reading," 3.

46. "Public Schools," 7. The statements support instruction about religion in public schools. For more on this topic see Marie Failinger's chapter, especially "Religion in Public Schools" (125–31).

47. LCA, "Church and State," 35.

48. CSLP, 2.

49. CSR, 3.

50. NCRG, 3.

51. NCRG, 4. Cf. LCA, "Church and State," 41–47; CSLP, 2; and CSR, 3–5. I will return in the next section to certain themes under how the state relates to the church's interest and in the final section to the church's contribution to the state.

52. CSR, 4.

53. "It is an historical fact that our government has generally been friendly toward religion while remaining officially neutral among the various religions" (LCA, "Church and State," 41). Susan Vallem in her chapter speaks of cooperation in social welfare from the nineteenth century on, 82–83.

54. CSR, 5. Cf. NCRG, 8; and the resolution on "Chaplaincies Supported by Government," ELCA Constituting Convention, 1987.

55. NCRG, 4, 7. A 1968 social statement made it stated policy that Lutheran social welfare programs "may properly enter into agreements with federal, state and local government to receive payment for services rendered or to accept, on a nonpreferential basis, grants or long-term loans." These services "should comply with the service stan-

dards set by government, professional agencies and the church." The statement appeals to functional interaction for its policy. See "The Church and Social Welfare," LCA, 1968.

56. CSR, 5–6. It continues: "Old age assistance grants, medical payments, hot lunches, grants for dependent children, higher educational benefits, and health and safety education are examples of such benefits to persons."

57. CSR, 4. One example of such a danger may be government attempts to distinguish between religious social agencies that are "pervasively religious" and those that are not, and to deny aid to the former. Since Lutheran agencies are usually perceived as not "pervasively religious," they may have an unfair advantage over some other religious agencies.

58. LCA, "Church and State," 47, also raises some concerns: "Even where such state aid is constitutionally legal, however, it may not always be socially desirable or ethically advisable. The church and its agencies must therefore decide in each case (1) if the integrity of the church's witness requires that the church itself pay for a given service, or (2) if the church may accept funds from the state for such a service, or (3) if the church considers that a particular service is the peculiar responsibility of the state alone. Prudentially, of course, any institution of the church that is the recipient of such public funds must face the fact that it takes the risk of being subject to governmental direction if it becomes financially dependent upon governmental financing." See Vallem, 87, on Lutheran social ministry, including the discussion on "Charitable Choice" legislation.

59. CSR, 6. This is the only statement that addresses this issue. CSR is also the only statement that refers to religious displays and ceremonies on public property. It considers that such matters are "best decided by the responsible authorities in each community" (7).

60. Ibid.

61. NCRG, 8. For more on governmental aid for parochial schools and on school voucher proposals, see Failinger, chap. 6, esp. "The State's Responsibility for Providing Education" (134–39).

62. NCRG, 2.

63. LCA, "Religious Liberty," 1968. This is the first and only Lutheran social statement that makes religious freedom its one explicit topic.

64. Ibid., 1.

65. Ibid.

66. Michael J. Sandel, "Freedom of Conscience or Freedom of Choice?" in *Articles of Faith, Articles of Peace*, ed. James Davison Hunter and Os Guinness (Washington, D.C.: The Brookings Institution, 1990), 75. Sandel argues that historically "free exercise of religion" referred to "the right to exercise religious duties according to the dictates of conscience, not the right to choose religious beliefs"(88).

67. See Roland Bainton, "The Development and Consistency of Luther's Attitude to Religious Liberty" *Harvard Theological Review* 22.2 (April 1929): 107–50. See also the chapters by Mary Jane Haemig (1) and Gary Simpson (2).

68. "Temporal Authority: To What Extent It Should Be Obeyed," in *LW* 45:105–6.

69. Ibid., 108. See Simpson, 35–36.

70. "Religious Liberty," 2. At this point the statement views the scope of religious freedom comprehensively, underscoring it is a right of both individuals and groups.

71. See the ELCA social statement "For Peace in God's World," 1995, which includes opposing religious persecution among human rights priorities (14). The statement reminds us that concern for religious liberty must have a global perspective.

72. "Religious Liberty," 2; CSR, 4–5, speak of state accommodation to religion: "The state, while not directly supporting or compelling religious teachings or practices, should be free to condition the exercise of coercive powers and be ready to adjust its programs in deference to the religious freedom and the religious expression of the people." The statements speak in different ways about legitimate government restrictions on religious liberty, but all agree that it "is not an absolute right; in every situation it must be weighed against other values before a decision is made" ("Religious Liberty," 3).

73. Cf. with George P. Fletcher's argument, *Basic Concepts of Legal Thought* (New York: Oxford University Press, 1996), 181–83: "The free exercise clause represents a frontal attack on the principle of applying the laws equally to everyone. What is so special about religious claims that they generate exemptions from statues that apply neutrally to everyone?" "There is no way to make headway on the constitutional concept of religion without first developing a theory about why the Constitution should wish to defer to religious commitments. The present tendency on the Court and among scholars is to think that the psychological intensity of religious beliefs requires us to accord these beliefs special protection. Forcing people to act contrary to their religious beliefs imposes a certain sort of harm, and this harm must be balanced against the state's interest in securing universal compliance" with generally applicable laws. "This way of thinking is deeply flawed" since other beliefs are as strongly held. Second, it is hard to imagine why an interest of the state should outweigh the religious commitment. Fletcher gives another account: "The imperative of loyalty to a higher power provides the most compelling account of our deferring to religious obligations. The religious life, as we know it in the West, is based on the individual's having loyalties to a transcendental authority. These loyalties preclude giving wholehearted allegiance to a secular authority." "The fundamental error, I submit, is the assumption that religious belief can be reduced to intensely and sincerely held beliefs that the believers label religious. Religious beliefs, so far as they are to be taken seriously, arise in congregations or communities of believers. They represent a submission to an external authority that commands obedience."

74. See above, 88 n. 51.

75. LCA, "Church and State," 44.

76. "Religious Liberty," 1, 3.

77. Ibid., 2, 3.

78. Ibid. 2.

79. In his study of Protestant churches' attitudes on church and state, Donald L. Drakeman writes, "Thus the Lutherans, too, have made a shift toward the strict separationist end of the spectrum." His observation is misleading for two reasons: (1) He bases his view only on what Lutheran churches said about school prayer; and (2) he assumes Lutherans followed the same path as churches that constituted the Protestant establishment at the beginning of the century. They did not because they began in a different place and were fighting a different battle. "The Churches on Church and State" in *The Churches' Public Role,* ed. Dieter T. Hessel (Grand Rapids, Mich.: Eerdmans, 1993), 272.

80. "Religious Liberty," 4. In speaking of the religious liberty rights of churches and religious organizations, the statement includes: "to give voice to its conscience on matters of public concern, whether from the pulpit, through formal resolutions or through other forms of communication" (2).

81. Public policy advocacy, for example, is one form of the church's public witness. For a discussion of different views toward advocacy, see *The Evangelical Lutheran Church*

in America and Public Policy Advocacy, ed. Roy J. Enquist (Chicago: Commission for Church in Society, ELCA, 1990).

82. "Prayer and Bible Reading," 2. The statement comes in the aftermath of the Supreme Court's rulings on prayer and Bible reading in public schools in 1963.

83. Ibid.

84. For a discussion on different ways the church influences culture and public life, see Robert Benne, *The Paradoxical Vision: A Public Theology for the Twenty-first Century* (Minneapolis: Fortress Press, 1995), 181ff.

85. Peter Berger and Andrew Greeley are two sociologists who convincingly argue against secularization theory.

86. See Richard John Neuhaus, *The Naked Public Square: Religion and Democracy in America* (Grand Rapids, Mich.: Eerdmans, 1984); Stephen L. Carter, *The Culture of Disbelief: How American Law and Politics Trivialize Religious Devotion* (New York: Basic Books, 1993); and Thiemann, *Religion in Public Life.*

87. Cf. Gilbert Meilaender, "'The Things Relevant to Mortal Life': Divorcing Augustine from Rawls," *The Journal for Peace and Justice Studies* 8.2 (1997): 63–68.

88. The quoted words come from Henry Melchior Muhlenberg's diary, June 24, 1747. He recorded what he had written in a church book in Lancaster, Pennsylvania. He wrote in his diary "that the subjects of His Majesty, George, in this country enjoy the free exercise of religion" and then describes Lutheran doctrine and practice. Quoted in Sydney E. Ahlstrom, *A Religious History of the American People* (New Haven: Yale University Press, 1972), 257.

89. See the chapters in the second part of this book for how these authors take up this task.

90. While I am in agreement with Simpson in preferring "integrity" to "separation," I do not find "companionship" to be an adequate replacement for "interaction." See the epilogue of his chapter, 50. The two-pronged principle of the social statements and the ELCA Constitution summarizes not only how the church views its relation with government but also how the church views government's relation to it and other religious bodies. Accordingly, Simpson's proposed replacement would have Lutherans expecting government to be their church's companion, which certainly is not the relationship prescribed by the First Amendment. The metaphorically rich notion of "companion" suggests a too cozy and friendly relationship for government to have with religious bodies as well as for the church to have with government. The noncommittal nature of "interaction" is an advantage for speaking of both sets of actors in a complex and often difficult relationship that seeks mutually agreed upon cooperation where both are properly engaged while recognizing that the relationship may also be marked by hostility, opposition, and conflict.

4. Promoting the General Welfare: Lutheran Social Ministry

1. Foster McCurley interview, Harrisburg, Pa., November 5, 1997.

2. Foster McCurley interview, Harrisburg, Pa., November 5, 1997; McCurley, *Serve the Lord: The Social Ministry of the Church* (Chicago: Division for Church in Society, Evangelical Lutheran Church in America, 2000).

3. Yehezkel Kaufmann, *The Religion of Israel from Its Beginnings to the Babylonian Exile,* trans. Moshe Greenberg (Chicago: University of Chicago Press, 1960), 320.

4. The Old Testament is an extended history of welfare as an expression of justice. Moses and the prophets emphasized the moral necessity of social and economic justice. Judaism was based on the concept of a God who was the creator of the universe, whose will was the supreme law for human action, and who commanded that people be kind, merciful, and just in their dealings with one another. The poor, widows, orphans, and strangers were to be given food and clothing. Gerald Handel, *Social Welfare in Western Society* (New York: Random House, 1982), 47. See also Frances Fox Piven and Richard Cloward, *Regulating the Poor: The Functions of Public Welfare* (New York: Vintage Books, 1993).

5. Carter Lindberg, *Beyond Charity: Reformation Initiatives for the Poor* (Minneapolis: Fortress Press, 1993), 22–24; Handel, *Social Welfare,* 48–49.

6. C. T. Dinmont, "Charity and Almsgiving" in *Encyclopaedia of Religion and Ethics,* vol. 3, ed. James Hastings (New York: Scribners, 1922), 362.

7. Brian Tierney, *Medieval Poor Law: A Sketch of Canonical Theory and Its Application in England* (Berkeley: University of California Press, 1959), 39.

8. Thomas Harvey, *Government Promotion of Faith-Based Solutions to Social Problems: Partisan or Prophetic?* (Washington, D.C.: Aspen Institute, 1997), 7–8.

9. Christine Pohl, "Hospitality from the Edge: The Significance of Marginality in the Practice of Welcome," *The Annual of the Society of Christian Ethics,* ed. H. Beckley. (Washington, D.C.: Georgetown University Press, 1998), 121–36.

10. Martin Luther, "Disputation of Doctor Martin Luther on the Power and Efficacy of Indulgences." See *LW* 31:29.

11. Jeannie Olson, *One Ministry, Many Roles* (St. Louis: Concordia, 1992), 97.

12. Mary Jane Haemig, chap. 1 and Gary Simpson, chap. 2.

13. Thomas Brady, "Luther's Social Teaching and the Social Order of His Age," in *The Martin Luther Quincentennial,* ed. G. Dunnhaupt (Detroit: Wayne State University Press, 1985), 285.

14. Martin Luther, "The Sermon on the Mount," *LW* 22:172.

15. Walter Von Loewenich, *Martin Luther: The Man and His Works* (Minneapolis: Augsburg, 1986), 242.

16. Lindberg, *Beyond Charity,* 100.

17. Olson, *One Ministry,* 100–102.

18. Martin Luther, "The Babylonian Captivity of the Church" in *Three Treatises: Martin Luther,* trans. A. T. W. Steinhauser (Philadelphia: Fortress Press, 1976), 248–49.

19. Horst Becker, former director of the Evangelical Lutheran Diaconewerk, Neuendettelsau, Germany, interview July 4, 1997.

20. Becker interview.

21. Olson, *One Ministry,* 257–64.

22. Beulah Compton, *Introduction to Social Welfare and Social Work* (Homewood, Ill.: Dorsey Press, 1980), 156–57.

23. Harvey, *Faith-Based Solutions,* 10.

24. Compton, *Introduction to Social Welfare,* 278–79.

25. Sidney Fine, *Laissez-Faire and the General Welfare State* (Ann Arbor: University of Michigan Press, 1964), 173.

26. George Forell, *Christian Social Teachings* (Garden City, N.Y.: Anchor Books, 1966), 360.

27. E. Clifford Nelson, *The Lutherans in North America* (Philadelphia: Fortress Press, 1975), 385–86.

28. Ibid., 378.

29. Walter Rauschenbusch, *Christianizing the Social Order* (New York: Macmillan, 1912), 24–25.

30. Nelson, *Lutherans in North America,* 392.

31. Marie Failinger, chap. 6.

32. Frank Fetter, "Subsidizing of Private Charities," *American Journal of Sociology* 7 (1901): 360. Also cited in Stephen Monsma, *When Sacred and Secular Mix* (Lantham, Md.: Rowman & Littlefield, 1996), 7. As Bernard Coughlin observed in 1965, "For over a hundred years there has existed in the United States a partnership between local governments and sectarian welfare." Bernard Coughlin, *Church and State in Social Welfare* (New York: Columbia University Press, 1965), 44.

33. Steven Smith and Michael Lipsky, *Nonprofits for Hire: The Welfare State in the Age of Contracting* (Cambridge, Mass.: Harvard University Press, 1993), 9.

34. "History of Bremwood," *Waverly (Iowa) Democrat,* 20 April 1989, and Jacob Schneider, *Our Portion of Manna,* self-published.

35. Stephen Monsma, "Government and the Religious Social Sector: A Happy Marriage or a Dysfunctional Partnership?" (unpublished monograph, 1996).

36. Monsma, *Sacred and Secular,* 40.

37. *Bradfield v. Roberts,* 175 U.S. at 298–99 (1899).

38. *Bowen v. Kendrick,* 487 U.S. at 602 (1988); Myles Stenshoel, chap. 5; Monsma, *Sacred and Secular,* 40. The Court cited *Bowen v. Kendrick* in a 1995 church-state case, *Rosenberger v. Rector.* In this case, the University of Virginia, which normally paid for the printing of student publications, refused to fund *Wide Awake,* a Christian publication. In a five to four vote, the Court decided, "We do not confront a case where, even under a neutral program that includes nonsectarian recipients, the government is making direct money payments to an institution or group that is engaged in religious activity."

39. John McCarthy and Jim Castelli, *Religion-Sponsored Social Service Providers: The Not-So-Independent Sector* (Washington, D.C.: Aspen Institute), 58.

40. Division for Church in Society, ELCA (1994).

41. Paul Wee, "Promoting the General Welfare—Without Welfare" (unpublished research, 1997).

42. U.S. Conference of Mayors Study on Hunger and Homelessness, 1998. This survey found that "overall demand for both emergency food and shelter grew during 1997 for most of the surveyed cities." An average increase of 16 percent in the number of requests for emergency food assistance (86 percent if cities reported an increase); 19 percent of the facilities reported lack of resources. Causes of hunger reported were low-paying jobs, unemployment, food stamp cuts, high housing costs, poverty or lack of income, and low benefits from public assistance. The study cited an overall 3 percent increase (59 percent of cities) in the number of requests for emergency shelter; causes of homelessness reported include substance abuse and lack of needed services, lack of affordable housing, mental illness, low paying jobs, domestic violence, and changes and cuts in public assistance.

43. Susan Kosche Vallem, "The Impact of Welfare Reform on Lutheran Social Ministry Organizations and Congregations" (unpublished research, 1998).

44. Support for faith-based organizations is found in the 1996 Personal Responsibil-

ity and Work Opportunity Reconciliation Act, P.L. 104–93, section 104: *Services Provided by Charitable, Religious, or Private Organizations,* signed into law August 1996, 87–99.

45. Welfare Information Network, *Issue Notes,* 2, 3 (March 1998).

46. John Stumme, chap. 3.

47. Luther, *WA* 51:241, in Foster McCurley, "Understanding Vocation in an LSMO" (unpublished paper presented at Pennsylvania State College, November 7, 1996).

48. George Hanusa, *Hope for All Generations: Lutheran Social Services of Iowa, 1870–1995* (Minneapolis: Kirk House, 1996), 116–17.

49. Welfare Information Network, *Issue Notes* (January 1998).

5. Religious Liberty: A Constitutional Quest

1. This chapter addresses four competing approaches used by the Supreme Court to apply the religion clauses: separation, accommodation, secular intent, and impact analysis. Other chapters refer to the language of "institutional separation and functional interaction" of church and state approved in statements of American Lutherans beginning in the 1960s. Casual identification of this language of the church with that of the courts tends to obscure rather than clarify the constitutional issues. Because of their differing definitions of "separation," the judicial battle has characteristically been *either separation or interaction,* while the theological imperative has been *both separation and interaction.*

2. 310 U.S. 296 (1940).

3. 330 U.S. 1 (1947).

4. 268 U.S. 510.

5. In the early twentieth century the Supreme Court's use of the amendment in a manner more protective of the rights of corporate "persons" than of individuals was characteristic. *Pierce* did, however, approve a role for parental rights in the education of children; their testimony was allowed to support the Society's proprietary rights.

6. 281 U.S. 370.

7. *Minersville School District v. Gobitis,* 310 U.S. 586 (1940).

8. *West Virginia Board of Education v. Barnette,* 319 U.S. 625 (1943).

9. *Everson v. Board of Education,* 330 U.S. 1 (1947).

10. 494 U.S. 872.

11. 508 U.S. 520.

12. The original intent of the clause forbidding any act of Congress "prohibiting the free exercise" of religion did not similarly limit the states. Given the implicit and explicit exemptions protective of religious practices and religious differences we have noted in the U.S. Constitution, one may well wonder whether this wording, so supportive of religious exercise, when added to the Fourteenth Amendment liberty protected against state action, can, as in *Smith,* legitimately be invoked to protect the rights of states to effectively *inhibit* the religious exercise of individuals and churches. Religious liberty is poorly protected when religion is officially ignored.

13. RFRA's purposes were based on its congressional "findings" that "(2) laws 'neutral' toward religion may burden religious exercise as surely as laws intended to interfere with religious exercise" and that "(4) in *Employment Division v. Smith* . . . the Supreme Court virtually eliminated the requirement that the government justify burdens on religious exercise imposed by laws neutral toward religion. . . ."

14. *City of Boerne v. Flores*, 521 U.S. 507 (1997). More specifically, the Court held that the congressional imposition of these standards upon state governments was not "appropriate legislation" under Section 5 of the Fourteenth Amendment to enforce the due process liberty protecting the First Amendment free exercise.

15. This is not to suggest that overt and intentional legislative inhibition of religious practices, as in the *Hialeah* case, is to be ignored; an ordinance intending to prohibit free exercise will, one may assume, often be effective. But so will many laws that do not on their face intend to do so. The one thing needful, the impact analysis approach suggests, is the practical effect of the legislation on religious liberty, whatever the intent of the legislators.

16. *Sherbert v. Verner*, 374 U.S. 398 (1963).

17. *Wisconsin v. Yoder*, 406 U.S. 205 (1972).

18. *Cantwell v. Connecticut*, 310 U.S. 296 (1940).

19. *Murdoch v. Pennsylvania*, 319 U.S. 105 (1943).

20. *Follett v. McCormick*, 321 U.S. 573 (1944).

21. *United States v. Ballard*, 322 U.S. 78 (1944). Ballard and other leaders of a professedly religious group known as the "I Am" movement had sought economic support for the group in publications sent by mail; they claimed to have experienced various spiritual revelations and to possess prophetic authority. One issue was the trial judge's instructions to the jury. He had said, in part: "The issue is: Did these defendants honestly and in good faith believe those things? If they did, they should be acquitted. I cannot make it any clearer than that. If these defendants did not believe those things, they did not believe that Jesus came down and dictated, or that Saint Germain came down and dictated, did not believe the things that they wrote, but used the mail for the purpose of getting money, the jury should find them guilty. Therefore, gentlemen, religion cannot come into this case." Thus the truth or falsity of the representations was not before the jury, as would have been the case in fraud trials not involving religious faith; but if religious truth was not at issue, sincerity of religious belief was. The Supreme Court agreed with the trial judge to exempt from consideration any question of truth or falsity of religious representations, but accorded no such exemption to the question of sincerity of belief.

22. 344 U.S. 94. While I emphasize the "impact analysis" aspect, *Kedroff* is one of the rare religion decisions equally supportable by all four rationales; the legislation invalidated was, I acknowledge, also vulnerable under the logic of separation, accommodation, and secular intent.

23. "Neutral principles" cases include *Presbyterian Church v. Mary Blue Hull Presbyterian Church*, 393 U.S. 440 (1969) and *Jones v. Wolf*, 99 Sup. Ct. 3020 (1979).

24. *Prince v. Massachusetts*, 321 U.S. 158 (1944).

25. *Goldman v. Weinberger*, 475 U.S. 503 (1986). The opinion of the Court by Justice Rehnquist upheld the refusal of a *Sherbert*-style exemption to permit Rabbi Goldman, then serving as an Air Force psychologist, to wear a yarmulke indoors. "Our review of military regulations challenged on First Amendment grounds is far more deferential than constitutional review of similar laws or regulations designed for civilian society. The military officials are under no constitutional mandate to abandon their considered professional judgment."

26. *U.S. v. Seeger*, 380 U.S. 163 (1965).

27. *Welsh v. United States*, 398 U.S. 333 (1970).

28. *Gillette v. United States, Negre v. Larsen,* 401 U.S. 437 (1971).

29. *Everson v. Board Education,* 330 U.S. 1 (1947) at 15.

30. Ibid.

31. *Rosenberger v. Rector and Visitors of University of Virginia,* 515 U.S. 819 (1995). The five-justice majority focused on the formal neutrality of the First Amendment's protection of speech and press and allowed student fees to subsidize a fundamentalist Christian student publication as the expression of one of many recognized student groups; secondarily the Court found the Establishment Clause compatible with this approach. The dissenters emphasized the Establishment Clause and the primacy of the separation imperative under that clause over any formally neutral secularity related to the First Amendment's general protection of expression.

32. *McCollum v. Board of Education,* 333 U.S. 203 (1948) at 209.

33. 333 U.S. at 247.

34. *Zorach v. Clauson,* 343 U.S. 306 (1952) at 315.

35. 343 U.S. at 313.

36. *Walz v. Tax Commission,* 397 U.S. 664 (1970). As applied to churches, a state exemption from taxes upon "real or personal property used exclusively for religious, educational or charitable purposes" was upheld; it did not, in Burger's Opinion of the Court, violate the religion clauses. This exemption, he argued, was less entangling of government and religion than the failure to exempt would be; it had the support of tradition and history. Such tradition-based legislation protective of religion is what we call "accommodation." Two years later in his *Lemon* test, Burger would continue to distinguish between "excessive entanglement," requiring separation, and the nonexcessive interaction that, combined with tradition, characterizes accommodation.

37. *Marsh v. Chambers,* 463 U.S. 783 (1983).

38. 343 U.S. at 311.

39. "Of Church and State and the Supreme Court," *University of Chicago Law Review* 29.2 (1961): 96. Prof. Kurland, despite his attempt to reconcile the two clauses, nevertheless referred to the "freedom and separation clauses" in this quotation, thus appearing to prejudice the cause of a valid conceptual unity.

40. E.g., *McGowan v. Maryland,* 366 U.S. 420.

41. *Braunfeld v. Brown,* 366 U.S. 599 (1961).

42. *Board of Education v. Allen,* 392 U.S. 236 (1968); *Mitchell v. Helms,* 530 U.S.793 (2000).

43. The "neutral principles" cases, n. 23 above.

44. *Zobrest v. Catalina Foothills School District,* 509 U.S. 1 (1993).

45. *Agostini v. Felton,* 521 U.S. 203 (1997), overturned *Aguilar v. Felton,* 473 U.S. 402 (1985).

46. *Lemon v. Kurtzman,* 403 U.S. 602 (1971) at 612.

47. Whether a general theory of the religion clauses is necessary or possible is of course debatable. I consider a two-clause general theory necessary to overcome the contradictions of the competing rationales of the Supreme Court's precedents and to maximize constitutional protection of religious liberty in the United States. Whether what is "necessary" is also possible may be the more difficult question. Political obstacles loom larger than other problems of law and logic.

48. *Torcaso v. Watkins,* 367 U.S. 488 (1961). Here the Court unanimously overturned Maryland's constitutional requirement that state officeholders declare "belief in the

existence of God." Torcaso had been refused his commission as a notary public because he was not willing to make the declaration.

49. For example, the *Welsh* conscientious objector case, n. 27 above.

50. Quoted in *Everson*, 330 U.S. 1 (1947) at 64.

51. Cf. Kurland's anomalous reference to "freedom and separation" clauses, n. 39 above.

52. As noted in our discussion of the need to reconcile the religion clauses, the incorporation of both establishment and free exercise liberties into the due process clause involves individuals in the protection of establishment as well as free exercise liberties; "persons" serve as surrogates for their faith communities.

53. Advocates of the various rationales of the religion clauses characteristically assert that their favored principle should be used because it protects religious liberty; thus whether it effectively protects freedom of religion in a given case is a legitimate and focal question.

54. *Sherbert v. Verner*, 374 U.S. 398 (1963) at 406.

55. If "neutrality" among religious options is to be the governmental goal in protecting religious liberty, it must be defined in terms that effectively and equitably protect the various religious options. Such is clearly not the case when, in the positive state, legislative unconcern or failure to anticipate the negative impact of a law upon particular religions is judicially approved as neutral, or when a decision providing protection under one religion clause does so by ignoring the burden it imposes upon another religion under the other clause.

56. Some Court observers include judicial protection of religious liberty via exemption as "accommodation"; we differentiate such judicial exemption from legislative accommodation and refer to it as "impact analysis."

57. *Board of Education of Kiryas Joel v. Grumet*, 512 U.S. 687 (1994).

58. The Kurland proposal, so tendentiously echoed by the current Court, was essentially an equal protection understanding of the religion clauses, arguing that government may not classify in terms of religion "either to confer a benefit or to impose a burden." One may agree that a governmental intent to help or to hurt religion is constitutionally forbidden without, however, excluding the "middle" as Kurland and similar secularists do when they forbid even that classification in terms of religion (exemplified, indeed, by the First Amendment religion clauses!) needed to provide effective religious neutrality. It is clearly not the case that the formal neutrality of ignoring religion provides equitable treatment vis-à-vis religious belief and religious unbelief. Such secularity, far from protecting religious liberty, effectively favors secularism over faith. An informed secular understanding of religious differences might, however, contribute to the right to differ religiously. Such a "neutral" reinterpretation of the *Lemon* test emphasizing the "effect" of legislation was the apparent thrust of Justice Thomas's plurality opinion in *Mitchell v. Helms*, 512 U.S. 793 (2000), approving the provision of computers and instructional equipment to parochial schools: "If the religious, irreligious, and areligious are all alike eligible for governmental aid, no one would conclude that any indoctrination that any particular recipient conducts has been done at the behest of the government."

59. However conceptually satisfying an impact analysis rationale of the religion clauses may appear, the case-by-case and religion-by-religion analysis it requires is undoubtedly a major discouragement to judges and justices. In 1963, when the Supreme

Court incorporated into the Fourteenth Amendment due process clause the Sixth Amendment right of a criminally accused person to a defense attorney in *Gideon v. Wainwright*, it freed itself and lower courts from the frustration of determining, case-by-case, whether special circumstances required the presence of counsel. By contrast, incorporation of the religion clause liberties has added greatly to the judicial burden; moreover, the impact analysis approach that the Court has sometimes used to maximize the protection of religious liberty is clearly the most burdensome of the four rationales we have surveyed.

60. In the 1970s the Court's impact analysis approach looked reasonably healthy and the Kurland religion blindness seemed to have run its course; in the late 1990s the opposite appeared to be true. While the justices are relatively immune to pressures of the moment, over time the Court tends to reflect the society of which it is a part. Perhaps a serious quest for effective religious liberty will be renewed. In the meantime, some protection of religious differences may derive from state constitutions and courts. Thus when the U.S. Supreme Court after its 1990 *Smith* decision failed to exempt some Amish citizens from Minnesota's statutory requirement of bright red safety triangles on their slow-moving buggies, the state's supreme court held that their religious exercise was protected under provisions of the Minnesota constitution; the Amish who found the red religiously offensive could safely substitute white reflective triangles.

61. See John T. Noonan, Jr., *The Lustre of Our Country* (Berkeley: University of California Press, 1998). Subtitled *The American Experience of Religious Freedom,* this work by an eminent Christian law professor and jurist discusses the constitutional developments we have encountered as affirmative contributions to U.S. and world history.

6. We Must Spare No Diligence: The State and Childhood Education

1. *Brown v. Board of Education,* 397 U.S. 483, 492(1954).

2. George W. Forell, "Luther and Conscience," in *Martin Luther: Theologian of the Church,* ed. William R. Russell (St. Paul, Minn.: *Word & World,* Luther Seminary, 1994); Gustav Wingren, *Luther on Vocation* (Philadelphia: Muhlenberg Press, 1957), 94–95.

3. Carl Esbeck, "A Typology of Church-State Relations," in *Religion, Public, Life and the American Polity,* ed. Luis E. Lugo (Knoxville: University of Tennessee Press, 1994), 11–12.

4. Ibid., 8.

5. Ibid.

6. Ibid., 21–22.

7. Ibid., 16–17.

8. Harold J. Grimm, "Luther's Impact on the Schools," in *Luther and Culture,* by George W. Forell, Harold J. Grimm, and Theodore Hoelty-Nickel (Decorah, Iowa: Luther College Press, 1960), 88–99.

9. Paul Althaus, *The Ethics of Martin Luther,* trans. Robert C. Schultz (Philadelphia: Fortress Press, 1972), 47–48, 54–56, 60, 99–100, 114–16; Forell, "The Political Use of the Law" in *Martin Luther: Theologian of the Church,* 92.

10. Althaus, *The Ethics of Martin Luther,* 61; Forell, "Luther and Political Life" in Forell et al., *Luther and Culture,* 48.

11. Lutheran Church in America (LCA), "Religious Liberty in the United States," (1968).

12. Grimm, "Luther's Impact on Schools," 81.

13. Ibid., 76.

14. Ibid., 85 ("Sermon on Keeping Children in School").

15. Ibid., 80.

16. See, e.g., John Witte Jr., "The Civic Seminary: Sources of Modern Public Education in the Lutheran Reformation of Germany," *Journal of Law and Religion* 12 (1995–96): 94.

17. Grimm, "Luther's Impact on Schools," 85, quoting Luther.

18. Sydney E. Ahlstrom, *A Religious History of the American People* (New Haven: Yale University Press, 1972), 641–42.

19. 262 U.S. 390 (1923); *Pierce v. Society of the Sisters* 268 U.S. 510, 534, 539 (1925).

20. *Wisconsin v. Yoder,* 406 U.S. 205, 233 (1972).

21. 310 U.S. 296, 303–4 (1940).

22. See *State v. Riddle,* 279 W.Va. 429, 265 S.E. 2d 359 (1981); *Hanson v. Cushman,* 490 F. Supp. 109, 115 (D. Mich. 1980); *Care and Protection of Charles,* 399 Mass. 324, 504 N.E. 2d 592 (1987), holding that parents may be required to submit their proposed curriculum and lesson plans for approval by the school superintendent.

23. See, e.g., *People v. Bennett,* 501 N.W.2d 106 (Mich. Sup. Ct. 1993); *State v. Lund,* 382 N.W. 2d 632 (N.D. 1986); *Hanson v. Cushman,* 490 F. Supp. 109 (W.D. Mich. 1980), upholding teacher certification requirement for parents home schooling their children.

24. *Care and Protection of Charles,* 399 Mass 324, 504 N.E.2d 592 (1987). Compare *State v. Whisner,* 47 Ohio St. 2d 181, 351 N.E.2d 750 (1976), holding that prescribing the number of instructional minutes and hours in the school day unduly burdens religious exercise.

25. 442 Mich. 226, 501 N.W2d 127 (1993).

26. *New Life Baptist Church Academy v. East Longmeadow,* 666 F. Supp. 293, 308 (D. Mass. 1987). This kind of challenge rarely happens at the college level, but see *N. J.-Phila. Presbytery of the Bible Presbyterian Church v. New Jersey State Board of Higher Education,* 514 F. Supp. 506 (N.J. 1981), holding that the state board cannot order a religious school without a degree-granting license to stop teaching activities.

27. Marilyn J. Harran, *Martin Luther: Learning for Life* (St. Louis: Concordia, 1997), 179; *LW* 45:353.

28. Both Luther's "Sermon on Sending Children to School" and "To the Councilmen of all Cities in Germany" evidence this concern. Gustav M. Bruce, *Luther as an Educator* (Westport, Conn.: Greenwood Press, 1979) 164–65.

29. *West Va. Bd. of Education v. Barnette,* 319 U.S. 624 (1943).

30. Lutheran Church in America, "Prayer and Bible Reading in the Public Schools" (1964), 1–2.

31. Cases on official school prayer include *Engel v. Vitale,* 370 U.S. 421 (1962), invalidating required school prayer; *Wallace v. Jaffree,* 472 U.S. 38 (1985), invalidating law requiring "meditation or prayer"; *Lee v. Weisman,* 505 U.S. 577 (1992), invalidating school-sponsored graduation prayer; and *Santa Fe Ind. School Dist. V. Doe,* 530 U.S. 290 (2000), invalidating school-sponsored prayer by student elected school body.

32. 319 U.S. 624, 642 (1943).

33. *Engel v. Vitale,* 370 U.S. 421 (1962), invalidating New York Board of Regents prescribed prayer for schoolchildren; *Abington School Dist. v. Schempp,* 374 U.S. 203 (1963), invalidating state law requiring the reading of a selection from the Bible and recitation of the Lord's Prayer; *Stone v. Graham,* 449 U.S. 39 (1980), invalidating a Kentucky law requiring the posting of the Ten Commandments in public school classrooms.

34. See Jay Alan Sekulow et al., "Proposed Guidelines for Student Religious Speech and Observance in Public Schools," *Mercer Law Review* 46 (1995): 1084–87 and cases cited therein.

35. "A Bill for Establishing Religious Freedom," reprinted in William Lee Miller, *The First Liberty: Religion and the American Republic* (New York: Knopf, 1986), app. I, 357–58.

36. 505 U.S. 577 (1992); 530 U.S. 290 (2000).

37. See *Lynch v Donnelly,* 465 U.S. 668, 688–89 (1984), J. O'Connor, concurring.

38. Miller, *First Liberty,* 13–16.

39. Ibid., 13, although Miller notes that this requirement was not enforced in Virginia. See also discussion of dissent in the southern colonies in Ahlstrom, *Religious History,* 188–99.

40. LCA, "Religious Liberty in the United States," 1.

41. LCA, "Human Rights: Doing Justice in God's World" (1978), 4.

42. LCA, "Prayer and Bible Reading in the Public Schools" (1964) 3.

43. American Lutheran Church, "The Nature of the Church and Its Relationship with Government," (1979), 3.

44. LCA, "Prayer and Bible Reading," 1.

45. Ibid., 1, 3.

46. Compare Miller, *First Liberty,* 358; with Luther's views on forcing religion on others see Roland H. Bainton, "The Development and Consistency of Luther's Attitude to Religious Liberty," *Harvard Theological Review* 22.2 (April 1929); and with "Religious Liberty," 1; LCA, "Prayer and Bible Reading," 3, 5.

47. LCA, "Prayer and Bible Reading," 3, 5.

48. Ibid. See also "Church-State Relations in the USA: A Statement of the American Lutheran Church" (Third General Convention, October 19–25, 1966).

49. "Christian Concern for General Education: A Statement of the American Lutheran Church," 3–4 (Seventh General Convention, October 12, 1974); "Public Schools and Religious Practices, Statement of ALC General Convention," 2–3 (Twelfth General Convention, October 20, 1984).

50. See, e.g., *Lamb's Chapel v. Center Moriches Union Free School District,* 508 U.S. 520 (1993), on a religious film series; *Good News Club v. Milford Central School,* 533 U.S. 98 (2001).

51. See *Equal Access Act,* 20 U.S.C § 4071–74 (1988); Sekulow, et al., "Proposed Guidelines," 1043–56.

52. Bruce, *Luther as an Educator,* 283–86. For instance, Luther suggested that teachers progress from teaching students the words of the text to discussions of their meaning, and then an explanation of the ideas in the text. Similarly, he encouraged students to use their creativity through play, discussions, debates, even dramatic presentations.

53. "Christian Concern for General Education," 2.

54. LCA, "Prayer and Bible Reading in the Schools," 4.

55. Martin Luther, "To the Christian Nobility of the German Nation Concerning the Reform of the Christian Estate," *LW* 44, ed. James Atkinson (Philadelphia: Fortress Press, 1966), 200. Quoted in Witte, "The Civic Seminary," 183 (cited in n. 16).

56. Among the rare exceptions is *Smith v. Board of School Commissioners of Mobile County,* 655 F. Supp. 939 (S.D.Ala. 1987).

57. *Citizens for Parental Rights v. San Mateo County Board of Education,* 51 Cal. App. 3d 1, 124 Ca. Rptr. 68 (1975).

58. 51 Cal. App. 3d at 24, 124 Cal. Rptr. at 86. This court refers to *Hopkins v. Hamden Board of Education*, 29 Conn. Super. 397, 289 A.2d 914 (1971), upholding a compulsory health course that included family life and sex education.

59. *Todd v. Rochester Community Schools*, 41 Mich. App. 320, 200 N.W.2d 90 (1972).

60. *Grove v. Mead School Dist. No. 354*, 753 F.2d 1528 (9th Cir. 1985).

61. See, e.g., *Malnak v. Yogi*, 592 F.2d 197 (3d Cir. 1979), aff'g 440 F.Supp. 1284 (D.N.J. 1977), holding that TM was a religion for purposes of the Establishment Clause and must be banned as an elective from the school curriculum.

62. 647 F. Supp. 1194 (E.D. Tenn. 1986), rev'd 827 F.2d 1058 (6th Cir. 1987), cert. denied, 484 U.S.1066 (1988).

63. 827 F.2d at 1062.

64. Ibid., 1066–67.

65. See *Grove v. Mead School Dist. No. 354*, 753 F.2d 1528 (9th Cir. 1985), child permitted to opt out; *Mozert v. Hawkins Co. Bd. of Education*, 579 F. Supp. at 1052; *Immediato v. Rye Neck School District*, 873 F.Supp. 846 (S.D.N.Y. 1995), no curricular opt-out right for purely secular reasons; see also *Medeiros v. Kiyosaki*, 52 Haw. 436, 478 P.2d 314 (1970), where the court held that there was no free exercise challenge to a film series on sex education where parents had the option of withdrawing their children from watching the film series.

66. Witte, "Civic Seminary," 194.

67. James B. Egle, *The Constitutional Implications of School Choice*, 1992 Wis. L. Rev. 459, 499 (1992), citing the Pennsylvania, Indiana, and New York constitutional provisions.

68. Bruce, *Luther as an Educator*, 212.

69. Ibid.; Luther, "A Sermon on Keeping Children in School" in *LW* 46, ed. Robert C. Schultz (Philadelphia: Fortress Press, 1967), 257.

70. Grimm, "Luther's Impact on the Schools" in *Luther and Culture*, 84–85.

71. *LW* 45:355.

72. Harran, *Martin Luther: Learning for Life*, 173–76, 181–83.

73. Statement of the Division of Education of the ELCA for Early Childhood Education Centers, Elementary and Secondary Schools 1–2 (Board of Directors, ELCA Division for Education, September 16, 1988).

74. ALC Stance on Christian Day Schools 4–6 (ALC Division for Life and Mission of the Congregation, undated).

75. 347 U.S. 483 (1954).

76. *Newsweek*, June 21, 1999, 64.

77. See ALC, "Christian Concern for General Education," 3.

78. Minority populations, in their view, will be left behind in the inferior public schools because they will not be able to afford the extra private school tuition or the additional effort involved in transferring out of the neighborhood school.

79. Grimm, "Luther's Impact on the Schools" in *Luther and Culture*, 80–84.

80. ELCA, Statement of the Division for Education, 2.

81. 330 U.S. 1 (1947).

82. *Mitchell v. Helms*, 120 S.Ct. 2530, 2539 (2000), federal funds used to lend educational materials and equipment to parochial schools permitted. This test derives from *Lemon v. Kurtzman*, 403 U.S. 602 (1972), on public payment for salaries, textbooks, and instructional materials; and *Agostini v. Felton*, 521 U.S. 203 (1997), permitting public employees to provide remedial education on-site to disadvantaged parochial school children.

83. See Laurence H. Tribe, *American Constitutional Law,* 2nd ed. (New York: Foundation Press, 1998), 1219–1220; *Zelamn v. Selman-Harris,* 122 S. Ct. 2460 (2002).

84. See Douglas Laycock, "A Survey of Religious Liberty in the United States," *Ohio State Law Journal* 47 (1986): 409, 443–46.

85. Ibid..

86. Ibid.

87. See Chester James Antieu, et al., *Religion Under the State Constitutions* (Washington, D.C.: Institute for Church-State Law, Georgetown University, 1965), 29–36.

88. Compare *Mueller v. Allen,* 463 U.S. 388 (1983) to *Zelamn v. Selman-Harris,* 122 S. Ct. 2460, 2465.

89. *Zelamn* 2466-67.

90. See Witte, "Civic Seminary," 193.

7. Love Thy Neighbor: Churches and Land Use Regulation

1. *Cornerstone Bible Church v. City of Hastings,* 740 F. Supp. 654 (D. Minn. 1990), affirmed in part and reversed in part, 948 F.2d 464 (8th Cir. 1991).

2. *Western Presbyterian Church v. Board of Zoning Adjustment,* 862 F. Supp. 538 (D.D.C. 1994).

3. *City of Boerne v. Flores,* 521 U.S. 507 (1997).

4. See Myles Stenshoel's essay, chap. 5, in this volume for his description of "impact analysis." I will use the phrase "free exercise exemptions" to describe the same legal doctrine.

5. The Religious Land Use and Institutionalized Persons Act, 42 U.S.C. § 2000cc. For further details about the rise of land use conflicts involving churches, see Robert W. Tuttle, "How Firm a Foundation? Protecting Religious Land Uses After Boerne," *George Washington Law Review* 68 (2000): 861.

6. See, for example, *Harrison v. St. Mark's Church,* 12 Pa. C. 259 (Phila. Ct. C.P. 1877); *Langan v. Bellinger,* 611 N.Y.S.2d 59 (N.Y. App. Div. 1994), nuisance actions against churches for bell-ringing. One commentator has argued that nuisance law—rather than the broader regulation of zoning law—should be the primary limitation on religious land uses. Shell Ross Saxer, "When Religion Becomes a Nuisance: Balancing Religious Land Use and Religious Freedom When Activities of Religious Institutions Bring Outsiders into the Neighborhood," *Kentucky Law Journal* 84 (1995–96): 507.

7. Martha A. Lees, "Preserving Property Values? Preserving Proper Homes? Preserving Privilege?: The Pre-Euclid Debate over Zoning for Exclusively Private Residential Areas, 1916–1926," *University of Pittsburgh Law Review* 56 (1994): 367.

8. *Village of Euclid v. Ambler Realty Co.,* 272 U.S. 365 (1926).

9. Edward M. Bassett, *Zoning: The Laws, Administration, and Court Decisions During the First Twenty Years* (New York: Russell Sage Foundation, 1940), 70; quoted in James E. Curry, *Public Regulation of the Religious Use of Land* (Charlottesville, Va.: The Michie Company, 1964), 8–9.

10. Laurie Reynolds, "Zoning the Church: The Police Power Versus the First Amendment," *Boston University Law Review* 64 (1985): 767.

11. *Corporation of the Presiding Bishop of the Church of Jesus Christ of Latter-Day Saints v. City of Porterville,* 203 P.2d 823 (Cal. Dist. Ct. App. 1949), appeal dismissed, 338 U.S. 805 (1949).

12. Douglas Laycock, "State RFRAs and Land Use Regulation," *University of California, Davis Law Review* 32 (1999): 755.

13. See Lucinda Harper, "Storefront Churches: The Neighbors Upscale Stores Don't Love," *Wall Street Journal*, 15 March 2000, B1. Even New York, a state that is among the most deferential to religious land uses, does not extend the same level of deference to religious uses in commercial districts. *Rhema Christian Fellowship v. Common Council of City of Buffalo*, 452 N.Y.S2d 292 (N.Y. Sup. Ct. 1982).

14. Daniel R. Mandelker, *Land Use Law*, 4th ed. (Charlottesville, Va.: Lexis Law Publishing: 1997), 275–81; Reynolds, "Zoning the Church," 784–85.

15. *Cornell Univ. v. Bagnardi*, 503 N.E.2d 509 (N.Y. 1986); *City of Colo. Springs v. Blanche*, 761 P.2d 212 (Colo. 1988); *Open Door Baptist Church v. Clark County*, 1998 WL 341968 (Wash Ct. App. June 26, 1998), affirmed, 995 P.2d 33 (Wash. 2000).

16. Mark W. Cordes, "Where to Pray? Religious Zoning and the First Amendment," *University of Kansas Law Review* 35 (1987): 697.

17. Mandelker, *Land Use Law*, 158. See also Cordes, "Where to Pray," 810–11.

18. Mandelker, *Land Use Law*, 479–91.

19. Angela Carmella, "Houses of Worship and Religious Liberty: Constitutional Limits to Landmark Preservation and Architectural Review," *Villanova Law Review* 36 (1991): 401, 436.

20. In addition to private foundation grants that may be available to assist historic church properties, some state historic preservation schemes permit public grants to historic religious properties. For further discussion of the constitutionality of government historic preservation grants to religious entities, see Ira C. Lupu and Robert W. Tuttle, "Historic Preservation Grants to Houses of Worship: A Case Study in the Survival of Separationism," *Boston College Review* 43 (2002): 1139–1176.

21. *The Nature of the Church and Its Relationship with Government* (New York: Lutheran Council in the U.S.A., 1979), 3.

22. Ibid., 3.

23. Luther contends that the state has a divinely ordained duty to safeguard the health, safety, and welfare of its residents. This duty requires the state to regulate the acts of all people, without regard to their office, who injure others. In his treatise "To the Christian Nobility of the German Nation Concerning the Reform of the Christian Estate," (*LW* 44:130–31). Luther condemns the clerical exemption from civil jurisdiction:

> [S]ince the temporal power is ordained of God to punish the wicked and protect the good, it should be left free to perform its office in the whole body of Christendom without restriction and without respect to persons, whether it affects pope, bishops, priests, nuns, or anyone else. . . . [W]hat then are the Romanist scribes doing with their own laws, which exempt them from the jurisdiction of the temporal Christian authority? It is just so that they can be free to do evil. . . .

24. *Sherbert v. Verner*, 374 U.S. 398 (1963).

25. The 1966 statement of the American Lutheran Church, "Church-State Relations in the USA," reads: "The Constitution denies to government the right to interfere with the person's exercise of his religion, provided that he does not offend public decency or tread upon the rights of others" (7). The 1968 statement of the Lutheran Church in America, "Religious Liberty in the United States," reads: "The religious liberty of a person or group may be limited by government only on the basis of an important and compelling public interest" (3).

26. Religious Land Use and Institutionalized Persons Act, 42 U.S.C. § 2000cc; Religious Freedom Restoration Act, 42 USC § 2000bb; held unconstitutional as applied to the states in *City of Boerne v. Flores*, 521 U.S. 597 (1997).

27. I explore the themes found in this section and the next at greater length in Tuttle, "How Firm a Foundation," 261.

28. See, for example, *Diocese of Rochester v. Planning Bd.*, 136 N.E.2d 827 (N.Y. 1956); Cordes, "Where to Pray," 705–6.

29 .*Corporation of the Presiding Bishop of the Church of Latter-Day Saints v. City of Porterville*, 203 P.2d 823 (Cal. Dist. Ct. App. 1949); Reynolds, 776.

30. See Tuttle, "How Firm a Foundation," 878–79.

31. *Porterville*, 203 P.2d at 825–26. These two features—the treatment of similar, non-religious, land uses and the burden on the church's ability to locate somewhere in the jurisdiction—turn out to be significant elements in the free speech/equal protection analysis detailed below, which provides an alternative to the *Sherbert* test for free exercise exemptions.

32. Curry, *Public Regulation*, 331–33, listing cases between 1947 and 1960 in which the U.S. Supreme Court refused to hear the appeals of religious uses raising constitutional objections to land use regulations.

33. *American Communications Association v. Douds*, 339 U.S. 382, 397–98 (1950), discussing *Corporation of the Presiding Bishop of the Church of Jesus Christ of Latter-Day Saints v. City of Porterville*, 203 P.2d 823, 90 Cal. App. 656 (Cal. App. 4th Dist. 1949), appeal dismissed, 338 U.S. 939 (1950). See Curry, *Public Regulation*, 331–32.

34. 699 F.2d 303 (6th Cir.), cert. denied, 464 U.S. 815 (1983).

35. Ibid. at 307.

36. R. Stark and L. Iannaccone, "Why Jehovah's Witnesses Grow So Rapidly," *Journal of Contemporary Religion* (December 1997): 133–57.

37. 859 F.2d 820 (10th Cir. 1988).

38. Ibid. at 825.

39. See, for example, *Grosz v. City of Miami Beach*, 721 F.2d 729 (11th Cir. 1983); *Christian Gospel Church v. City and County of San Francisco*, 896 F.2d 1221 (9th Cir. 1990).

40. Christopher Eisgruber and Lawrence Sager, "The Vulnerability of Conscience: The Constitutional Basis for Protecting Religious Conduct," *University of Chicago Law Review* 61 (1994): 1245, 1259–60.

41. See Ira C. Lupu, "The Failure of RFRA," *University of Arkansas, Little Rock Law Journal 20* (1998): 575, 603–4.

42. Laycock, "State RFRAs," 759.

43. Frederick Mark Gedicks, "The Normalized Free Exercise Clause: Three Abnormalities," *Indiana Law Journal* 75 (2000): 77.

44. *Church of the Lukumi Babalu Aye v. Hialeah*, 508 U.S. 520 (1993). The decision draws from a number of constitutional grounds, particularly the Free Exercise Clause, but equal protection analysis seems to be at the heart of the majority opinion in the case.

45. *Lukumi Babalu Aye*, 508 U.S. at 535–39.

46. *Cornerstone*, 948 F.2d 464, 471.

47. Ibid. 464, 470–72.

48. See, for example, *Niemotko v. Maryland*, 340 U.S. 268 (1951), public preaching; *Lovell v. City of Griffin*, 303 U.S. 444 (1938), proselytizing.

49. *Good News Club v. Milford Central School*, 121 S.Ct. 2093 (2001); *Lamb's Chapel v. Center Moriches Union Free School Dist.*, 508 U.S. 384 (1993); *Widmar v. Vincent*, 454 U.S. 263 (1981).

50. *Ward v. Rock Against Racism*, 491 US 781, 799 (1989).

51. *Cornerstone*, 948 F.2d at 469–70, the city had provided only "conclusory and speculative" affidavits to support exclusion of the church from the business district. Contrast the court's scrutiny in *Cornerstone* with two other cases: *Lakewood, Ohio Congregation of Jehovah's Witnesses v. City of Lakewood*, 699 F.2d 303 (6th Cir. 1983), and *Messiah Baptist Church v. County of Jefferson* 859 F.2d 820 (10th Cir. 1988), both of which involve exclusion of churches from a particular zone. In each case the court first determined that the zoning exclusion did not rise to the level of a "substantial burden" on free exercise (under the *Sherbert* strict scrutiny test), but never considered the intermediate scrutiny demanded when regulations impose an indirect burden on free speech (as such exclusion clearly involves).

52. *City of Renton v. Playtime Theaters*, 475 US 41, 53 (1986).

53. *Lakewood*, 699 F.2d at 307. In this constricted reading of the reasonable alternatives requirement, the *Lakewood* court is in line with the Supreme Court's treatment of the requirement in adult theater cases, where the court has permitted cities to place substantial limits on sites available to adult uses.

54. *Grosz v. City of Miami Beach*, 721 F.2d 729 (11th Cir. 1983); *Christian Gospel Church v. City and County of San Francisco*, 896 F.2d 1221 (9th Cir. 1990); Ann L. Wehener, "When a Home Is Not a Home but a Church: A Proposal for Protection of Home Worship from Zoning Ordinances," *Capital University Law Review* 22 (1993): 491.

55. *Love Church v. City of Evanston*, 671 F. Supp. 508 (N.D. Ill. 1987).

56. *Lakewood*, 699 F.2d at 307. In rejecting economic considerations, the court's opinion is consistent with Supreme Court rulings in adult theater zoning cases.

57. *Village Lutheran Church v City of Ladue*, 997 S.W.2d 506 (Mo. Ct. App. 1999); *Open Door Baptist Church v. Clark County*, 995 P.2d 33 (Wash. 2000).

58. See *C.L.U.B. v. City of Chicago*, 2001 U.S. Dist. LEXIS 3791 (N.D. Ill. 2001).

59. *Islamic Center of Mississippi v. City of Starkville*, 840 F.2d 293 (5th Cir. 1988).

60. *City of Lovell v. Griffin*, 303 U.S. 444 (1938), invalidating ordinance that required permit before distributing literature; *Cantwell v. Connecticut*, 310 U.S. 296 (1940), invalidating permit requirement for solicitation; *Shuttlesworth v. City of Birmingham*, 394 U.S. 147 (1969), invalidating permit requirement for public demonstrations; *City of Lakewood v. Plain Dealer Publishing Co.*, 486 U.S. 750 (1988), invalidating permit requirement for placing newspaper boxes on public property.

61. See, for example, *The Jesus Center v. Farmington Hills Zoning Board of Appeals*, 215 Mich. App. 54 (1996); *Stuart Circle Parish v. Board of Zoning Appeals*, 946 F. Supp. 1225 (E.D. Va. 1996); *First Assembly of God v. Collier County*, 20 F.3d 419 (11th Cir. 1994).

62. Mandelker, *Land Use Law*, § 5.14.

63. The requirement that the accessory use must be subordinated to the primary use would provide some check on unfettered development of religious property, as would the continuing possibility of private nuisance actions brought by the church's neighbors.

64. Something like this determination belongs behind the judgment, in *First Assembly v Collier and Daytona Rescue Mission*, 885 F. Supp 1554 (M.D. Fla. 1995), that denial of permission for a homeless shelter as an accessory use does not constitute a "substantial burden" on the free exercise of religion. That is, feeding the homeless is not a "core" religious activity. See *Western Presbyterian Church v. Board of Zoning Appeals*, 862 F. Supp. 538 (D.D.C. 1994); *Jesus Center v. Farmington Hills*, 215 Mich. App. 54 (1996), where "customary" was initially translated as "what other churches do."

65. See, for example, *Western Presbyterian, Jesus Center,* and *Stuart Circle Parish.*

66. See Rev. John W. Wimberly Jr, "A Law unto Themselves," *George Washington Law Review* 68 (2000): 953.

67. *Keeler v. Cumberland,* 940 F. Supp. 879 (D.Md. 1996); *St. Bartholomew's v. City of New York,* 914 F.2d 348 (2d Cir. 1990), cert. denied, 499 U.S. 905 (1991).

68. *Society of Jesus v. Boston Landmarks Commission,* 409 Mass. 38, 564 N.E.2d 571 (1990).

69. *First Covenant Church v. City of Seattle,* 787 P.2d 1352 (Wash. 1990), vacated and remanded, 499 U.S. 901 (1991), holding reinstated, 120 Wash. 2d 203, 840 P.2d 174 (1992).

70. *St. Bartholomew's,* 914 F.2d 348 (2d. Cir. 1990), cert. denied, 499 U.S. 905 (1991).

71. *Keeler,* 940 F. Supp. 879 (D.Md. 1996).

72. The *First Covenant* holding was extended in *First United Methodist Church v. Hearing Examiner,* 129 Wash. 2d 192, 930 P.2d 318 (1997) and *Munns v. Martin,* 131 Wash. 2d 192, 930 P.2d 318 (1997).

73. *Society of Jesus,* 409 Mass. 38, 564 N.E.2d 571 (1990).

74. *West Virginia v. Barnette* 319 U.S. 624 (1943), exemption of students from the flag salute; *Wooley v. Maynard* 430 U.S. 705 (1977), exemption of motorists from displaying the motto "Live Free or Die" on their license plate.

75. *NLRB v. Catholic Bishop,* 440 U.S. 490 (1979); see also *Lynch v. Donnelly,* 465 U.S. 668, 687 (1984), O'Connor, concurring.

76. The New York City Landmark ordinance contains an exemption for changes to landmarked structures by non-profit institutions (including churches) when such changes are necessary to maintain the utility of the structure for the institution's non-profit purposes.

77. 438 U.S. 104, reh'd denied, 439 U.S. 883 (1978), denying constitutional claims of owners of Grand Central Terminal, who were refused permission to build an office tower on top of the landmarked Terminal.

78. Religious Land Use and Institutionalized Persons Act, 42 U.S.C. 2000cc.

79. See *C.L.U.B. v. City of Chicago,* 2001 U.S. Dist. LEXIS 3791 (N.D. Ill.); *City of Chicago Heights v. Living Word,* 2001 Ill.LEXIS 243 (Ill. Sup. Ct.).

80. Both *C.L.U.B.* and *Living Word* attest to the limited benefits of state RFRAs in land use cases: not only did the churches draw from RLUIPA, but they also relied on the Illinois RFRA, but the courts' response to both the federal and state claims was the same: zoning limits on churches do not impose a substantial burden on religious exercise.

81. See, for example, *Ehlers-Renzi v. Connelly School of the Holy Child,* 224 F.3d 283 (4th Cir. 2000), upholding Montgomery County, Maryland's exemption of religious schools from special use permit requirement against Establishment Clause challenge.

82. *Boyajian v. Gatzunis,* 212 F.3d 1 (1st Cir. 2000). The Dover Amendment can be found at Mass. Gen. Laws Ch. 40A § 3.

83. *Texas Monthly v. Bullock,* 489 U.S. 1 (1989).

84. *East Bay Asian Local Development Corporation v. California,* 24 Cal. 4th 693, 13 P.3d 1122 (2000). The challenged regulations can be found at Cal. Gov't Code §§ 25373 and 37361.

85. As we saw in the discussion of *Society of Jesus,* restrictions on the design of worship space or other theologically expressive architecture would already be governed by free speech analysis, so the exemption chiefly works to alleviate other burdens.

86. *East Bay,* 13 P.3d at 1134, 1154 & n.8. See also 16 USC 470a, providing that federal

historic preservation grants may be made to religious properties "provided that the purpose of the grant is secular, does not promote religion, and seeks to protect those qualities that are historically significant."

87. "The Nature of the Church and Its Relation with Government," 3.

Index of Cases

Index of Names and Subjects